SELECTED CLIMBS IN THE
CASCADES
VOLUME I

SELECTED CLIMBS IN THE
CASCADES
VOLUME I
Second Edition

JIM NELSON
PETER POTTERFIELD

THE MOUNTAINEERS BOOKS

Published by
The Mountaineers Books
1001 SW Klickitat Way, Suite 201
Seattle, WA 98134

First edition 1993. Second edition 2003.

Published simultaneously in Great Britain by Cordee, 3a DeMontfort Street, Leicester, England, LE1 7HD

Manufactured in the United States of America

Project Editors: Christine Ummel Hosler, Kris Fulsaas
Copyeditor: Kris Fulsaas
Cover and book design: The Mountaineers Books
Layout artist: Jennifer LaRock Shontz

Cover photograph: *Ed Cooper on the summit of Mount Challenger, August 2001*
(Photo by Jim Nelson)
Frontispiece: *Dan Cauthorn on the summit of Early Morning Spire, with the Triad above his helmet* (Photo by Mark Kroese)

Library of Congress Cataloging-in-Publication Data
Nelson, Jim, 1954-
    Selected climbs in the Cascades / Jim Nelson and Peter Potterfield.—
2nd ed.
        p.   cm.
Includes index.
    ISBN 0-89886-767-3 (pbk.)
    1. Mountaineering—Washington (State)—Guidebooks. 2.
Mountaineering—Cascade Range—Guidebooks. 3. Washington
(State)—Guidebooks. 4. Cascade Range—Guidebooks. I. Potterfield,
Peter. II. Title.
    GV199.42.W2 N45 2003
    796.52'2'09797—dc21

                                            2002153641

CONTENTS

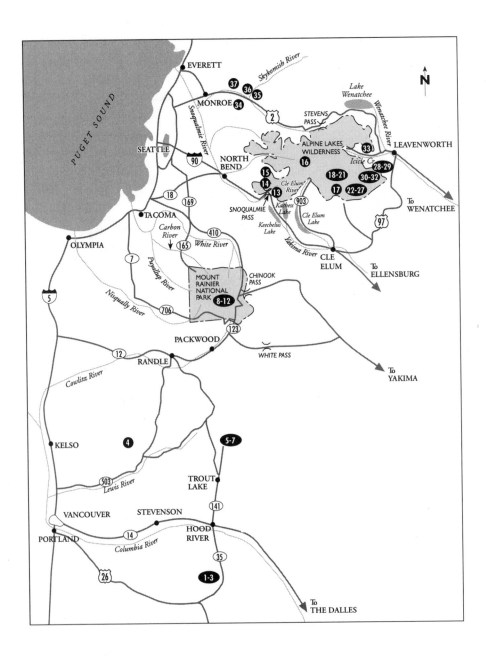

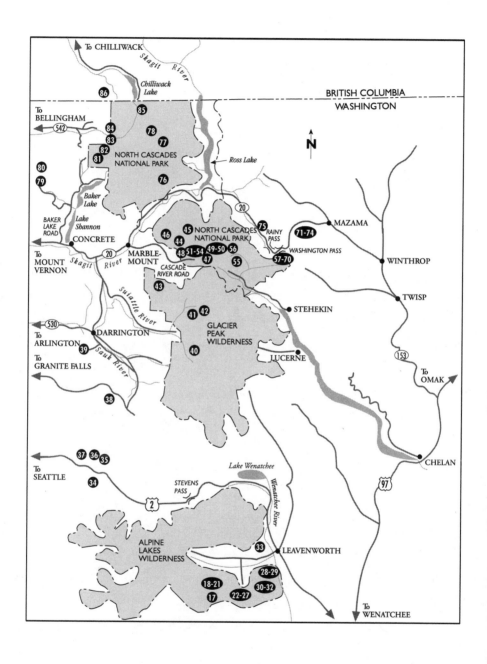

ACKNOWLEDGMENTS

The authors wish to thank copy editor Kris Fulsaas for her skilled and thorough work on our manuscript. She improved the book immensely. Claire Hagen Dole's careful review of the material proved essential for its accuracy and substance. We wish to thank Fred Beckey for his permission to use some first-ascent information gathered by him. This generous gesture saved us hours trying to duplicate his scholarly research.

We also wish to thank those who contributed to this project with information, photographs, suggestions, and encouragement. The enthusiasm that others showed for this climbing guide was gratifying and inspirational as we worked to compile accurate information.

For providing route suggestions, firsthand descriptions of routes, photos, and other crucial assistance in putting together this book, we wish to thank Dan Aylward, Steve Baldwin, Dave Bale, Paul Baugher, Alex Bertulis, Dave Betts, Max Block, Tim Bonnet, Jim Bourgeois, Jane Bromet, Stim Bullitt, Bryan Burdo, Bruce Carter, Joe Catellani, Dan Cauthorn, Geoff Childs, Ed Cooper, John Cooper, Robert Cordery-Cotter, Sean Courage, Darrell Cramer, Carl Diedrich, Jim Dockery, Mike Dole, Mick Fenn, Cal Folsom, Phil Fortier, Glen Frese, Don Goodman, Keith Gunnar, Colin Haley, Paul Hickenbottom, Roy Holland, Greg Jacobson, Pete Keane, Tim Kelly, Larry Kemp, Matt Kerns, Morris Kittleman, David Knoll, Viktor Kramar, Bob Kroese, Mark Kroese, Cliff Leight, Kit Lewis, Bill Liddell, Jim Martin, Tim Matsui, Tom Miller, Forrest Murphy, Bart Paull, Matt Perkins, Bill Pilling, Yale Preston, Norm Reid, Walt Reissig, Dale Remsberg, Steve Risse, Jim Ruch, Leonard Russell, Andreas Schmidt, John Sharp, Carl Skoog, Gordy Skoog, Mark Shipman, Kurt Smith, Fred Stanley, Matt Stanley, Brian Sullivan, Steve Swenson, Brian Voigt, Jack Voigt, Mark Westman, Dave Whitelaw, Dave Hirst (at the USGS Ice and Climate Project, for retrieval and printing of the Austin Post photographs), Kelly Bush at North Cascades National Park, Mike Gauthier at Mount Rainier National Park, and Rick Kirschner and Gail Purifoy, who work for the government agencies responsible for managing the Cascades and who thoughtfully reviewed our work to ensure that the regulations presented are accurate and up-to-date.

Index Peaks, and US 2, from the east (Photo by Jim Nelson)

INTRODUCTION

Ten years have passed since the publication of *Selected Climbs in the Cascades*. When the first edition of this climbing guide hit the bookshelves in 1993, it was the tangible manifestation of a new idea for the Cascades: a carefully compiled source of information for climbers with a singular goal—not to be comprehensive but, rather, to steer climbers to outstanding routes in the Cascades. It was our intent to highlight the finest, most aesthetic, and most enjoyable of Cascades climbing routes, regardless of difficulty. A climb did not have to be really hard, or really easy, to be in the guidebook. Subjective though it was, the resulting compilation seemed to strike a nerve; many of the climbs became Cascades favorites.

In fact, the warm reception of that guidebook was one of the factors that inspired us to do it once again for volume II, which we finished in 1999, and for this revised edition of the original volume. More than just a substantial overhaul and update of the initial book—reflecting input received during the past decade—this new edition is also an excuse for us to add many more pages to the original book, and considerable new material, including nearly a dozen new routes.

Much like the first volume, this edition contains a familiar mix of walk-ups, snow climbs, scrambles, wilderness alpine routes, hard rock climbs, ice climbs, and strenuous mixed climbs. (The sport climbing section is unique to volume II, which we will update when it is time.) The idea of a qualitative climbing guide, one that dares to rate climbs by appeal, not by difficulty or type of climbing, was new to the Cascades at the time *Selected Climbs in the Cascades* was published. A review in a major climbing magazine took us to task for including the Southwest Couloir on South Early Winters Spire, noting that the climb was "too easy" to be included in such a book. However, since that route description was published, the Southwest Couloir has seen hundreds of ascents and has introduced many aspiring alpine climbers to the joys of snow-filled couloirs, and set them up for more ambitious steep gullies, such as Triple Couloirs on Dragontail Peak. That was the whole idea, and that is why we will continue to recommend routes on the basis of their merit as fun, quality climbs.

That answers questions such as: What on earth is Mount Daniel or Ruth Mountain doing in the same guidebook as Girth Pillar on Mount Stuart, or the North Buttress of Bear Mountain? We put a high value on alpine ambience and quality climbing, regardless of the level of difficulty, and that seems to go against guidebook trends. It seems we are just contrarians by nature, an attitude that mirrors the gnarly and diverse character of the Cascades themselves. But we have not shied away from really hard climbs either. The criterion is merely this: that the route be an outstanding one.

As we did in volume II, we have in this edition highlighted some of the good

Climber on the distinctive rime "ice" that traditionally forms on Mount Hood in winter (Photo by Joe Catellani)

climbing to be found in the accessible Interstate 90 corridor. Long snubbed as "Low-Quality Pass," the area around Snoqualmie Pass in fact harbors outstanding routes, such as Chair Peak and the Tooth. The Improbable Traverse on Guye Peak is a really decent alpine rock climb just a hour or so from Seattle. Pointing out climbs like that is part of what this book is all about, because many Cascade climbers live in the big metropolitan areas around Puget Sound, and because climbers do not always have a weekend or a week to punch more deeply into the range. Whether we are successful or not is up to those many active climbers who go frequently into the Cascades, and who are not shy about giving us suggestions, feedback, and aggressively opinionated responses to what they find in these pages.

The way in which this new edition was put together differs radically from that of our first: this is more than ever a collaborative effort on the part of the climbing community. We have heard from climbers all over the Cascade Range who have a favorite climb, discovered a new one, or tried a variation of an old favorite that they think should be included in a qualitative Cascades guide. So, more than our first book, this volume reflects what we have learned over a decade of conversation. In that regard, this book can be considered not just ours, but one with the viewpoints of many active Cascades climbers.

And ten years later, the process by which we received information is completely different, reflecting a decade of technological innovation. Rather than scraps of notes on legal pages and Polaroid prints of slides, the information from other climbers now comes in the form of emails, digital images, and forwarded websites, a wholly more satisfactory and efficient way to disseminate information. We wonder when guidebooks such as this one will be supplemented by subscription-based websites, wherein climbers will merely print out a continually updated version of a particular climb description, replete with approach maps and climbers topos. Our guess is, that is not far off.

But in the meantime, we hope this new edition continues to provide useful information for climbers who enjoy the unique mountain environment of the Cascades. Our intention is to produce a guidebook for climbers of all abilities, a guidebook full of practical, useful information on the best climbs in the range, the kind of information that enables the reader to make intelligent decisions about what and where (and when) to climb. That way, every climber can make the most of his or her time spent in the Cascades.

How to Use This Book

Each of the eighty-six routes chosen for *Selected Climbs in the Cascades, Volume I, Second Edition* is described in detail, with the following components:

An overview of the peak or climbing area describes the setting and, often, climbing history. A brief section on special considerations (if any) relates either potential hazards, or permits and/or restrictions that may be imposed on the climber by management agencies such as the U.S. Forest Service or the National Park Service.

For each route, an overview provides a descriptive portrayal of the route, including its virtues and other noteworthy characteristics. Then, for each route, a summary provides information on first ascents, elevation, difficulty, time required, equipment required, and appropriate climbing season. The summary is followed by a detailed approach description—including highway and trail instructions where necessary—and a detailed description of the climbing route. Finally, each route concludes with a description of the descent.

In addition to the above descriptions, photographs and maps provide invaluable information on both the approach and route. The photographs are self-explanatory; the "climbers topos" or diagrams amount to route descriptions in their own right, providing detailed information on rock features and climbing routes. See the climbers topo key this page.

The **difficulty** ratings should be familiar to most climbers. The overall difficulty of a route is given as a "grade," ranging from the easiest (Grade I) to the most committing and difficult (Grade V).

Technical free-climbing difficulty is given here in the "Yosemite Standard," class 1 through class 5. Class 1 and class 2 climbs are basically walk-ups or scrambles that require no technical skills; class 3 climbing begins to involve finding and using holds, but still is not really technical and no rope is usually required. Class 4 climbing is technically easy, with ample holds, but can be steep and exposed; a rope is often useful when climbing class 4 ground.

Class 5 climbs are rated 5.0 through 5.14, depending on technical difficulty. This book sometimes rates climbs as "low 5th class," because in practice the distinctions between, say, 5.0 and 5.2 are often difficult if not impossible to discern. In that same vein, "mid-5th-class climbing" denotes technical difficulties from 5.4 to 5.6. Climbs rated 5.9 and up obviously require a higher standard of climbing proficiency.

The difficulty of climbing on direct aid is rated A1 (denoting straightforward nailing or chock placements) to A4 (for awkward, insecure placements, bat hooks, bashies, and other marginal aid).

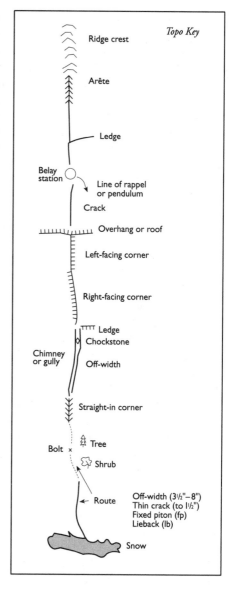

Topo Key

Ridge crest
Arête
Ledge
Belay station
Line of rappel or pendulum
Crack
Overhang or roof
Left-facing corner
Right-facing corner
Ledge
Chockstone
Chimney or gully
Off-width
Straight-in corner
Bolt x
Tree
Shrub
Route
Off-width (3½"–8")
Thin crack (to 1½")
Fixed piton (fp)
Lieback (lb)
Snow

Ice-climbing difficulty ratings are as follows: WI denotes water ice, and is rated in difficulty from 1 to 5, with WI 5 representing the most difficult climbing. AI denotes alpine ice, such as névé or glacial ice or compacted snow, and is rated similarly.

In a deviation from standard practice, this book also rates the *approach* to the climb. While unconventional, this is a practical and useful thing to do, for in the Cascade Range, the approach is frequently the most challenging part of the climb. Approaches are rated by "Grade," with Grade I the easiest—a simple, short, nonstrenuous approach, such as the 45-minute walk to a route at Washington Pass—and Grade V the most difficult, such as the grueling 2 days of torture required to get in to Mount Challenger. Note that except for Mount Hood in Oregon and Slesse Mountain in British Columbia, all climbs are located in Washington State—so the state/province in which cities and highways are located is not specified except for Hood and Slesse.

The **time** required to do a route is given as a round-trip time for multiday climbs, and/or one-way time to the summit. Remember, the one-way time is from the *car to the summit* (not round trip) unless otherwise noted. Other time estimates are provided where useful, such as split times on long volcano routes. The fast end of the time range represents the authors' estimate for a fast, fit party of strong climbers; the slow end of the range represents the estimate for an average party of weekend climbers.

The **equipment** summary covers the basic hardware requirements for each route, such as rock, ice, and snow protection; crampons where steep or hard snow may be expected; and two ropes when long rappels are useful.

A further word on ropes: unless otherwise described, a rope is assumed to be a standard 50-meter (160-foot) climbing rope. (Note that throughout the text, rope measurements are given in meters, not feet, to reflect standard climbing practices.) Where appropriate, the authors have suggested the use of longer (60-meter/197-foot) ropes, or sometimes shorter ropes. This is helpful information when weight considerations or the necessity of long rappels become a factor.

Important note: The equipment list does not include safety gear such as helmets, avalanche beacons, ropes, prusiks, rescue pulleys, proper clothing, and first-aid supplies. It is assumed the climber is sufficiently skilled and experienced to know when to wear a helmet, carry a rope, or take along crevasse-rescue equipment.

Some of our recommendations on **seasons** are obvious. For example, Chair Peak's North Face is recommended for December through March, with the idea that it is a fine winter route but not a worthy summer route. Note that State Highway 20, the North Cascades Highway, is closed in the winter.

For other routes, we offer a range for what usually is the normal summer season, when access and route conditions are reasonable for most parties. For example, for Ingalls Peak we give June through October as the primary season: the road typically opens just before Memorial Day, but unless you are very clever about reading snow conditions and start very early, the approach becomes an unpleasant postholing adventure. July through September usually provide the easiest approach conditions as well as a reasonable shot at good climbing weather. In some years, sunny (though short) days run into late October, so most years, the best climbing is found June through October.

We note, where appropriate, routes on which experienced parties with winter-climbing skills might contemplate doing what normally is a summer route in winter conditions.

Still other routes—the Tooth's South Face, for example—have proven to be popular year-round, so we note that. (For the Tooth, that is because of its good access and aesthetic appeal.) But in any given year, favorable weather conditions may exist for only 150 days, so it is up to the climber to assess both approach and route conditions as they change with the seasons.

The Cascades

It is not possible to describe in a few pages the character of the mountains that make up the Cascades—the range is

Climbing ranger Bruce Carter carrying a climbing-camp composting-toilet lid (Photo by Tracey Wiese)

too big, the mountains too diverse and too changeable by season. There are, however, some generalizations about the range that are useful to those without extensive experience in it.

If *Selected Climbs in the Cascades, Volume I, Second Edition* seems to start with easier climbs and progress steadily toward more difficult climbs, that is because the book reflects the nature of the Cascade Range. As one moves from south to north, the character of the Cascades gradually changes until it reaches the dramatic climax of the North Cascades, where many of the hard, interesting climbs in this book can be found. The southern section of the book is preoccupied with volcanoes—Hood, Adams, and Rainier. North of Snoqualmie Pass, the nonvolcanic character of the Cascades emerges with the likes of Mounts Index and Stuart. Finally, in the northernmost 80 miles, the North Cascades' awesome peaks—such as Dome, Forbidden, and Eldorado Peaks and Mount Challenger—reach the range's rugged climax. It is not hard to see why this northernmost section of the Cascades, with more than 500 glaciers and almost 100 square miles of ice, holds inordinate interest for climbers.

The Cascades are still wild, at least in places. Many of the climbs in this book are, therefore, hard to get to, and not just because they are far from any drivable roads. Particularly in those areas of the Cascades north of State Highway 20 (North Cascades Highway), the terrain between the road end and the climb is likely to be exceedingly rugged and so thickly overgrown with vegetation that cross-country travel is arduous and time-consuming. For climbers accustomed to mountains and climbing areas with easier access, this extra effort can sap energy and will. But these sorts of difficulties are part of climbing in the Cascades, and should be planned for accordingly. The unsavory obstacles that lie between the climber and the chosen mountain are one reason why there are still places of solitude in the Cascades. Luna Peak, for instance, is the appealing climb it is precisely because it is so well protected. Of the three possible approaches, all either involve notorious bushwhacking; are long, unreasonably strenuous, or technically dangerous; or all of the above.

The heavily glaciated nature of the Cascades presents unique climbing opportunities and obvious dangers. The ice-clad slopes of Mount Rainier, Mount Baker, and Mount Shuksan in particular are rich in routes and outstanding climbing experiences. But more climbers are killed or injured on those peaks than all the other Cascades combined. The obvious lesson is that to venture onto these mountains without appropriate skills invites trouble.

Permits and the Cascade Climber

If the Cascades are still wild, they are not as wild as they used to be. In fact, certain areas of the range face serious problems of overcrowding. The Alpine Lakes Wilderness Area bears the double whammy of outstanding backcountry and close proximity to the urban population centers of western Washington. The result is extreme visitation pressures on popular areas such as the Enchantment Lakes Basin and Colchuck Lake, necessitating stringent permit requirements. The impact on climbers, who must share these areas with other backcountry users, is that they must reserve campsites months in advance and take their chances with weather. Climbers going into Prusik Peak or Temple Ridge, for example, should reserve summer and fall permits by early spring, or face the uncertainties of the daily permit "lottery."

The permit system has undoubtedly taken away some of the freedom normally associated with climbing. No longer can climbers simply watch the weather and, when it looks good, pick up and go climb a popular peak such as Colchuck, or even Forbidden. And no one associated with the management of the national forests and wilderness areas expects it to get any better. In fact, it is a safe bet that permits will be harder to get in the future. If day-use quotas are instituted on the Mountaineers Creek approach to Mount Stuart, that would effectively put a ceiling on the number of climbers who could do routes on the mountain. For now, the best advice is to contact the appropriate ranger station for the area in which you wish to climb to ascertain that access is permitted.

The inevitable result of the permit system to manage overcrowding has been that climbers have altered behavior patterns to get around the regulations. One obvious example is that routes that were formerly overnight trips have been turned into long day trips. Climbers headed for Forbidden Peak often forgo the usual camp in Boston Basin, camping instead by the car and doing the climb in a long day from the road. Even if such measures usually are required only during busy times, notably Saturday night, such creativity will serve the climber well when venturing into these prime— and therefore popular—areas in the years to come.

Thoughtful backcountry managers, such as Kelly Bush of North Cascades National Park, make this point: climbers should understand that the trigger for increasing regulations often is climber impact on wilderness land. While monitoring impacts and measuring soil loss in heavy-use areas such as Boston Basin, Bush says, the Park Service might have to consider such draconian measures as day-use quotas and designated camps in formerly open camping zones if the situation gets worse. So even the "creativity" of such strategies as bombing up to Forbidden for a day climb will only delay the inevitable. But Bush hopes that through a common desire to keep the Cascades wild, climbers will adopt stringent low-impact techniques, and practice them religiously. This is clearly the only way to go. And remember, it is against National Park Service policy to place bolts or fixed protection within any national park.

Probably the most sweeping permit news to emerge since *Selected Climbs in the Cascades* was first published is the institution of the trailhead parking pass, now known as the Northwest Forest Pass, required for all U.S. Forest Service trailheads and some trailheads in North Cascades National Park. This required pass, $5 per day or $30 per year from date of purchase, is good for the Mount Baker–Snoqualmie, Okanogan, and Wenatchee National Forests. Much like Sno-Park passes, these passes are necessary to avoid tickets at trailheads into most sections of the Cascades. Always ask at a ranger station if you are in doubt.

There remain, however, places in the range that harbor secrets. The Pickets, for instance, protected by unsavory and time-consuming approaches, epitomize Cascades wilderness. In recent years, more and more people have ventured into these remote, storybook mountains—a big change from the '70s and '80s, when a handful of climbers had the place to themselves. And yet a party can still visit this area and see no other climbers for days. A number of good climbs in the Pickets can be found in this book, but the area remains, to a certain extent, terra incognita. There are fine rock climbs and alpine routes that simply have yet to be discovered.

Wilderness Ethic

In this day of vanishing wilderness, disappearing forests, and heavy use of the Northwest backcountry, it is incumbent on the alpine climber to camp and climb with minimum impact. "Leave no trace" is the mantra. Good sense and wilderness ethics, as well as management agencies, mandate that climbers and all backcountry users follow a few simple but important guidelines:

Do not camp on vegetation. Camp on snow, rock, or bare ground, in that order.

Take proper care with sanitation. One of the biggest high-country problems is human waste, which presents aesthetic as well as health problems. Where available, use sanitation facilities—and know *how* to use them. Put no trash, tampons, or other garbage in any outhouse facilities, particularly the composting toilets of North Cascades National Park. Where packing out human waste is not required, or in other areas where there are no facilities, follow these practices:

At lower elevations, in the forest and trail zone, it is acceptable to dig a cat hole (4–8 inches deep, 4–6 inches diameter) at least 200 feet from water, campsites, and trails.

Higher up, the elimination of waste requires more attention and effort. In the alpine zone, talus fields can be used when no other option is present: smear the excrement on rock where ultraviolet light can break it down and rain can wash it away. Never place human waste near streams or drainages that eventually feed into streams.

Burying waste in a snowfield is ludicrous: the snowfield soon melts out, revealing a disagreeable, bespoiling presence, or it drains into a stream, contaminating it;

or some other backcountry user unknowingly camps on the site, perhaps using your latrine for a water source. Never excrete on snow—or a glacier—if it can be avoided.

In North Cascades National Park, rangers encourage climbers to eliminate waste before venturing higher on climbs where waste is more difficult to deal with. On overnight trips where the high camp is on a glacier—such as the Easton on Mount Baker or more remote routes on Mount Rainier—the climber must be inventive. Park rangers began handing out the dreaded "blue bags" there for use in alpine areas where either the composting toilet is not melted out or there is none. Backcountry ranger Kelly Bush says she especially encourages the use of "blue bags" for areas such as Eldorado Creek and Boston Basin, which are focal-point base camps in this book. Packing out human waste in plastic bags—a realistic consideration for some other land management agencies as well—requires an attitude shift. There are no deposit barrels in North Cascades National Park, unlike at Mount Rainier, so the climber must carry this cargo back to the trailhead. These considerations demand real behavior modification on the part of all climbers to avoid seeing good climbing areas bespoiled by human excrement.

One solution may be to encourage construction of technologically advanced alpine toilets in busy areas. Get involved: lobby agencies, raise money and awareness, do whatever it takes to help solve this problem, or suffer greater regulation.

Travel in small groups. Group size is already limited in Northwest wilderness areas and national parks; in parts of North Cascades National Park, six is the maximum group size in some areas. In most other Cascades wilderness areas, the limit is eight or twelve. Make it a practice to climb in parties of two and three and four, not bigger parties that concentrate impacts. Know the size limit for the area in which you are traveling.

Pack out *everything* you bring in. There is never a good reason to violate this rule.

Be aware that *Giardia* can be found virtually everyplace in the Cascades. The only safe course of action is to treat all water, filter it, or boil it for 1 minute.

To climbers, by nature iconoclastic and irreverent, rules and regulations have often seemed unnecessary or counterproductive. But in this particular time of the planet, regulations are unavoidable. Enjoy the mountains, but take care of them. Make it your responsibility. As a user, take seriously your stewardship of the Cascades so these wonderful mountains will remain a place of beauty, pleasure, and renewal.

—*Jim Nelson, Peter Potterfield*

A Note About Safety

Climbing involves unavoidable risks that every climber assumes. The fact that a route is described in this book is not a representation that it will be safe for you. Routes vary greatly in difficulty and in the amount and kind of experience and preparation needed to enjoy them safely. Some routes may have changed or deteriorated since this book was written. Also, of course, climbing conditions can change from day to day, due to weather and other factors. A route that is safe in good weather, or for a highly conditioned, properly equipped climber, may be completely unsafe for someone else or under adverse conditions.

—*The Mountaineers*

MOUNT HOOD

▲ *Palmer Glacier/South Side* ▲ *Yocum Ridge* ▲ *Sandy Headwall*

Mount Hood is one of the most frequently climbed big mountains in the United States. Sometimes called the Mount Fuji of North America, the volcano's pleasing daggerlike shape as seen from nearby Portland—and much of Washington and Oregon, for that matter—attracts novices and experts alike. Most climbers come to Mount Hood for the relatively straightforward ascent of the normal route, a few for the more remotely situated or technically challenging climbs elsewhere on the peak. But by any route, Mount Hood offers an outstanding mountaineering experience, with the ambience of a big peak and summit views south to the Sisters and Mount Jefferson, and north across the Columbia River to Mounts St. Helens, Adams, even Rainier and beyond on a clear day.

The South Side route on Mount Hood (Photo by Austin Post, USGS)

Hood is unique among the major Cascades volcanoes. Because of the busy ski area on its southern flank, and the need to get skiers there reliably in all weather, access to the south side of the mountain is unequaled for a peak of this size. This outstanding approachability means that many climbs on the mountain can be done in a day, round-trip, without a high camp. This easy accessibility means that the main or South Side route, which follows the Palmer Ski Lift to 8,500 feet, sees literally thousands of ascents each year. But there are other, better, less-traveled routes that can also be reached via the Timberline area, an unusual situation that opens up quality climbs on this big mountain to day trips.

The inevitable complaints about crowds on the popular South Side route spurred the Forest Service to threaten in 1999 to limit the population of climbers allowed there. But legions of Hood's faithful uprose en masse, squelching that effort. So the south side remains well populated, but those who come frequently to climb Hood know there is an easy cure for overcrowding: choose a route that is more technically demanding, such as Yocum Ridge or Sandy Headwall; one on the north side of the peak, such as Cooper Spur, where relatively few climbers go; or a less-traveled route such as Leuthold Couloir. In fact, choosing *any* route other than the Palmer Glacier/South Side eliminates crowd problems.

The routes recommended here make for a sampler for the peak, including the ever popular South Side route, the more challenging Sandy Headwall, and the quite technical Yocum Ridge.

The numbers of climbers attracted to Mount Hood can give the mountain the illusion of a moderate outing—a big-time climbing experience with little potential for grave consequences. Paul Hickenbottom, for instance, tells of spending 2 days in alpine splendor and isolation on the lovely Sandy Headwall route, only to reach the summit to find a volleyball game in progress attended by a couple of dogs who had managed the 35- to 45-degree chute up the south side.

But the carnival-like atmosphere that can prevail on Mount Hood belies the fact that the mountain is as dangerous as any of the Cascade volcanoes. The potential for bad weather, reduced visibility, and altitude-related dangers makes the ascent of this 11,000-foot mountain by any route a serious undertaking. Climbers attempting the peak should be well versed in crevasse rescue and glacier travel, know the signs of altitude sickness, and exercise good judgment. Every climber should carry a compass (a compass *and* an altimeter is even better) and know how to descend the South Side route in poor visibility. Safety on Hood is an issue that moved to the forefront in the wake of the 1986 tragedy, when eleven students were killed when they were caught high on the peak by bad weather. Conditions played a part in the accident in spring 2002, in which one rope of two climbers lost footing on an icy section and fell, careening into other ropes, setting off a chain-reaction accident that killed three climbers. Conditions change rapidly, which is why Hood demands respect by any route, as do all the Cascade volcanoes.

There's more to Mount Hood than a high, volcanic summit. If you're looking for accessible, reliable ice climbing or mixed climbing, Mount Hood's Illumination Rock offers multiple single-day routes. Located at an elevation that provides consistently freezing temperatures and a full range of aspects (east, south, west, and north), it almost always has something in condition November through April. Wayne Wallace notes that "I-Rock," the sixth highest summit in Oregon, holds varied mixed rock and ice routes up to six pitches long. "It is the perfect one-day playground for the alpinist." In addition to its easy access and minimal avalanche danger, the rock enjoys a six- to seven-month-long season. The best routes start at the downhill toe of the rock itself and end near the west summit. At least eleven new routes have been climbed in the M3-M6 range, and each are attractive climbs that reliably "come in." Wallace notes that he has found the best conditions on the rock in November-December and March-April.

Special Considerations: Climbers approaching Mount Hood from the south must self-register for their attempts at Timberline Lodge; climbers approaching Hood from the north must self-register for a Mount Hood Wilderness backcountry permit at the trailhead. For up-to-date information and regulations on all Mount Hood routes, call the Mount Hood Information Center (503-622-7674); for south-side routes, call the Zig Zag Ranger District (503-622-3191); for north-side routes, call the Hood River Ranger District (541-352-6002). Northwest Forest Pass required to park at the trailhead for north-side approaches.

For those without climbing experience—or those unfamiliar with the high-altitude, glaciated environment on Mount Hood—the authors recommend contacting the concessioned guide service, Timberline Mountain Guides (541-312-9242). Besides climbing instruction and ascents by a variety of routes, the guide service offers the added incentive of a snowcat ride to 8,500 feet on the South Side route. It is a great way for climbers new to Cascade volcanoes to get a feel for what it is like.

Those who choose to climb Mount Hood on their own should be aware that, along with the fun climbing and interesting environment, the mountain harbors lethal dangers that require skill and experience to meet.

1 PALMER GLACIER/SOUTH SIDE GRADE II

Also known as the Hogsback or Regular route, this, the most popular route on a very popular mountain, presents few technical difficulties and more than a few peculiarities on its 5,300-foot climb from Timberline Lodge to the summit. The first 2,500 feet follows the well-traveled route (to the right or east of the ski area) toward Silcox Hut, then up under the towers of the Palmer Ski Lift, the highest in the Cascades and one that affords skiing year-round. The lifts give rise to some unexpected dangers: beware of the grooming machine. It can run you down in the dark of an alpine start, and if you walk in the groomed snow, the person driving the groomer will yell obscenities at you. This is not your average 11,000-foot mountain.

The route can be done much of the year (it is most appealing from winter through July) by climbers with appropriate experience; late in the season the route can become dangerously icy. The year-round approach made possible by the plowed road to Timberline Lodge and the ski lifts on Hood's south side make this route feasible in winter when conditions permit. Difficulties include 35- to 45-degree snow, glacier travel, and altitude.

One of the authors climbed the route with pioneering Cascades photographer Keith Gunnar—at night—under a full moon so bright it never became necessary to

The summit gully or "Chute" on Hood's South Side route (Photo by Joe Catellani)

Climbers at approximately 7,000 feet on the Palmer Glacier/South Side route (Photo by Keith Gunnar)

turn on the headlamps. The summit was attained just as the sun rose to warm the solitary splendor, a rare thing on Mount Hood. It was a beautiful moment—so much so Keith captured it on film for an REI catalog cover. Certain they were the highest people in Oregon, the pair got a scare when the snow underfoot suddenly moved, and some guy who had bivied up there popped out of his sleeping bag asking what time it was. Shaken, they turned to descend, only to be met by the unnerving sight of literally hundreds of climbers coming up "the Chute" and the final, steep slope in an en masse Saturday morning ascent. Go midweek if you can.

First ascent ▲ W. L. Chittenden, James Deardorff, W. L. Buckley, L. J. Powell, Henry Pittock, August 1857

Elevation ▲ 11,235 feet

Difficulty ▲ Grade II; 35- to 45-degree snow, glacier travel, altitude

Time ▲ 4–8 hours one-way, car to summit

Equipment ▲ Ice ax, crampons, wands

Season ▲ May-July

Approach (Grade I): Drive US 26 to the town of Government Camp, Oregon; take Timberline Road to Timberline Lodge and park in the lower parking lot (5,920 feet). The climbers register is near the entrance to the day lodge.

Route: From the east side of Timberline Lodge, climb approximately 1 mile through the trees (do not climb up the groomed ski slopes) toward the Silcox Hut, approximately 7,000 feet. Continue climbing (stay well east of the ski area) another

Climber on the Hogsback in winter (Photo by Joe Catellani)

mile to the end of the Palmer Ski Lift (approximately 8,500 feet); from the end of the lift, climb toward the right (east) side of Crater Rock. Climb up and around the east side of the rock to the high ridge of snow leading from Crater Rock toward the summit (known as the Hogback or Hogsback). Follow this feature to the bergschrund, which can usually be turned from either side if no convenient snow bridges are at hand. A steep (35-degree) gully known as the Chute leads through prominent rock towers to the summit ridge.

Descent: Descend the climbing route. It is essential that climbers on Mount Hood know how to descend this route in poor visibility. A frequent mistake made by climbers descending this route in bad weather is to move straight downhill, assuming that will take them back to Timberline Lodge. A fall-line descent, however, causes the climber to veer southwesterly (toward Zigzag Canyon) and therefore completely miss the top of the ski lifts and the safe route back to Timberline Lodge.

If you are caught high on Mount Hood in bad weather, descend from the summit to Crater Rock and climb down and around the left (east) side of the rock. Once below Crater Rock, follow magnetic south (the direction indicated by the southerly end of a magnetic compass needle); this vector, which involves considerable sidehilling, takes the climber very close to the top of the ski lifts and the Silcox Hut; from there, the ski lifts or snowcat tracks can be followed back to Timberline Lodge.

2 YOCUM RIDGE GRADE IV; AI 3

When Mount Hood is viewed from the west, on a winter's day with the low-angled light slanting across the mountain, a jagged ice-covered ridge descends toward the viewer: Yocum Ridge. Yocum Ridge is a narrow rock ridge composed (some would say barely composed) of extremely loose rock. This route, therefore, is safe to climb only when the rock is covered and glued together by the rime ice that characteristically forms on Hood, and that means only in winter or early spring. Under ideal conditions, the ridge is totally white and daytime temperatures are below freezing. Climbing Yocum Ridge in the right conditions is like a quick trip to Alaska: the crest is spectacular and the gullies and flutings on the ridge give the route a big-mountain atmosphere.

Mount Hood from the west, with Sandy Glacier Headwall: A. Yocum Ridge (climb 2); B. Sandy Headwall (climb 3). (Photo by Austin Post, USGS)

Bill Pilling on Yocum Ridge (Photo by Matt Perkins)

Named after O. C. Yocum, a Mount Hood guide during the early part of the twentieth century, the ridge's rotten rock repulsed attempts for many years. Finally, in 1959, Fred Beckey, showing the original thinking that made him the most accomplished alpinist in North America, figured out that the only safe way to do the climb was during the winter. With partner Leo Scheiblehner, a skilled ice climber from Austria who settled at Crystal Mountain where his family owns the Alpine Inn, Beckey made the first ascent of this long-sought route in April 1959.

Northwest climber Bill Pilling reports that Galen Rowell, who was stormed off the ridge while training for his 1975 attempt on K2, said Yocum Ridge was the hardest alpine ice climb in the Northwest—with steep snow to 60 degrees, glacier travel, and altitude. And despite a growing number of ascents per year and a fairly moderate rating, the route still carries a fearsome reputation, largely because most of the climbing is on the distinctive rime that forms on Hood. It is a different kind of ice that demands extra care and some experience on the part of would-be climbers. Belays and anchors in the rime are often unreliable, and shaky tool placements require confident surefootedness. While water ice might be found (take a few ice screws), most of the climbing is on snow or rime ice. Bollards or snow pickets pounded into the rime are the best anchors for the route; alpine picks seem to work best in the rime, but frequently one must clear the top surface and use the shaft of the ice tool.

The ridge does have a convenient bailout route: one can come down Leuthold Couloir from the saddle at about half height if the weather turns or conditions become unfavorable. And like many routes on Hood, a predawn start enables a fit party to do the route in a long day from Timberline Lodge, unusual for a climb of this seriousness.

First ascent ▲ Fred Beckey and Leo Scheiblehner, April 1959
Elevation ▲ 11,235 feet
Difficulty ▲ Grade IV; AI 3; steep snow to 60 degrees, glacier travel, altitude
Time ▲ 1–2 days round trip; 8–10 hours one-way, car to summit
Equipment ▲ Ice ax, crampons, 2 ice tools
Season ▲ January–May

Approach (Grade II): Follow the approach to Timberline Lodge given for climb 1, Palmer Glacier/South Side.

Route: From the east side of Timberline Lodge, climb approximately a mile through the trees (do not climb up the groomed ski slopes) to the Silcox Hut, approximately 7,000 feet elevation. Continue climbing another mile to the end of the Palmer Ski Lift (at approximately 8,500 feet). From the top of the Palmer Ski Lift, ascend to the left (west) toward Illumination Rock and reach Illumination Saddle (9,320 feet). Descend the north side of the saddle to the flats at the head of the Reid Glacier. Cross to the north side of the Reid, then contour west (at approximately 8,000 feet) on to the moderately angled western end of Yocum Ridge. Walk up moderate slopes of the lower ridge until it steepens beneath the first gendarme. There are at least two variations to pass the first gendarme.

Option 1: The first, and easiest, is to pass it on the north side by traversing down and left across snow and ice or mixed terrain until you can see steep snow-and-ice ramps (approximately 60 degrees) heading toward the notch between the first and second gendarmes. Climb the ramps to a ledge on the north side of the notch, then go left up a spectacular "half-pipe" gully leading onto the upper part of the second gendarme.

Option 2: The second option around the first gendarme is the more technical south flank. Traverse snow and ice to the right to a belay station beneath a hanging gully. Climb a steep ice (some mixed ground) wall to gain entry to the gully, then follow gullies and ribs up and right to a belay near the ridge crest at the west end of the notch between the first and second gendarmes. Follow the narrow crest forming the notch for one sensational pitch to reach the upper slopes of the second gendarme.

From the upper slopes of the second gendarme, climb down into the notch between the second gendarme and the next small tower. (Teams with double or twin ropes can fashion a bollard on the second gendarme for a back belay for the second climber on the down-climb into the notch.) From the notch, rappel 150 feet down the north side onto a steep snow slope. (A big sling can be placed over the small tower to serve as a rappel anchor.) Traverse the snow slope east and up to the broad snow saddle separating the steep upper buttress from the lower arête.

Cross the saddle to the south side of the ridge and follow the base of the rimed-up rocks high on the left bank of Leuthold Couloir. After a few hundred feet passing above fearfully steep chimneys and rime pillars, turn left up a gully and reach the crest again after several pitches. Follow the easy but spectacularly narrow crest to where it meets the summit ridge at the Queens Chair. Walk the beautiful snow ridge to the summit.

Descent: From the summit, find the top of the chute leading down to the South Side route (see Descent for climb 1, Palmer Glacier/South Side).

3 SANDY HEADWALL GRADE III

A steep snow-and-ice climb of distinction, the Sandy Headwall is a more serious route than the South Side, requiring a higher level of experience and mountaineering skills to deal with the steep snow and/or ice to 45 degrees, glacier travel, and altitude. The route takes a direct line up the west face of the peak; as the climber goes higher, the slope gets steeper and steeper and the ridges close in to give this snow-and-ice route a serious, satisfying alpine feel. Like all such routes, conditions can vary tremendously. But climbers should be prepared for snow with short sections of hard water ice higher up, until the crest of the ridge is reached and the summit attained via snow slopes. The Sandy Headwall offers an outstanding route to the summit and, out-of-the-way and more difficult to reach, an excellent way to escape the crowds elsewhere on the mountain.

First ascent ▲ Joe Leuthold and Russ McJury, June 1937
Elevation ▲ 11,235 feet
Difficulty ▲ Grade III; steep snow and/or ice to 45 degrees, glacier travel, altitude
Time ▲ 1–2 days round trip
Equipment ▲ Ice ax, crampons, second ice tool
Season ▲ May–June; rockfall danger increases later in season

Approach (Grade II+): Follow the approach to Timberline Lodge given for climb 1, Palmer Glacier/South Side.

Route: From Timberline Lodge, follow the South Side route (climb 1) up the Palmer Glacier; near the top of the lifts, veer left and climb to Illumination Saddle (9,320 feet) just above Illumination Rock. From the saddle, drop down to the Reid Glacier and continue across. Traverse around the foot of Yocum Ridge onto the Sandy Glacier, or climb over the lower section of Yocum Ridge (approximately 8,600 feet) and onto the Sandy Glacier.

Traverse left (north) across the Sandy Glacier to its head, and ascend the headwall. Follow steep slopes (to 45 degrees) up to where the route narrows (stay left of the upper buttress of Yocum Ridge). Climb up the "hourglass" to the point where upper Yocum Ridge meets Cathedral Ridge, and ascend the snow slopes of the upper ridge to the summit.

Descent: Follow the same descent as for climb 1, Palmer Glacier/South Side.

MOUNT ST. HELENS ————————

▲ *Monitor Ridge and Swift Glacier*

The chief allure of climbing this shattered volcano is the glimpse over the rim into "the hole," at the smoking, pulsating lava dome in the crater of this living mountain. The nontechnical route up the moderate slopes holds great appeal for climbers of all abilities who wish to take in this unusual sight, and has become a favorite for ski ascents as well.

Even though Mount St. Helens is not considered a difficult climb, this blown-apart mountain harbors hazards, some of them out of the ordinary for Cascade volcanoes. Its relatively high elevation, irregular and frequently snow-covered slopes, and rapidly changing weather conditions can prove dangerous to those not properly experienced or equipped. In addition to the avalanche hazard that can exist on the route in early season, dangerous conditions may exist at the rim as well. Cornices

Mount St. Helens from the south, showing the Monitor Ridge climbing route (Photo by Austin Post, USGS)

frequently form around the rim; take care to avoid them. Rockfall is another real hazard around the highly unstable rim. The potential for rapidly changing weather and poor visibility underscores the fact that Mount St. Helens is as hazardous as any of the Cascade volcanoes, even if it is somewhat lower.

Mount St. Helens is a mountain completely different from what it was before its explosive eruption in 1980, but only the old-timers remember that. Even in its truncated state, however, the mountain remains interesting. The views into the crater itself make up for what the mountain now lacks in climbing challenges since it lost more than 1,000 feet of altitude and a cubic mile of material in the eruption. Climbers doing the peak may wish to make side trips for up-close views of the blast zone, the blown-down forest, Spirit Lake, Coldwater Ridge, and other areas affected by the cataclysmic event.

Special Considerations: Permits are required for climbing Mount St. Helens. Obtain reservations for climbing permits from the Mount St. Helens National Volcanic Monument headquarters (360-247-3900; 360-247-3961 climbing hot line) near the town of Amboy, located on State Highway 503 east of Woodland. The number of climbers allowed on the mountain is limited; obtaining a permit reservation in advance is recommended for anytime between April and October. Without an advance reservation, it may still be possible to obtain a climbing permit the day before the climb by applying for one of a limited number (currently fifty) of "next-day" permits available each day. These permits are sold at Jack's Restaurant and Store (360-231-4276) on Highway 503, 23 miles east of Woodland. The "lottery" is held each day at 6:00 P.M. (arrive 10 minutes early) for permits good for the next day. (If demand does not exceed supply, permits may be available for the same day on a first-come, first-served basis.) The permit fee is $15 per person, per climb, year-round. Rangers aggressively enforce the rules on St. Helens, ticketing anyone without a permit above 4,800 feet and assessing a $100 fine. Sno-Park permit and Northwest Forest Pass required.

Keep in mind that Mount St. Helens is an active volcano. In addition to the usual risks of mountaineering, climbers on the mountain expose themselves to hazards of volcanic activity that cannot always be predicted. Volcanic activity advisories are posted at the climbers register.

4 MONITOR RIDGE AND SWIFT GLACIER GRADE II+

It is ski mountaineers who account for much of this route's popularity, and the south-facing slope is conducive to the formation of stable, forgiving "corn snow." The route on Mount St. Helens is relatively gentle as backcountry ski routes go, but it is big enough to be interesting: a 4,000-foot fall-line ski run will put a smile on any ski mountaineer's face. Ascents can be made on skis with skins, if conditions permit.

First ascent ▲ Unknown
Elevation ▲ 8,365 feet
Difficulty ▲ Grade II+; snow slopes to 25 degrees
Time ▲ 5–8 hours one-way, car to summit
Equipment ▲ Ice ax, crampons
Season ▲ March-June

Climbers on the crater rim of Mount St. Helens (Photo by Keith Gunnar)

Approach (Grade I): There are two starting points, Climbers Bivouac and, in winter or in times of heavy snowpack, Marble Mountain Sno-Park.

Climbers Bivouac: Drive Interstate 5 to Woodland; take exit 21 and head east on State Highway 503. Continue on Highway 503 through the hamlet of Cougar until it becomes Forest Road 90; 5 miles beyond Cougar, turn left on FR 8300. Continue on FR 8300 for approximately 3–4 miles to a fork; bear slightly left, leaving FR 8300, onto FR 8100. Drive 1.5 miles on FR 8100 to its intersection with FR 830; turn right on FR 830 and drive for 3.5 miles to Climbers Bivouac at 3,740 feet (car camping here, but no water).

Take Ptarmigan Trail No. 216A; for the first 2 miles and 1,000 feet, follow the well-marked path through lush green forest (snow in early season). Then climb up to timberline (6,600 feet) on the snow slopes of Monitor Ridge toward the summit, about 4.5 miles from the trailhead.

Marble Mountain Sno-Park: On plowed FR 8300 at the fork at FR 8100, continue on FR 8300 3 miles to the Sno-Park (2,700 feet).

From the west side of the parking area, follow the Swift Creek Trail No. 244B north, joining trail No. 244, still called the Swift Creek Trail. At 2.5 miles from the Sno-Park, the route emerges above timberline (6,600 feet).

Route: In late season, with the snow cover gone, the route from timberline ascends a series of lava flows that form steep and unstable boulder fields, talus, and scree, followed by 1,000 feet of loose and erodible volcanic ash. If you go at this time of year, follow the route marked by wooden posts, thus protecting returning vegetation.

In winter or in times of heavy snowpack, the route from timberline is via Worm Flows winter route. Above timberline, cross to the west side of Swift Creek immediately upstream from Chocolate Falls, and climb north along the first ridge system west of Swift Creek. This ridge trends slightly westward, joining the Monitor Ridge route at about 7,500 feet. An unbroken snow slope leads to the top for the final 800–900 feet. This route can be used when a winter snowpack prevents the higher start, but be aware of changing snow conditions and possible avalanche danger.

Descent: Descend the climbing route; skis or snowboard recommended.

MOUNT ADAMS ━━━━━━━━━━━━━━━━━━━━━━━━━━━

▲ *South Spur* ▲ *Mazama Glacier and the Castle* ▲ *Adams Glacier*

Second in height only to Mount Rainier, Mount Adams' gigantic bulk is revealed late in the year for the rubble heap it is. But its situation and altitude make it irresistible, and the routes recommended include perhaps the easiest route up any of the Cascade volcanoes (next to Mount St. Helens), as well as a steep glacier climb on what is surely the grandest of the mountain's many big glaciers. The views from Mount Adams' huge summit plateau feature the Goat Rocks peaks and Mount St. Helens nearby, Mount Rainier to the north, and, across the Columbia, the southern Cascades—Mount Hood, Mount Jefferson, and the Sisters on a clear day. The south side route is an excellent ski outing in May and June.

Mount Adams definitely shows a gentle side, but climbers should be wary. Any climb of a Cascade volcano can present altitude problems, but Mount Adams, at more than 12,000 feet, begins to touch the danger zone where altitude sickness can turn lethal quickly. Climbers should be able to recognize the symptoms of altitude-related edemas—pulmonary and cerebral—and be ready to descend rapidly if such a condition is suspected.

A greater danger to climbers on Mount Adams may be the possibility of being caught in a whiteout. Even on the "walk-up" south side route, inexperienced climbers should be aware of the potential for rapidly changing weather and deteriorating visibility. Neophytes are often aghast at the speed with which clouds can form, making it difficult to see a ropemate, much less find the right route off the mountain. Be prepared; carry a compass (an altimeter in conjunction with a compass is even better) and wands, and make prudence the better part of valor when the weather shows signs of changing.

Special Considerations: Permits are required for backpackers and climbers entering the Mount Adams Wilderness Area from the south, but obtaining them is easy: merely self-register and pick up a permit at all popular trailheads. The Forest Service asks climbers to sign in and sign out at either the Cowlitz Valley Ranger District (360-497-7565) in Randle or the Mount Adams Ranger District (509-395-2501) in Trout Lake. Call either ranger station for information and up-to-date regulations. Northwest Forest Pass required.

Climbers on Mount Adams' South Spur (Photo by Mark Kroese)

5 SOUTH SPUR GRADE I

The South Spur, South Rib, or so-called Standard route, which is approached from Cold Springs, is—along with climb 4 on Mount St. Helens—one of the easiest and safest routes up any of the Cascade volcanoes. This is a nontechnical route, so much so, in fact, that to many climbers it is just too boring. It is basically a long, long snow slog that does not require so much as a rope. The route ascends snowfields to the false summit (late in the year, trails beaten down by mules and horses carrying sulphur on this route in the 1930s are still visible) before climbing up to the summit plateau. This is a good choice of route for climbers new to the Cascades who wish to gain experience on volcanoes.

First ascent ▲ Henry Coe, Phelps, Julia Johnson, Sarah Fisher, 1863 or 1864
Elevation ▲ 12,276 feet
Difficulty ▲ Grade I; moderate snow slopes, altitude
Time ▲ 1–2 days round trip; 4–7 hours one-way, car to summit
Equipment ▲ Ice ax, crampons, snowshoes or skis in early season, wands
Season ▲ May-August; can be icy in late season

Approach (Grade II): From State Highway 141 at the town of Trout Lake, drive north on a road signed "Mount Adams Recreation Area." Continue north, following signs to Morrison Creek Campground; continue on Forest Road 8040 to its end at Cold Springs Campground (5,600 feet). Find the trailhead for the South Climb Trail.

Route: Hike approximately 3.5 miles on the South Climb Trail to the Crescent Glacier and on to the "Lunch Counter," a distinctive shoulder plateau that some climbers use as a high camp (approximately 9,400 feet). Ascend north toward the false (south) summit at 11,657 feet and on across the summit plateau to the true or middle summit.

Descent: Descend the climbing route.

6 MAZAMA GLACIER AND THE CASTLE GRADE II+

A more appealing and less crowded variation on the south side of the mountain is approached via Bird Creek Meadows, and ascends the Mazama Glacier to the false summit. This variation has a higher camp, is more interesting, and includes views down into the Klickitat Glacier icefall on the ascent. The Mazama route also encourages the 2-hour detour over to the Castle. A prominent outrider peak, the "Little Tahoma" of Mount Adams, and an extraordinary viewpoint from its flat summit, the Castle is the resting place of the ashes of Claude Rusk, who did so much pioneering on the mountain. Keith Gunnar, a prolific Cascades photographer and devotee of this route, says, "I would never climb Adams without doing the Castle—it is the frosting on the cake, a really neat place."

First ascent ▲ Unknown
Elevation ▲ 12,276 feet
Difficulty ▲ Grade II+; glacier travel
Time ▲ 1–2 days round trip; 4–7 hours one-way from high camp
Equipment ▲ Ice ax, crampons; snowshoes or skis in early season
Season ▲ May–August; can be icy in late season

Approach (Grade II+): Follow the approach to Cold Springs Campground given for climb 5, South Spur.

From Cold Springs Campground, hike the South Climb Trail approximately 1.2 miles to Round the Mountain Trail (6,200 feet); turn right and follow Round the Mountain Trail for approximately 2 miles to Bird Creek Meadows. From the meadows, ascend the lower slopes of old moraines to a small pass or notch in the ridge

Mount Adams from the south: A. South Spur (climb 5); B. Mazama Glacier (climb 6).
(Photo by Austin Post, USGS)

Daniel Kroese, age twelve, on the summit of Mount Adams (Photo by Mark Kroese)

(Early Morning Ridge) between the Mazama and Klickitat Glaciers. This little pass (8,350 feet), known as Sunrise Camp, makes the ideal high camp for the Mazama route.

Note: A more direct driving approach to Bird Creek Meadows is no longer practical due to heavy restrictions on entering the Yakama Indian Reservation. Contact the Trout Lake ranger station for up-to-date information (see Special Considerations, above).

Route: From Sunrise Camp, ascend the right side of the Mazama Glacier, usually uncrevassed but slightly steeper (to 25 degrees) than the South Spur route. On the way up, be sure to clamber up on Early Morning Ridge, which separates the Mazama Glacier from the rugged Klickitat Glacier, for good views into the icefall below. Climb the Mazama Glacier to the false summit, and follow the regular South Spur route from there.

Side trip to the Castle: From the false summit, traverse across the lower summit ice field to the obvious rocky, blocky prominence. Scramble loose, unappealing gullies to the flat summit—almost an acre of pumice—and the monument to early climber Claude Rusk. From the Castle, traverse back to the false summit to pick up the South Spur route to the summit, or take the more direct, more challenging, and more interesting route directly up the ice field to the summit.

Descent: Descend the climbing route.

North Ridge

The Adams Glacier on Mount Adams (Photo by Austin Post, USGS)

7 ADAMS GLACIER GRADE III

An interesting climbing route on a big and very broken glacier tumbling down a narrow corridor between rock walls from Mount Adam's expansive summit plateau, this is certainly one of the best climbs on the mountain. Suitable only in early season, the most challenging part of the route is the steep icefall at midheight. A moderate approach and magnificently scenic camps (views to Mount St. Helens, Mount Rainier, the Goat Rocks, and the tumbling Adams Glacier itself) in Adams Glacier Meadows make this a memorable package.

First ascent ▲ Fred Beckey, Dave Lind, Robert Mulhall, July 1945
Elevation ▲ 12,276 feet
Difficulty ▲ Grade III; ice and snow to 45 degrees, glacier travel, altitude
Time ▲ 2–3 days round trip; 4–7 hours one-way from high camp
Equipment ▲ Ice ax, crampons, ice screws and/or pickets, second ice tool
Season ▲ May-July; not recommended for late season

Approach (Grade II+): From US 12 at the town of Randle, drive southeast 32 miles on Forest Road 23; turn left on FR 2329, passing Taklakh Lake in 2 miles and reaching the parking area and trailhead (4,600 feet) in 5.7 miles.

Climber in the icefall of the Adams Glacier, Mount Adams (Photo by Joe Catellani)

Mount Adams from the north, showing the North Ridge descent route
(Photo by Ed Cooper)

Hike the Killen Creek Trail No. 113 through open forest and meadows; in 3.5 miles cross the old Pacific Crest Trail and, just beyond, the current Pacific Crest Trail (6,100 feet). The trail here and beyond is hard to follow, and in early season may be obscured by snow; a map and compass are strongly advised.

In 5.5 miles enter the broad expanse of open, rolling meadow (approximately 6,900 feet) directly beneath the northwest face of the mountain, a beautiful spot and one in which it is very easy to lose one's bearings. Pay attention to where the trail enters and leaves the meadows. There is ample water and outstanding views from camps that look directly into the tumbling Adams Glacier.

Route: From high camp in the meadows, hike southeasterly over moraines and/or snow to the foot of the Adams Glacier (approximately 7,000 feet). The long lower section of glacier is quite moderate for at least the first mile. As the way steepens, the glacier begins to break up into a profusion of crevasses—some quite large—that change from year to year. From the base of the icefall, the route skirts the worst of the broken area on either side, depending on conditions, with the usual route ascending the right side of the icefall, then veering left as the glacier eases, to gain the crest of the summit plateau. The true summit lies a long trudge (0.5 mile) away across the huge summit plateau to the south.

Descent: Descend the nontechnical North Ridge back to the meadows; be prepared for short sections of steep snow and unstable pumice while descending the North Ridge.

MOUNT RAINIER

▲ *Disappointment Cleaver/Ingraham Glacier* ▲ *Little Tahoma* ▲ *Emmons Glacier*
▲ *Liberty Ridge*

Mount Rainier is by far the most coveted summit in the Cascade Range. At 14,410 feet, just 84 feet lower than highest-in-the-Lower-48 Mount Whitney, this glacier-clad volcano towers above Seattle and much of the Northwest countryside. With the largest system of glaciers in the United States (outside Alaska), the giant hulk of a mountain carries 35 square miles of ice. Mount Rainier's familiar shape and looming presence are a virtual symbol of the Cascades and the Northwest. This far-reaching visibility makes it a prime destination for novices and expert mountaineers alike. Mount Rainier is a tremendous resource for climbers, offering great mountaineering experiences of many different kinds: routes recommended here embody the variety of climbs on the peak, ranging from the least-technical route on the mountain to the standard glacier route, and an airy ridge. A novel ice climb on Observation Rock, a route on Little Tahoma—the third-highest peak in the Cascades—complete the menu of Rainer routes offered here, and demonstrate how varied the climbing can be on this big mountain.

Mount Rainier from the south, showing the approach to Camp Muir and the winter or alternative route to Little Tahoma (Photo by Mike Gauthier)

If the mountain's allure is irresistible, it can also exact a deadly toll. The thousands of tourists who gather at Paradise on a sunny weekend in August see only one side of Mount Rainier's character. The benign aspect the mountain projects on a clear summer day is misleading, for conditions can quickly turn grim. More climbers, hikers, and casual visitors have been killed on this mountain than on all other Cascades peaks combined.

With more than 11,000 official summit attempts per year as of 1999 (about half are successful), it is easy for those not familiar with climbing in the Cascades to get the mistaken notion that climbing Mount Rainier is not a serious challenge. On the contrary; high altitude, active glaciers, avalanches, falling rock and ice, and—most serious of all—rapidly changing weather combine to create a hazardous environment. Mount Rainier, in fact, makes a realistic and appropriate training ground for expeditions to Denali and the Himalaya precisely because of its altitude, glaciation, and potential for bad weather. Perhaps the greatest danger on the mountain is the possibility of whiteout conditions, leaving climbers lost on dangerous terrain. Be prepared, use good judgment, bring a map and compass (a compass in conjunction with an altimeter or a GPS device is even better), bring bivy gear, and know that an ascent of Mount Rainier by any route should be undertaken with the utmost respect. Climbers should be aware that avalanche hazard related to summer storms is always possible above 10,000 feet.

Mount Rainier is a rewarding but strenuous experience. Prior conditioning is essential for an enjoyable ascent. On Rainier, good physical conditioning and a steady pace are the best recipe for success on both technical and nontechnical routes. Acclimatization to altitude is equally important but, and if one lives near sea level, more difficult to achieve. In that case, the best solution is to take 2 or 3 nights to reach the summit instead of 1; this technique aids in adjustment to the thinner air and generally makes the climb something other than a grim physical ordeal. At more than 14,000 feet, Mount Rainier can present potentially lethal altitude problems. Headaches, nausea, lassitude, and generalized malaise are common symptoms of altitude sickness; much more dangerous are pulmonary edema and cerebral edema, both potentially fatal. Learn to recognize the symptoms, and descend at once if either of these conditions is suspected.

Other maladies can plague climbers while attempting Rainier. Sunburn may be the most common. Climbers must take care to protect all exposed body parts with a sunscreen rated at SPF 15 or higher. Dehydration is another common ailment; be sure to consume at least three quarts of water per day, more if you feel you need it. Clear urine is a good indicator of proper hydration. Glacier goggles must be worn to prevent snow blindness.

With those caveats in mind, it is worth emphasizing that Mount Rainier is a lot of fun. An attempt by a fit party climbing within its comfort level of skill can be extraordinary, an experience on the volcano's high, icy slopes that will linger in the memory.

From Mount Rainier, Little Tahoma stands as an impressive sentinel of rock that divides the Emmons and Ingraham Glaciers. Climbers ascending one of Rainier's two most popular routes, the Disappointment Cleaver or Emmons/Winthrop Glacier, enjoy dramatic views of Little Tahoma's jagged west ridge and steep north face.

Special Considerations: For novice climbers on Rainier, the authors strongly recommend hiring a guide. Presently, there are five guide services that the National Park Service permits to lead summit climbs. Rainier Mountaineering Inc. (206-569-2227) is the oldest and the only concessioned guide service, offering 1-day climbing schools with 2-day summit attempts throughout the summer on the Disappointment Cleaver route. Four other guide services hold conditional use permits, and lead summit climbs up the Emmons Glacier: Alpine Ascents International (206-378-1927), American Alpine Institute (360-671-1505), Cascade Alpine Guides (800-981-0381), and Mount Rainier Alpine Guides (360-569-2604). All services have limited space, and interested parties should contact them in the winter to schedule climbs for the following spring and summer.

Climbers choosing to go it on their own should be adept at crevasse rescue before venturing high on the mountain, have solid glacier-travel skills, and make prudence the better part of valor when the weather changes for the worse. The choice of route should correspond to the team's skills and experience, not just the most proficient member of the team. Snow, ice, and glacier climbs change dramatically throughout the year on Mount Rainier. In the spring and early summer, climbers can expect ample snow cover, which intensifies the avalanche and crevasse hazards. Later in the summer and fall, however, the glaciers become hard and icy and the routes are longer and more circuitous. Teams should be prepared for varied conditions. *Mount Rainier: A Climbing Guide* (The Mountaineers, 1999), written by lead climbing ranger Mike Gauthier, is an excellent resource full of firsthand information that is very useful to independent climbers.

All climbers in Mount Rainier National Park who intend to go above Camp Muir or Camp Schurman or travel on glaciers must register and fill out a climber information card prior to the climb. Climbing permits can be obtained at Longmire, Paradise, White River, and Carbon River ranger stations. Call the backcountry information desk (360-569-4453) or check the website *(www.nps.gov/mora)* for information on permits. "Self-registration" is allowed only in the fall, winter, and early spring. Limits have been established for many of the high camps (110 people per night at Camp Muir; 35 people per night at Camp Schurman) and remote alpine areas on the mountain. Inquire about permits and limits before arriving. Mount Rainier now has a backcountry permit reservation system; call the backcountry information desk. Sixty percent of the allowable sites can be reserved; the rest are available on a first-come, first-served basis. There is a $20 fee for the assurance and the park will require you to prepay your $15 per person climbing fee up front.

Climbing fees currently are $15 per person, or climbers may purchase an annual climbing permit for $25. (Note: Fees are expected to rise in 2003.) Revenue from this climbing fee, unlike other park fees, actually stays in Mount Rainier National Park and benefits climbers directly. These funds help pay for the helicopter flights to remove human-waste barrels on the mountain, for new state-of-the-art solar toilets at the high camps, and for staffing climbing rangers at the high camps.

Climbers should understand that Mount Rainier National Park is popular and heavily used. To keep the park as pristine as possible, the Park Service has restrictions

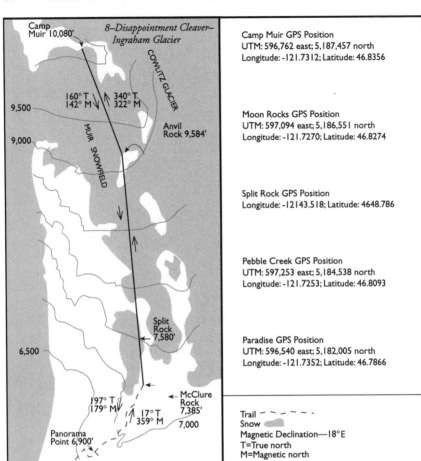

Camp Muir 10,080'

8–Disappointment Cleaver–Ingraham Glacier

COWLITZ GLACIER

9,500

160° T 142° M | 340° T 322° M

Anvil Rock 9,584'

9,000

MUIR SNOWFIELD

6,500

Split Rock 7,580'

McClure Rock 7,385'

197° T 179° M | 17° T 359° M

7,000

Panorama Point 6,900'

Glacier Vista

To Paradise

Camp Muir GPS Position
UTM: 596,762 east; 5,187,457 north
Longitude: -121.7312; Latitude: 46.8356

Moon Rocks GPS Position
UTM: 597,094 east; 5,186,551 north
Longitude: -121.7270; Latitude: 46.8274

Split Rock GPS Position
Longitude: -12143.518; Latitude: 4648.786

Pebble Creek GPS Position
UTM: 597,253 east; 5,184,538 north
Longitude: -121.7253; Latitude: 46.8093

Paradise GPS Position
UTM: 596,540 east; 5,182,005 north
Longitude: -121.7352; Latitude: 46.7866

Trail - - - - - -
Snow
Magnetic Declination—18°E
T=True north
M=Magnetic north

GPS coordinates are provided in UTM and
Decimal Degrees (DD) and are in NAD1927.

Climbing ranger Mike Gauthier at Mount Rainier National Park reminds climbers that the information in the map above can save lives as having to descend from Camp Muir in bad weather is fairly common. To the compass vectors and GPS positions provided by the Park Service, veteran Rainier guide Dave Hahn suggests using Split Rock as a waypoint above Pebble Creek, as it is never covered in snow; when you find the rock on the descent, you know you go left. (Locations for Split Rock and Moon Rocks are useful only if one can recognize the landmarks, which aren't obvious.)

regarding party size, camping areas, and sanitation practices to help preserve the wilderness integrity of the park. Use the toilets at the popular high camps. If there is no toilet, regulations require climbers to "blue bag" their human waste. Used bags can be deposited in barrels at key locations along popular routes. Talk to a ranger, call the backcountry information desk, or check the website for information and up-to-date limits and regulations.

8 DISAPPOINTMENT CLEAVER/INGRAHAM GLACIER
GRADE III

Undoubtedly the most popular route on Mount Rainier, this one starts from the main visitors area at Paradise and is the principal route used by the concessioned guide service, Rainier Mountaineering Inc. The route is characterized by the moderate Muir Snowfield to the 10,000-foot level (known as Camp Muir), where there is a guide hut, a ranger station, a public shelter, and outhouse facilities. From Camp Muir, the summit-day route crosses the Cowlitz and Ingraham Glaciers and then ascends the cleaver dividing the Emmons and Ingraham Glaciers.

First ascent ▲ Unknown, probably Stevens and Van Trump via Gibraltar Ledges
Elevation ▲ 14,410 feet
Difficulty ▲ Grade III; 30- to 35-degree snow and ice, glacier travel, altitude
Time ▲ 2–4 days round trip; 6–10 hours one-way from Camp Muir
Equipment ▲ Ice ax, crampons, snow anchor, wands
Season ▲ May-August

Approach (Grade III+): Enter Mount Rainier National Park through the Nisqually entrance via State Highway 706 and drive to the large parking lot near the Paradise Inn

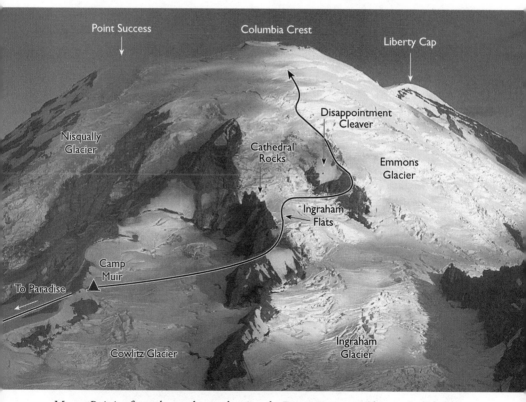

Mount Rainier from the southeast, showing the Disappointment Cleaver–Ingraham Glacier route from Camp Muir (Photo by Mike Gauthier)

Climber descending the dusty rubble of Disappointment Cleaver toward the Ingraham Glacier (Photo by Mike Gauthier)

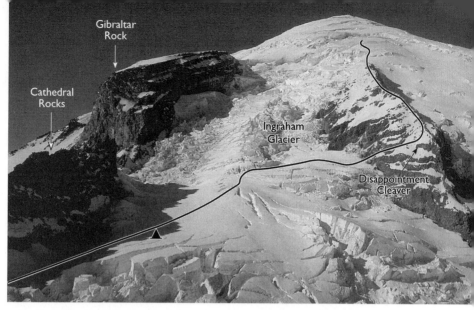

Ingraham Glacier, showing route details on the upper Disappointment Cleaver route
(Photo by Mike Gauthier)

(5,420 feet). The climbing ranger station where permits are obtained is in the small A-frame on the north side of the lot. Find the paved trail that starts on the north side of the large parking lot.

Follow the Skyline Trail for 1.5 miles to the long switchback on Panorama Point (6,900 feet) and the junction with the Pebble Creek Trail (snow in early season). Continue 0.5 mile via the Pebble Creek Trail or on snow to the edge of the permanent snowfield (Muir Snowfield), which can be crevassed in late season. Climb up toward Gibraltar Rock (trending north, then northwest) to Camp Muir (10,080 feet), approximately 4.5 miles from Paradise. A stone shelter (can be crowded and noisy), level ground—most of it on snow—for tents, an outhouse, guide service facilities, and a ranger station (staffed in season) are found at Camp Muir, with good views to the south all the way to Oregon.

Route: From Camp Muir, traverse east across the Cowlitz Glacier; find the climbers path (at approximately 10,400 feet; snow in early season) on the east side of the Cowlitz where it meets a rocky ridge. Climb the boot track or snow up and over the pumice ridge known as Cathedral Rocks through the middle of three gaps, reaching the Ingraham Glacier at 10,800 feet. Climb to Ingraham Flats at 11,100 feet (good camping; privacy screens and barrels for human waste), traversing onto Disappointment Cleaver above its base at approximately 11,300 feet. Find the boot track (snow in early season) in scree and pumice that switchbacks up to the top of the cleaver (12,400 feet). Be careful to avoid rockfall from other parties, particularly lower on the cleaver. Parties should complete the traverse under the Ingraham icefall and onto the spine of the cleaver as quickly as possible.

From the top of the cleaver, ascend the Ingraham Glacier in a westerly direction, negotiating crevasses as necessary. The route varies from year to year; when in doubt, follow the guide service's "sidewalk," an obvious trail beaten down by guided parties. The true summit (Columbia Crest) lies across the crater to the northwest.

Descent: Descend the climbing route.

9 LITTLE TAHOMA GRADE II+

At 11,138 feet, Little Tahoma (commonly referred to as "Little T") weighs in as Washington State's third-highest summit. Its significance, however, is often dwarfed because it has such a popular neighbor, Mount Rainier.

An ascent up Little Tahoma's standard route is relatively straightforward and simple. Climbers are warned that all rock on the peak should be viewed with distrust. Little Tahoma is actually the remains of a once larger and higher Mount Rainier. Eruptions, mudflows, and years of glaciation have eroded Rainier's original mass, leaving Little Tahoma a satellite peak. Therefore its rock, like Rainier's, is volcanic, loose, and crumbly. Despite these warnings, the climb is aesthetically pleasing and provides outstanding views of Rainier's east face. It also should be noted that Little Tahoma is a great ski descent in the early season.

First ascent ▲ J. B. Flett and Henry H. Garrison, August 29, 1894 (via East Shoulder); first ski ascent: Paul Gilbreath and J. Wendell Trosper, April 1933

Elevation ▲ 11,138 feet

Difficulty ▲ Grade II+; snow and ice to 35 degrees

Time ▲ 1–2 days round trip

Equipment ▲ Ice ax, crampons

Season ▲ Winter–early season via Paradise; early season–June via White River

Approach (Grade III): Most climbers approach Little Tahoma from White River, but approaching from Paradise is another viable option, and the only option in winter or early spring.

Climber approaches the top of Little Tahoma in spring conditions
(Photo by Mike Gauthier)

Skier approaches Little Tahoma, Mount Rainier (Photo by Andreas Schmidt)

Via White River: Enter Mount Rainier National Park through the White River entrance via US 410; drive 2 miles from the park entrance to a parking lot just beyond the Fryingpan Creek bridge (3,800 feet). The trail starts across the highway.

For the first 2 miles, the trail ascends gradually through old-growth forest to a point overlooking Fryingpan Creek, and at 3 miles passes a large avalanche debris zone. The last mile to Summerland (5,998 feet) follows a steep switchback through meadows that in season are rife with flowers. Continue above Summerland on the

Snowboarder on the Fryingpan Glacier approaching Little Tahoma on Mount Rainier (Photo by Mike Gauthier)

Wonderland Trail for approximately 0.3 mile, leaving the trail at 6,100 feet and heading uphill in a southwesterly direction. Skirt rocky cliffs on the right (northwest) while climbing south to Meany Crest (7,000 feet), and then ascend southwesterly onto the eastern edge of Fryingpan Glacier near Point 7573. Ascend the Fryingpan Glacier in a southwesterly direction to a saddle just south of Point 9323 and just north of Point 9194 on Whitman Crest, which marks the divide between the Fryingpan and Whitman Glaciers. There is camping at the notch (9,000 feet), or on the flats just west of the notch. This area can be icy late in the season.

Via Paradise: For winter or early-season attempts, prior to the opening of the White River entrance, start at Paradise. Climb as though headed to Camp Muir from Paradise (see climb 8, Disappointment Cleaver/Ingraham Glacier). From 8,600 feet on the Muir Snowfield, below Moon Rocks, traverse northeast below Anvil Rock onto the upper Paradise Glacier. Once you have rounded below Anvil Rock, head northeast and traverse across the Cowlitz Glacier toward Cathedral Rocks, avoiding the crevasse fields below 8,400 feet. Cross Cathedral Rocks, a rock cleaver that divides the Cowlitz Glacier from the Ingraham Glacier, at a gap near 8,450 feet. Once on the Ingraham, continue north and east across the glacier as crevasses allow toward a prominent notch near 8,800 feet. Crossing through that notch leads to the Whitman Glacier. Continue up the Whitman Glacier toward Little Tahoma's summit via the standard route.

Route: Once through the notch (9,000 feet) between the Fryingpan and Whitman Glaciers, head west and ascend the Whitman Glacier west toward the summit of

A climber begins descending from the summit of Little Tahoma. (Photo by Mike Gauthier)

Little Tahoma. The slope angle gradually increases as you climb to the head of the glacier at approximately 10,300 feet. The final 800 feet of the route, depending on the snow cover, ascends class 2–3 rock that is notoriously loose. Though the climbing is nontechnical, use caution, as nothing is trustworthy.

Descent: Descend the climbing route.

10 EMMONS GLACIER GRADE III

Probably the least-technical route on Mount Rainier, the Emmons Glacier offers the majesty and beauty of sunrise from high on the mountain while calling for only straightforward glacier-climbing skills and good judgment. The route's high camp is located at Camp Schurman (9,500 feet), and the summit-day route proceeds directly up the "corridor" of the Emmons Glacier, taking the least-crevassed line among the big glacier's huge and yawning crevasses.

First ascent ▲ Warner Fobes, George James, Richard Wells, August 1884
Elevation ▲ 14,410 feet
Difficulty ▲ Grade III; snow-and-ice slopes to 40 degrees, glacier travel, altitude
Time ▲ 2–4 days round trip; 6–12 hours one-way from Camp Schurman
Equipment ▲ Ice ax, crampons, snow anchors, wands
Season ▲ May-August

Approach (Grade II+): Enter Mount Rainier National Park through the White River entrance via US 410; drive 5 miles from the park entrance to the White River bridge and turn left into the White River Campground (4,350 feet). Find the Glacier Basin trailhead in the upper end of the campground.

Follow the trail for 3.1 miles to Glacier Basin (5,900 feet). Good camping is available here, and it makes a good acclimatization camp on a 3-day ascent, which

Overview of Mount Rainier from the east, showing the Emmons Glacier route in its entirety (Photo by Mike Gauthier)

is recommended. (A workable itinerary for sea-level-based climbers is to start late on the first day, bivy at Glacier Basin, climb to high camp at Emmons Flats on the second day, and finally make a summit attempt on the third day.)

From Glacier Basin, a climbers path leads out of the basin toward Inter Glacier; ascend the steep snowfield to Inter Glacier, and ascend the glacier (bearing slightly left) to 8,800 feet. Parties should be roped here; numerous crevasses falls, including a fatality, have occurred on the Inter Glacier. Traverse left between Mount Ruth and Steamboat Prow and descend onto the Emmons Glacier at 8,800 feet. Climb up the

Climbers in low-visibility conditions on the Emmons Glacier, Mount Rainier
(Photo by Mike Gauthier)

Emmons Glacier beside the cliffs of Steamboat Prow to the ranger station, outhouse facilities, and tent city at Camp Schurman (9,500 feet). Camp here, or, for slightly more privacy and a somewhat shorter summit day, climb higher to the slightly sloping Emmons Flats (10,200 feet), where decent tent sites can be dug. Probe for

Climbers on the Emmons Glacier, Mount Rainier, with Little Tahoma, the third-highest peak in the state of Washington, in the background (Photo by Mike Gauthier)

Climbers between 12,000 and 13,000 feet on the Emmons Glacier route on Mount Rainier (Photo by Mike Gauthier)

crevasses before making camp and do not venture unroped beyond the probed area.

Route: From high camp at either Camp Schurman or Emmons Flats, climb southwesterly directly up the Emmons Glacier as crevasses allow. The first half of the route—the so-called "Corridor"—is usually relatively unbroken. Above 12,000 feet, navigate around crevasses as required; the bergschrund can be a problem, particularly later in the season, but most years it can usually be outflanked or crossed via a snow bridge. The summit lies around the crater rim to the north.

Descent: Descend the climbing route.

Climbers on the Emmons Glacier, Mount Rainier, working their way through a crevasse field (Photo by Mike Gauthier)

11 LIBERTY RIDGE GRADE V

On this route, more than 5,000 feet of steep (40- to 50-degree) snow and ice on a prominent ridge rise grandly to bisect the impressive north face of Mount Rainier. Flanked on either side by the mountain's huge summit seracs and ice cliffs, Liberty Ridge is a stupendous place—and, because of its position, a relatively safe and sane place—in a world of violent chaos. As with all snow-and-ice climbs, conditions play a major factor in the difficulty rating: freezing temperatures overnight usually result in the best conditions, and generally the months of May and June are best (weather permitting). With almost a mile of steep snow or ice, Liberty Ridge should be considered a route requiring serious commitment, which means there is some difficulty of retreat. Add changeable weather and the potential for altitude-related illness, and the climb takes on a serious nature. But an ascent of Liberty Ridge under good conditions is a wonderful climb with spectacular views into the Willis Wall. Good camping and bivy skills, and the ability to travel light, serve the climber well on Liberty Ridge.

Climbers should take note that on this climb they are not summiting from high camp with day packs, but carrying all their gear up and over a 14,000-foot mountain. This adds to the strenuousness of the climb. In addition, there is definite rockfall hazard in late season (or warm weather) on Liberty Ridge; for that reason the route is best done early in the season. But underestimating the severity of early-season weather on Mount Rainier can be lethal. Exhaustion, hypothermia, and falls occurring while trying to force a retreat off the ridge have accounted for recent fatalities. Avalanche must also be considered in May and June. While Paradise may have spring conditions, the 45-degree slopes on Liberty Ridge may be quite unstable. All climbers in the Cascades should be aware that statistically they are just as likely to be killed by an avalanche in May as any other month of the year.

Crossing the Carbon Glacier approaching Liberty Ridge (Photo by Mark Kroese)

Thumb Rock

Carbon Glacier

Carbon Glacier

Liberty Ridge from the north (Photo by Mike Gauthier)

Liberty Cap

The summit of Mount Rainier; the crater is 1,300–1,400 feet across.
(Photo by Keith Gunnar)

First ascent ▲ Ome Daiber, Arnie Campbell, Jim Borrow, September 1935; first winter ascent: climbers unknown, January 1976
Elevation ▲ 14,410 feet
Difficulty ▲ Grade V; 50-degree snow or ice, glacier travel, altitude
Time ▲ 3–4 days round trip; 6–12 hours one-way from Thumb Rock
Equipment ▲ Ice ax, crampons, snow anchors, ice screws; shovel and transceiver in early season
Season ▲ May–early July

Approach (Grade III): There are two approaches commonly used to reach the Liberty Ridge route.

Via White River/Glacier Basin: Enter Mount Rainier National Park through the White River entrance and follow the approach to Glacier Basin given for climb 10, Emmons Glacier. (A workable itinerary for sea-level-based climbers is to start late on the first day, bivy at Glacier Basin, climb to high camp at Thumb Rock on the second day, and finally make a summit attempt on the third day.)

From Glacier Basin, follow a climbers path leading toward Inter Glacier; at approximately 6,500 feet take a climbers path veering right (northwest), climbing to

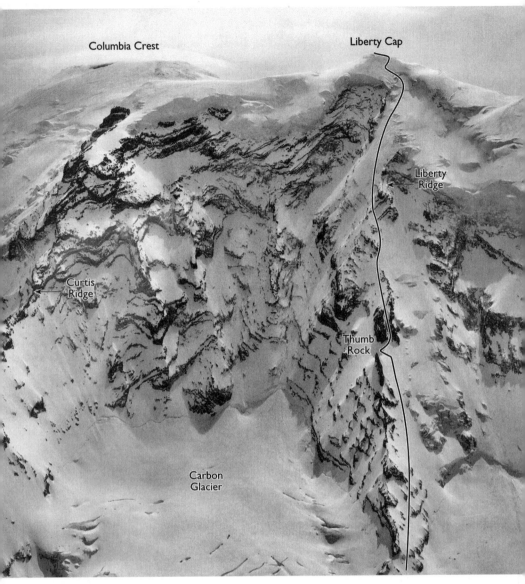

Liberty Ridge route in winter conditions (Photo by Robert Krimmel, USGS)

St. Elmos Pass (7,400 feet). From the pass, a long traverse begins: cross the Winthrop Glacier at approximately 7,200 feet to the broad lower slopes of Curtis Ridge. Traverse talus and scree across Curtis Ridge until able to drop down onto the Carbon Glacier at 7,200 feet, aiming for the toe of Liberty Ridge (8,600 feet).

Via Carbon River/Ipsut Creek: Enter the park through the Carbon River entrance via State Highway 165; drive to the road end at Ipsut Creek Campground (2,300 feet). Find the trailhead at the upper end of the parking lot.

Eric Bilski at 12,000 feet on Liberty Ridge (Photo by Cliff Leight)

Follow the trail and in 0.25 mile, go left (east) on the Wonderland Trail. In a little more than 3 miles, cross the Carbon River on a bridge; just beyond the bridge, take the right (uphill) fork to the small meadows known as Moraine Park. Just above the meadows (6,100 feet), leave the Wonderland Trail and ascend southeast on moraine until able to reach the Carbon Glacier between 7,000 and 7,500 feet. Climb the glacier, aiming for the toe of Liberty Ridge (8,600 feet).

From either approach, most parties climb the right side of Liberty Ridge (snow or scree) to the small campsite at Thumb Rock (10,750 feet).

Route: From Thumb Rock, ascend the ridge up and right via 40- to 45-degree snow-and-ice slopes, or take the left-hand "chute" route. Continue climbing snow slopes along the crest, passing the final prominent rock band ("Black Pyramid") at 12,000 feet on the left (east). Continue climbing the ridge to the Liberty Cap Glacier. Find a route across the bergschrund (may require steep snow-and-ice climbing) to reach Liberty Cap, Mount Rainier's northwest summit at 14,112 feet. From Liberty Cap go east, then south across the broad summit plateau to the true summit (Columbia Crest).

Descent: The descent is usually made via the Emmons Glacier (see climb 10).

Dan Nordstrom, with short skis, after descending the Emmons Glacier route following a carryover from a climb of Liberty Ridge (Photo by Gordy Skoog)

The ridge leading from Castle Peak toward Unicorn Peak, Tatoosh Range
(Photo by Peter Potterfield)

UNICORN PEAK ———————————————

▲ *South Side*

Unicorn Peak, the highest of the Tatoosh peaks that stand due south of Paradise on Rainier's southern flank, is also the most dramatic climbing objective in the "miniature" range. Standing slightly off and to the east from its companion Tatoosh Range peaks, Unicorn Peak shows a striking profile when viewed from the Castle or Pinnacle Peak, the more common Tatoosh destinations. The stark watchtower formation or "horn of the unicorn" is an appealing summit tower of this nearly 7,000-foot peak. A long snow ridge, with a high point known as Foss Peak, connects Unicorn with the Castle. Unicorn can be incorporated into a traverse of the range (starting from Plummer, or from the more distant Eagle Peak, even farther west), but it is big enough and interesting enough to make a worthwhile ascent on its own.

Like Pinnacle, Plummer, and Castle, Unicorn feels bigger than it is because Rainier looms above, lending a high-mountain ambience that powerfully changes the character and feel of the climb. Devotees of this range freely admit they are drawn back to these peaks by the irresistible presence of the mighty volcano and the atmosphere it lends.

Special Considerations: At present, day climbs in the Tatoosh Range do not require registration; overnight trips do, with a backcountry permit. Permits, information, and registration forms can be obtained at Longmire, Paradise, and Carbon River ranger stations. Talk to a ranger or call the backcountry information desk (360-569-4453) for information and up-to-date regulations.

Mount Rainier National Park is heavily used. Please protect the backcountry by obeying all park regulations regarding party size, camping restrictions, and sanitation practices.

12 SOUTH SIDE GRADE II

Unicorn has the appeal of being the highest, biggest, and arguably most interesting of all the Tatoosh peaks, and with the bonus of best viewpoint. It has an interesting approach via Bench Lake and Snow Lake, some circuitous routefinding, and a satisfying finish on rock. Good access on a road plowed for most of the year (during winter months, the road is usually plowed only as far as Narada Falls) extends the season for this climb, despite avalanche danger.

First ascent ▲ Unknown
Elevation ▲ 6,917 feet
Difficulty ▲ Grade II; 5.6 or 4th class; snow to 30 degrees
Time ▲ 3–5 hours one-way, car to summit
Equipment ▲ Ice ax, crampons, 50-meter rope for rappel
Season ▲ April–mid-June

Approach (Grade I+): The Tatoosh Range is approached via the Bench Lake Trail, which can be reached from either the west or the east.

From the west: Enter Mount Rainier National Park through the Nisqually entrance via State Highway 706, and proceed east past Longmire ranger station (all services) toward Paradise. From the junction of the road leading to Paradise, drive 1 mile east of the Reflection Lakes parking lot (4,860 feet) to the Bench Lake trailhead (4,550 feet). In winter or early season, the road may be plowed only as far as Narada Falls, which adds approximately 6 miles to the approach to the trailhead.

From the east: Enter the park through the Stevens Canyon entrance via State Highway 123, and proceed west for 16.5 miles to the Bench Lake trailhead (4,550 feet). In winter or early season, Highway 123 may be closed.

From either approach, follow the Bench Lake Trail as it ascends slightly, traversing meadows as it winds around pleasant Bench Lake, still quite close to the road. Ascend a small rise and drop into the Snow Lake drainage (despite the ups and downs along the trail, both lakes are at nearly the same elevation as the trailhead). Snow Lake (4,675 feet) is at the bottom of a steep-walled cirque; pass the lake on its right (west) side, where the trail ends at the south end of the lake. From here, moderately steep slopes (beware slide danger) lead up and out of the basin onto a steep snowfield/bench. Snow slopes (talus and heather in late season) lead to a low point on the ridge (6,500 feet elevation).

Descending Unicorn Peak
(Photo by Mike Dole)

This saddle can also be reached from the other Tatoosh peaks. From Castle Peak, make a long traverse east along the ridge, over or around the high point known as Foss Peak, to reach the saddle at 6,500 feet.

Route: From the saddle, the route begins to move almost completely around the mountain as it ascends. Scrambling with occasional steep steps leads to gentle but exposed slopes on the south flank of Unicorn (cliff bands below) that open onto a broad ridge near the final summit tower. Travel east along the narrowing ridge (some scrambling) to the base of the rock climb on the southeast side of the summit tower, which is approximately 90–100 feet high. Ascend straight up past the fixed pin (awkward moves) to the summit (5.6), or start the final pitch farther to the right for a low-5th- and 4th-class finish.

Descent: Descend the climbing route via one rappel and down-climbing.

GUYE PEAK

▲ *Improbable Traverse*

Guye Peak has a couple of strikes against it, right from the start: a well-deserved reputation for poor rock, and its modest elevation. But in spite of being one of the lowest peaks in the Snoqualmie Pass region, it is still a very striking mountain, especially from the west. Guye boasts the irresistible qualities of very easy access and that steep wall you cannot ignore, so it is logical to look for quality routes here.

The peak is quite prominent from its position on the north side of Interstate 90, right at Snoqualmie Pass. The mountain has a particularly striking profile as one approaches from the east: a classic pyramid with the steep west face in profile forming the left-hand skyline.

Because its prominence and accessibility make it so appealing, the peak has seen serious exploration. Winter routes have been tried on the south side, where there are a number of mediocre rock routes, but the search for quality is largely futile on this side, as evidenced by the lack of popular climbs. The rock on Guye, as a whole, is generally a step or two below the quality of what can be found on the nearby Tooth (see climb 14) or Lundin Peak (see volume II). One could say Guye Peak is, in fact, famous for loose rock.

The Improbable Traverse is the exception that proves the rule. While there is some loose stuff on the Improbable Traverse, the route has rock as good as any on the peak. It is precisely because the rock here is "good enough" that this climb has become perhaps the most popular out of a half dozen other routes on the west face. In winter, appealing moderate mixed snow-and-rock climbs can be found on the south rib of Guye Peak. The "back side" (east side) is a popular snowshoe climb (or summer hike) from Commonwealth Basin.

Guye Peak was first climbed by Don Blair, Forest Farr, Norval Grigg, Jim Martin, and Art Winder in May 1931, but they didn't use the Improbable Traverse.

Special Considerations: At present, permits are not necessary to climb on Guye, or anywhere at Snoqualmie Pass. For more information, contact the North Bend ranger station (425-888-1421).

SEE DETAIL

Guye Peak, showing the Improbable Traverse route (Photo by Jim Nelson)

13 IMPROBABLE TRAVERSE GRADE III

This route is on the most appealing face of Guye Peak, which adds to the interest. And if the shape of it draws you in, it is the one or two pitches of high-quality climbing on clean rock that make it worthwhile. This climb has some champions who say the quality of the climbing makes up for the lack of quality rock. Stim Bullitt, for whom the route is a favorite, claims one distinctive feature for the Improbable Traverse: status as the nearest technical alpine rock climb to a summit within its radius from Seattle. Perhaps the chief rival to that claim is the big rock buttress on the west side of Mount Si, with routes put up by Andy Dappen and Pete Doorish. But whether he is right or not, Bullitt's remark underscores the big draw of this route on Guye.

First ascents ▲ Dave Hiser and Mike Borghoff, 1960; first winter ascent:
Kit Lewis, 1975
Elevation ▲ 5,168 feet
Difficulty ▲ Grade III; 5.8
Time ▲ 4–6 hours one-way, car to summit
Equipment ▲ Medium rack
Season ▲ May–October (winter ascents possible)

Approach (Grade I): Drive Interstate 90 to Snoqualmie Pass and take exit 52; cross
under the freeway by heading north and follow Alpental Road for approximately 0.5
mile (well before the ski area) to a road leading to a housing development on the
right. Drive Ober Strasse Road to a private parking lot adjacent to the talus field
below Guye's west face. Park where it is legal and where it will not annoy the locals;
no-parking signs may make it necessary to park at the intersection of Alpental Road
and Ober Strasse (3,100 feet).

Walk up through the housing
development to the base of the large
rockslide/talus field under the west
face of Guye Peak. Ascend the talus
slope directly to near the base of the
main wall on its right (south) side. This
is a loose talus field, but short.

Route: The climb begins with 200
feet of dirt-, moss-, and debris-covered
slabs leading to some scree-covered
ledges. Fortunately the difficulty is
mostly 3rd class and occasional 4th
class, as there are no good cracks for
protection on this section. The roped
climbing usually begins here. **Pitch 1**
wanders up approximately 100 feet,
ending at a tree belay on the right. The
climbing here is mostly 4th and low
5th class, with occasional bits of mid-
5th. Solid cracks for protection are
occasionally available, but there is
quite a bit of loose rock to contend
with as well. You should also expect
some moss and dirt on these three or
four pitches leading to Lunch Ledge.

Pitch 2: From the tree, continue
left a bit, then up again. There is a
belay with slings around blocks at
approximately 100 feet, and a bit left
(north). Difficulty is up to mid-5th

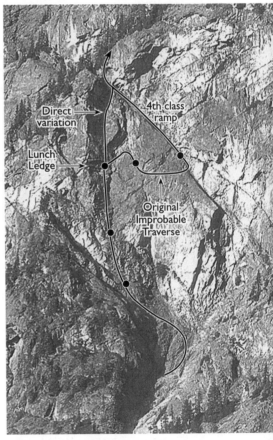

The Improbable Traverse route
(Photo by Jim Nelson)

Morris Kittleman on the Improbable Traverse, Guye Peak (Photo by Jim Nelson)

class. **Pitch 3:** More funky climbing (up to mid-5th class) continues to a nice belay below a small roof at Lunch Ledge (under the smaller of two overhangs) in 150 feet. There is a nice berry bush with fruit in season, and a good view of the "traverse" pitch.

Pitch 4: The quality of the rock improves greatly at this point. The rock is solid and clean for the two pitches across the main wall. Begin with moves right (5.7) and up to ledges. Continues right, then down a bit to a nice alcove stance. This is a short pitch, approximately 50 feet. **Pitch 5:** The "traverse" pitch begins with 5.8 moves, protected by two thin knifeblade pitons, followed by more balance climbing rightward. Stay low at first (off-route piton above), until able to climb easily up to slightly

Jim Nelson on the Improbable Traverse, Guye Peak, with Lake Keechelus in the background (Photo by Morris Kittleman)

higher ledges (5.6). The pitch continues across this ledge until steeper climbing with nice in-cut holds (5.7) leads to a large 4th-class ramp. **Pitch 4 direct variation** from Lunch Ledge: Climbing the straight-in face crack (5.8) directly up the face bypasses the Improbable Traverse pitches and rejoins the route above the ramp.

Pitches 6 and 7: A large 4th-class ramp leads up and left into trees and the end of the difficulties. Most parties will pack away the rope and rock shoes here, and scramble to the top.

Descent: From the summit, traverse to the north for a short distance (east of the ridge crest to begin), then climb on the ridge crest over two false summits before picking up the climbers track and hiking toward the Guye-Snoqualmie saddle, where a climbers trail leads down and west. Hike left down the climbers trail on the northwest flank of the peak to Alpental in a couple of quick miles.

THE TOOTH ──────────────────

▲ *South Face*

With its proximity to Interstate 90 and Seattle population centers, the Tooth is a good conditioning climb, and an authentic alternative for more ambitious climbing when time is limited. Set above pretty Source Lake in the Alpental valley, the Tooth's low elevation and southerly aspect combine to create a climb that comes into condition very early in the season, as well as drying very quickly following snow- or rainstorms.

Wilderness does not apply to the environs. Located close to the rapidly developing Snoqualmie Pass recreational/bedroom communities, the Tooth's summit views offer dramatic contrast: into the Alpine Lakes and Henry M. Jackson Wilderness Areas to the north, or down to Interstate 90 and trucks lumbering up the grade, with a patchwork of clear-cuts south and east.

Special Considerations: At present, permits are not necessary to climb on the Tooth, or anywhere at Snoqualmie Pass. For more information, contact the North Bend ranger station (425-888-1421). Northwest Forest Pass required.

14 SOUTH FACE GRADE II

A short, interesting route (with a "crux" pitch—the term hardly applies—that offers two distinct options) leading to a nicely exposed and satisfyingly jagged summit, this all-season climb is fun, close, easily gotten to, and habit-forming. Starting at tight little Pineapple Pass, the South Face is usually climbed in four pitches, all but one of which are enjoyable ones on pretty good rock. On the key final pitch, choose "the ramp" (the "catwalk") or "the face," or do one, rope down, and then do the other.

First ascent ▲ C. L. Anderson and Herman P. Wunderling, September 1928

Elevation ▲ 5,604 feet

Difficulty ▲ Grade II; 5.4

Time ▲ 4–7 hours one-way, car to summit

Equipment ▲ Small rack to 2 inches; ice ax in early season

Season ▲ Year-round (avalanche potential in winter on approach)

Approach (Grade II): Drive Interstate 90 to Snoqualmie Pass and take exit 52; cross under the freeway by heading north and follow Alpental Road to the parking lot for the Snow Lake trailhead (3,100 feet).

The Tooth from the southeast, showing Pineapple Pass (Photo by Jim Nelson)

Pineapple
Pass

Pineapple
Pass

The Tooth, South Face, from the south (Photo by Jim Nelson)

Follow the trail along the right-hand (east) side of the valley 2 miles, to a junction where the old trail is labeled Source Lake Trail and continues left. A new Snow Lake Trail branches off right (east), but do not take it. Continue upvalley on the old trail to the talus field above Source Lake. Make a descending traverse to the base of the cliff (3,750 feet). Follow the climbers track along the base of the cliff to an obvious talus field (4,400 feet). Find the boot track on the left edge of the talus field and follow it into the basin east and below the Tooth. Climb up to the small notch south of the prominent gendarme at the base of the route. Climb through the notch down and around the west side of the gendarme. Ascend 3rd-class rock to Pineapple Pass (the obvious notch) at the base of the climb (5,200 feet).

Route: From tiny Pineapple Pass, ascend a crack and large, steep blocks (5.3) to the belay ledge at the base of a steep wall and the end of the 100-foot **first pitch. Pitch 2** ascends a steep wall with balance climbing (5.3) 60 feet to a good ledge with an obvious tree anchor. (These first two pitches, both low 5th class, are sometimes combined).

The **third pitch,** least technical, follows ledge systems through trees and short steps 160 feet to the base of the final wall. For the **final pitch,** climb the ramp (exposed low 5th class), traversing left (west) past the distinctive fixed ring pin to easier ground and the summit. One can also climb directly up and right from the fixed pin (5.6) to the summit.

Bob Kroese on the Tooth, South Face, in winter (Photo by Mark Kroese)

Descent: Descend the route via a series of single-rope rappels; pitch 3 can be down-climbed.

A second good descent route is via the North Ridge. From the summit, follow ledges west (and below) the North Ridge crest, until able to down-climb (4th class) or rappel a short section into a short gully. Follow this gully down (west) until it is possible to traverse (south) below the west face back toward the South Face.

CHAIR PEAK
▲ *North Face*

Close to the urban centers of western Washington and easily reached by interstate highway, Chair Peak has long been a popular destination for climbers. Views from the summit include Mounts Rainier and Stuart and the Cascades crest, notably Chimney Rock. Most come to do the loose and somewhat dangerous standard (Northeast Buttress) route in summer. The whole peak is notorious for loose rock during summer, and several tragedies have occurred due to rockfall.

East
Face

Northeast
Buttress

North
Face

Climbers approaching the North Face of Chair Peak in winter (Photo by Jim Nelson)

However, winter conditions greatly reduce rockfall potential on the mountain. It is in winter that the proximity and accessibility of Chair Peak, and greater safety from rockfall, make it particularly appealing. With favorable snow conditions, Chair Peak offers a variety of fun winter mixed climbs: the Northeast Buttress is a challenging mixed climb, especially its lower half; the East Face Direct offers a Grade IV pillar of ice, followed by more mixed climbing. While other routes on Chair Peak have also been climbed in winter, because the North Face does not see the sun, it consistently offers safer and better ice conditions than the other winter routes. However, it is on the approach to climb the North Face that one should pay particular attention to snow conditions, specifically avalanche potential. Conditions will vary greatly.

Special Considerations: At present, permits are not necessary to climb on Chair, or anywhere at Snoqualmie Pass. For more information, contact the North Bend ranger station (425-888-1421). Northwest Forest Pass required.

15 NORTH FACE GRADE III

While the North Face has been climbed in summer, it is as a winter snow-and-ice climb that this popular and appealing route deserves attention. This winter route on a true north face of moderate steepness offers four pitches of snow-and-ice climbing over varied terrain.

First winter ascent ▲ Kit Lewis, Charlie Hampson, Rob Harris, Greg Jacobson, January 1975

Elevation ▲ 6,238 feet

Difficulty ▲ Grade III; 50- to 70-degree ice

Time ▲ 6–12 hours one-way, car to summit

Equipment ▲ Skis or snowshoes, 2–3 rock pitons, ice screws, crampons, ice tools, small wired nuts, 60-meter rope

Season ▲ December–March or April

Approach (Grade II–III): The difficulty of this approach varies, depending on snow conditions. Drive Interstate 90 to Snoqualmie Pass and take exit 52; cross under the freeway by heading north, and follow Alpental Road north 2 miles to the upper parking lot (3,240 feet).

Hike upvalley, staying left (south) of the creek, to the head of the valley above Source Lake. This area is prone to avalanche. Use extreme caution. Stable snow conditions above here are a must—if snow conditions are poor, abandon the climb and go somewhere else. If conditions are stable, climb open slopes up and right to a bench at 4,500 feet. Continue up and left into the basin below the east face of Chair Peak at 5,200 feet. A small snow-covered pinnacle in the basin is a good place to leave skis or snowshoes for the descent. Climb a short snow gully up and right for 300 feet to gain the northeast ridge leading to the Northeast Buttress. Follow the ridge to nearly the base of the mountain, until able to traverse several hundred feet toward the middle of the face. Beware of avalanche potential on this large slope.

Route: The route begins in the center of the face with some steep snow climbing that leads to a left-facing open book. The **first pitch** is 60- to 70-degree ice, with

Jens Keiler on a winter climb of the East Face of Chair Peak (Photo by Gordy Skoog)

Rob Harris and Kit Lewis making the first winter ascent of Chair Peak's North Face
(Photo by Greg Jacobson)

ice-screw protection. The **second pitch** is a runout of approximately 200 feet of 50-degree snow to a tree anchor. The next 150 feet utilizes a half dozen tree anchors for protection. The **final pitch** is 50- to 70-degree snow and ice leading to a small col 30 feet below the summit.

    Descent: From the small col, climb southeast up and over a false summit into a south-facing couloir. Descend 200 feet until able to traverse left (north) to the col. Rappel east over the cornice into a steep, narrow gully leading back to the bowl below the east face and to your skis or snowshoes.

MOUNT DANIEL

▲ *Daniel Glacier*

A classic Cascades crest alpine peak located in the heart of the central Cascades, Mount Daniel offers outstanding views from its snowfields and glaciers: Mount Stuart, Chimney Rock, Bears Breast, Mount Rainier, and others can be seen along the spine of the range. Approached via good trails, Mount Daniel makes a particularly enjoyable outing, and one with a long season. Unlike many climbs, the mountain retains its appeal late in the year, and in fact makes a good candidate for an October climb, suitable for the short days and reached through miles of colorful foliage. The emphatic, rugged plug of Cathedral Rock and still waters of pretty little Peggys Pond make pleasing backdrops to the climb.

    Special Considerations: For destinations into the Alpine Lakes Wilderness Area that are approached from the Salmon la Sac Road, permits are not required in advance. Self-register at the trailhead. While all wilderness-area regulations—such as a maximum party size of twelve—apply, permits into Peggys Pond are not required. For information and up-to-date regulations, contact the Cle Elum ranger station (509-674-4411). Northwest Forest Pass required.

16 DANIEL GLACIER GRADE II

The route up Mount Daniel presents few technical difficulties while rewarding the climber with a moderate approach, a scenic camp, and an interesting route. The way up includes a short stretch of moderately steep glacier and a long, high traverse across the mountain's upper slopes to reach the true summit. Peggys Pond is a very pretty and fragile spot; take every precaution to protect the area, including respecting the ban on fires.

First ascent ▲ Middle Peak and/or East Peak: Mountaineers party, August 1925 (likely climbed previously by surveyors)
Elevation ▲ 7,960 feet
Difficulty ▲ Grade II; 35-degree snow and/or ice
Time ▲ 1–2 days round trip; 4–8 hours one-way from Peggys Pond
Equipment ▲ Ice ax, crampons
Season ▲ May-October

Approach (Grade II+): Drive Interstate 90 east of Snoqualmie Pass and take exit 80; proceed 3 miles to Roslyn. From Roslyn, follow State Highway 903 (Salmon la

Mount Daniel from the north (Photo by Austin Post, USGS)

Sac Road) through the hamlet of Ronald and on to Salmon la Sac, approximately 16 miles from Roslyn. Just before crossing the Cle Elum River, turn right on Forest Road 4330 toward Fish Lake. Drive for approximately 12 miles, past Fish Lake (also known as Tucquala Lake) to a fork near the end of the road. Take the left spur for a couple of hundred feet to the trailhead (3,350 feet).

Hike the Cathedral Rock Trail No. 1345, crossing the Cle Elum River on a bridge and reaching Squaw Lake in 2.5 miles. Continue up through open timber and heather to Cathedral Pass at 4.25 miles (5,500 feet) and the intersection with the Pacific Crest Trail. Near the end of the first switchback west of Cathedral Pass, turn left (west) onto the Pacific Crest Trail and hike less than 0.5 mile to another intersection. At this intersection, do not descend on the Pacific Crest Trail toward Deep Lake. Instead, turn right (northwest) onto Trail No. 1375, passing Cathedral Rock on its west side and arriving at Peggys Pond (5,560 feet) in an appealing hollow between Cathedral Rock and Mount Daniel, about 3 hours from the trailhead.

Route: From the saddle near Peggys Pond, ascend west over talus (snow in early season) and glacial remnants, keeping right of the large rock in the center of the basin. Ascend the Hyas Creek Glacier toward the East Peak, then turn northwesterly to climb snow slopes to the crest of the ridge (approximately 7,200 feet) extending east from the East Peak. Climb closely under the East Peak on its right (north) side, traversing between large crevasses on the Daniel Glacier to reach the saddle on the ridge between the East Peak and the Middle Peak. Climb along the broad ridge/summit plateau, passing the Middle Peak on its left (south) side to reach the true summit several hundred yards beyond.

Descent: Descend the climbing route.

Doug Gantenbein on the Daniel Glacier climbing toward the saddle between the East and Middle Peaks (Photo by Peter Potterfield)

Ingalls Peaks from the southeast (Photo by Jim Nelson)

INGALLS PEAK, NORTH PEAK ————————————

▲ South Ridge

This sunny, south-facing ridge rises above a lunarlike basin of weird red rock. The peak offers views right into the huge flank of Mount Stuart, which towers majestically just across Ingalls Creek to the east. Ingalls Peak makes an outstanding day climb (or alternative destination when foul weather cancels out a bigger climb elsewhere in the range). Because summer comes early to the area, the climbing season is long, making the peak a good climb early in the season. The approach, characterized by straightforward hiking on good trails, is part of Ingalls Peak's appeal. The only caveat to the climber is to beware hot days: the approach is fully exposed to summer sun, so start early.

Special Considerations: Ingalls Peak is within the Alpine Lakes Wilderness Area, but at publication date, permits are not required for camping. Self-register at the trailhead. All campsites in the basin must be 200 feet from Ingalls Lake, and fires are not permitted. Call the Leavenworth ranger station (509-548-6977) for information and up-to-date regulations. Northwest Forest Pass required.

17 SOUTH RIDGE GRADE II; 5.4

The approach route climbs from the trailhead in the Teanaway Valley to scenic Ingalls Pass, then down into the basin holding Ingalls Lake and a chaos of boulders and broken rock. A short hike and scramble lead to the base of the three-pitch South Ridge. This short but pleasant climb ascends obvious, easy cracks in sound rock; the mid-5th-class route is more face climb than ridge climb. The climb is so much fun that, once on top, some climbers are tempted to rope down and do it once more before hiking out.

East
Ridge

Ingalls Peak, North Peak, from the south, showing the South Ridge climbing route
(Photo by Jim Nelson)

First ascent ▲ Keith Rankin and Ken Solberg, May 1941
Elevation ▲ 7,662 feet
Difficulty ▲ Grade II; 5.4
Time ▲ 4–8 hours one-way, car to summit
Equipment ▲ Small rack to 2 inches
Season ▲ June-October

Approach (Grade II): Drive Interstate 90 to 22 miles east of Snoqualmie Pass and take exit 85 at Cle Elum onto State Highway 970. At 5 miles from I-90, turn west onto the Teanaway River Road (follow North Fork) and drive to its end (22 miles from Highway 970) and the Longs Pass trailhead (4,243 feet).

Take the Longs Pass Trail No. 1229 1.5 miles to the intersection with the Ingalls Lake Trail No. 1390. Take the left-hand branch onto Ingalls Lake Trail to Ingalls Pass

Sean Courage avoids the crowds with an off-season trip to Ingalls; here he warms his hands on the South Ridge of the North Peak. (Photo by Andreas Schmidt)

(6,500 feet). From the pass, follow the trail down and across the basin toward the lake. Leave the trail short of the lake (at approximately 3 miles from the intersection with the Longs Pass Trail), and angle west across rocky terrain (scree and talus) toward the saddle between the north and south peaks and the distinctive Dog Tooth Crags (7,300 feet).

Route: From just below the ridge at the base of the Dog Tooth Crags, climb the prominent red slab via cracks (5.2) to a belay on a large ledge. A short pitch ascends easily to the base of the upper slab, climbed via crack climbing and face holds to another broken ledge. The climb follows the west side of the ridge crest to the summit.

Descent: Rappel the route or descend the peak by down-climbing and scrambling on the west side until able to traverse back to the east and the base of the climb.

Ingalls Peak can be a busy place, especially when club climbers converge on the South Ridge. (Photo by Dave Betts)

MOUNT STUART

▲ *Ice Cliff Glacier* ▲ *Girth Pillar* ▲ *North Ridge* ▲ *Stuart Glacier Couloir*

Big, distinctive, centrally located, and easily viewed from many summits, the Mount Stuart massif is one of the highest nonvolcanic peaks in the Cascades, and carries on its slopes some of the best, most varied ground for Northwest climbers.

Veteran climber Jim Donini was so impressed the first time he saw Mount Stuart, he moved to Leavenworth and opened a climbing school to take advantage of the "perfect granite and the perfect weather." There is no better mountain in the range for long, high-quality alpine climbs. Challenging routes on very good rock, broken glaciers, narrow couloirs, and airy, truly spectacular ridges are just some of what this mountain has to offer. The four recommended routes include all of the above.

These climbs on Stuart can be approached by one of the two routes described below, and often by both. Because walking around Stuart is no passing matter, the choice of descent route can depend on which approach is used.

The Cascadian Couloir descent is recommended for climbs approached from the south (Teanaway River Road/Ingalls Lake Trail). Climbers who approach from the north (Icicle Creek Road/Mountaineer Creek Trail) may wish to descend the Sherpa Glacier, certainly a more technical descent route, but a good option in early season.

*Mount Stuart, with Sherpa Peak, from the north: A. Ice Cliff Glacier (climb 18);
B. Girth Pillar (climb 19); C. North Ridge (climb 20); D. Stuart Glacier Couloir
(climb 21). (Photo by Jim Nelson)*

Special Considerations: The Mountaineer Creek valley is snow-covered until
early June in most years. The trailhead and lower valley begin to melt out most years
in May. Permits are required for camping and backcountry travel in the Alpine Lakes
Wilderness Area, which includes most of Mount Stuart and the approaches for the
Ice Cliff Glacier route. Call or visit the Leavenworth ranger station (509-548-6977)
for information and up-to-date regulations. The best advice is to obtain your permits
early or take your chances with the low-percentage daily permit "lottery," held
summer mornings at 7:45 A.M., in which the few remaining permits are handed out
on the spot. Northwest Forest Pass required.

18 ICE CLIFF GLACIER GRADE III–V

The Ice Cliff Glacier occupies a dramatic hanging valley, very alpine and deeply
enclosed by the impressive walls of the northeast face and Girth Pillar of Mount
Stuart. There is really no other place in the range like this high glacial cirque, where
there is that much broken ice surrounded by that much steep rock.

Conditions are critical on this route: as for all snow-and-ice climbs, conditions on the climb vary dramatically over the course of the climbing season. This is considered an excellent route choice for a winter ascent of Mount Stuart. Winter and spring hold by far the best climbing conditions. By midsummer the route becomes much more serious, with more ice climbing and the added risk of serac collapse and icefall danger. By September, this high glacier cirque can be a dangerous place, and the climb an authentic Grade V. In the rough-and-tumble early 1970s, this climb was a cult favorite for hard-man ice climbers who chose to climb it at its most demanding condition—in September or October. Most climbers take a more reasonable approach to the climb now, doing it earlier in the season.

First ascent ▲ Bill and Gene Prater, Dave Mahre, August 1957; first winter ascent: S. Reilly Moss, 1975

Elevation ▲ 9,415 feet

Difficulty ▲ Grade III–V, depending on season; steep snow and ice to 50 degrees, glacier travel

Time ▲ 1–3 days round trip

Equipment ▲ Ice ax, crampons, 1–3 ice screws, snow pickets or deadmen, small rack of rock protection to 2 inches

Season ▲ January-June

Approach (Grade III+–IV): The difficulty of this approach varies, depending on snow conditions for March-May trips when parts of the road are closed. From US 2 at the western edge of Leavenworth, turn south onto Icicle Creek Road and drive 9.2 miles to Bridge Creek Campground. (The road is plowed to here in winter. Expect to walk, ski, or snowshoe from this point before about mid-April). Drive south (left) across the bridge and continue 3.5 miles to the Stuart Lake/Mountaineer Creek trailhead (3,400 feet).

The trail follows the left (east) side of Mountaineer Creek for 2 miles before crossing to the west side. At 3 miles the trail forks, with the left branch going to Colchuck Lake. Continue straight (south) past the fork; proceed up Mountaineer Creek another mile, past swamps and back into timber. The main trail switchbacks to Stuart Lake. Leave the trail at the first switchback (left/south) and cross the creek immediately. This is the branch of Mountaineer Creek that comes from Stuart Lake. Traverse across benches above the main branch of Mountaineer Creek for 0.25 mile until able to drop 100 feet to the creek beyond the swampy area. Find the climbers track along the creek and continue up the gentle valley 1.5 miles to where the valley steepens abruptly. Climb up and right (west) through talus and open forest to enter the upper valley. Another 0.5 mile through forest and beyond a small swamp leads to good campsites (5,400 feet) directly below the Sherpa and Ice Cliff Glaciers.

Route: From the good campsites just below the Ice Cliff Glacier, follow the crest of the moraine to the base of the North Ridge. Ascend a series of steps to just under the threatening ice cliff (7,200 feet). Climb the ice cliff itself on either the extreme right side or extreme left side of the cliff; the right side is best in late season when it is possible to climb a slabby rock pitch (5.8) to reach a ledge that leads back left, above the danger from icefall and into the upper cirque.

Dan Cauthorn on the Ice Cliff Glacier
(Photo by Jim Nelson)

Once on the upper glacier, traverse to the obvious Ice Cliff Couloir (the bergschrund is usually climbed to the right or west). Climb the gully (to 50 degrees), taking the right branch near the top.

The ridge is corniced in spring, when the climb is usually done. It is recommended to establish a rock belay before tackling the difficult cornice pitch leading onto the southeast slopes below the false summit. Beware snowballing of crampons on these steep snow slopes as the route traverses around the left (south) side of the false summit (8,950 feet). Climb more steep, exposed slopes (if crampons are balling up, these slopes can be treacherous, because there is no runout; take necessary precautions) to the crest of the east ridge just below the summit. Follow the ridge to the summit.

Descent: Since this route is usually climbed early in the year, it makes sense to approach from Mountaineer Creek and descend the Sherpa Glacier. From the summit, descend 3rd-class rock of the east ridge (just right/south of the crest); after several hundred feet on or near the crest of the ridge, descend south toward Ingalls Creek for 150 feet, and begin traversing east to a point 250 feet below the false summit (8,950 feet). From this point, climb upward for 10 feet (5.0) through blocks to a ledge system traversing east and around the false summit. This ledge system leads to the western edge of a large snowfield on the southeast slopes of the false summit. A descending traverse east leads past the top of the Ice Cliff Glacier couloir and onto the top of the Sherpa Glacier couloir (8,700 feet).

Careful down-climbing (north) of this 40-degree couloir for approximately 1,500 feet leads to a bergschrund crossing (8,000 feet); find a way across the 'schrund and onto the Sherpa Glacier. (A rappel or two are necessary to negotiate the 'schrund in late season.) Keeping to the left (west) edge of the glacier, descend to rock slabs (snow in early season) below. Continue down rock slabs (3rd and 4th class). Avoid the gully on the right (east) side of the slabs (except in winter, when the gully is a safe and fast descent route) because of icefall danger. Stay to the left (west) side of the slabs to the bottom of the slabs; from there make a rappel from the handy trees to reach the talus below. Retrace the approach route back to Mountaineer Creek and the trail.

19 GIRTH PILLAR GRADE V; 5.11C, OR 5.10 AND A1

This is a modern, strenuous route featuring 5.11 crack climbing on clean granite in an uncommonly wild setting, with awesome views down steep walls into a high glacial cirque and steep icefall. The climb is guarded by an approach over what can be a very problematic glacier. Climber Kit Lewis, no stranger to hard climbs, calls this route not *one* of the best he has done in the Cascades, but *the* best.

Jutting out from the rest of the east face like a ship's prow, the Girth Pillar hangs high above the Ice Cliff Glacier cirque with dizzying views across the glacier-polished slabs of the northeast face to the North Ridge. Formed by the junction of two vertical slabs of clean granite, this climb ascends the north-facing of the two walls. Following a steep crack system for 400 vertical feet, these three pitches of 5.10–5.11 climbing form the crux of the climb. Straightforward pack hauling and excellent protection on solid rock allow the climber to focus his or her energies solely on the difficult and strenuous climbing.

Access to the Pillar is via the troublesome Ice Cliff Glacier, which becomes more and more problematic as the season progresses. By September it can become a major ice climb in itself. June and early July seem to be the best times for the ascent—warm enough for pleasant rock climbing but early enough for the glacier to be relatively straightforward. The pillar itself, steep and exposed, is dry twelve months of the year. There is a good bivy site at the base of the pillar, about five pitches above the glacier.

Major rockfall in 1994–95 altered the lower part of this route. The long, narrow scar is plainly visible from the moraine and also the North Ridge. The upper portion of the route is not changed.

First ascent ▲ Kit Lewis and Jim Nelson, July 1984; first free ascent: Dan McNerthney and Tim Wilson, July 1985; first winter ascent: Kit Lewis and Jim Nelson, February 1986

Elevation ▲ 9,415 feet

Difficulty ▲ Grade V; 5.11c, or 5.10 and A1

Time ▲ 2–4 days round trip

Equipment ▲ Ice ax, crampons, ice screws, rock protection to 3 inches, lightweight aiders, haul rope

Season ▲ June-August

Approach (Grade III+): Follow the Icicle Creek Road/Mountaineer Creek Trail approach given for climb 18, Ice Cliff Glacier.

Route: Follow the Ice Cliff Glacier route (climb 18) up to the upper cirque. Once on the upper glacier, traverse to the obvious Ice Cliff Couloir (past possible bergschrund problems at 7,800 feet). From the base of the couloir, climb up and left around a large block into a gully that turns into a corner system. Make a difficult move (wet; 5.8) to the right, out of the corner, to a ledge and easier ground leading in two pitches to a ledge at the base of the pillar. The ledge makes a good spot for a bivy.

The **first pitch** of the pillar proper starts in the corner at the right-hand base of the pillar. Climbing cracks to the left of the corner, climb to a small ledge. **Pitch 2** climbs a straight-in hand crack (5.7 turning to 5.10) past a small ledge that can be used as a belay to divide the pitch. The **third pitch** climbs a crack (5.10) directly up,

Kit Lewis on Girth Pillar (Photo by Jim Nelson)

then moves left (5.11) to a final corner crack that leads to the top of the pillar. The final **four pitches** are moderate (to 5.8) to the false summit. Follow the east ridge to the true summit.

Descent: If the route is climbed early in the season, it makes sense to descend the Sherpa Glacier (see climb 18, Ice Cliff Glacier, Descent). For climbers making a late-season ascent, the Teanaway River Road/Ingalls Lake Trail approach permits a descent via Cascadian Couloir:

From the summit, descend 3rd-class rock of the east ridge (just right/south of the crest); after several hundred feet on or near the crest of the ridge, descend south toward Ingalls Creek for 150 feet, and begin traversing east to a point 250 feet below the false summit (8,950 feet). From this point, climb upward for 10 feet (5.0) through blocks to a ledge system traversing east and around the false summit. This ledge system leads to the western edge of a large snowfield on the southeast slopes of the false summit. Descend along the right (west) edge of this snowfield 1,000 feet to a large bench on a shoulder (8,200 feet). From here follow trails (snow in early season) down and right (west) into Cascadian Couloir. Scree and sandy boot tracks lead down and into the woods along Ingalls Creek. Find Ingalls Creek Trail and follow it right (west) 0.5 mile to the obscure but critical intersection with the Longs Pass Trail. Cross Ingalls Creek and climb the steep trail to Longs Pass and on over the other side to the trailhead at the Teanaway road end.

20 NORTH RIDGE GRADE IV; 5.9

This route offers twenty pitches of climbing on solid rock, much of it delightfully exposed on a narrow ridge crest, all of it with spectacular views of the nearby environs of Mount Stuart, including Sherpa, Colchuck, and Argonaut. Add the real possibility of weather better than that elsewhere in the Cascades, and an appropriate sense of commitment, and you have the North Ridge, one of the best routes in the range.

Dan Cauthorn on the North Ridge of Mount Stuart; Stuart Glacier and Goat Pass below (Photo by Jim Nelson)

Dividing the Ice Cliff Glacier from the Stuart Glacier, the North Ridge rises abruptly at two-thirds height, forming a steep buttress (the Great Gendarme) and the crux of the route. The long ridge presents the classic alpine climbing dilemma: to carry over with bivy gear or go lightweight in the hope that the greater speed will see you off the route by dark. Good arguments can be made for either stratagem, but since pack hauling is feasible on only the two gendarme pitches, climbers planning to bivy should be prepared for technical climbing with an extra ten to twenty pounds, more if rock shoes are worn and boots carried. In either case, strong rock-climbing skills are necessary in completing this long climb and lengthy descent safely.

The climber must decide on a strategy when planning for this desirable climb. An approach from the south via the Teanaway Valley allows for a descent via Cascadian Couloir and an efficient return to the car. Approached from the north via Mountaineer Creek valley, the way is more direct but, unless one of the technical north-side descent routes is taken, the climber is left with a long walk around the mountain back to the car.

Mount Stuart from the north in early summer (Photo by Jim Nelson)

Stuart Glacier

First ascent ▲ John Rupley and Don Gordon, September 1956; first winter ascent: Craig McKibben and Jay Ossiander, March 1975; first ascent via Great Gendarme: Fred Stanley and Jim Wickwire, July 1964; first free ascent of Great Gendarme: Dave Stutzman and Bob Plum, July 1978

Elevation ▲ 9,415 feet

Difficulty ▲ Grade IV; 5.9; rock climbing, glacier travel, steep snow

Time ▲ 2–3 days round trip

Equipment ▲ Ice ax, crampons, medium rack to 3¹/₂ inches

Season ▲ July–September

Approach (Grade III+): Follow the approach to Ingalls Lake given for Ingalls Peak, North Peak (see climb 17, South Ridge). From the outlet of Ingalls Lake (north end), descend for 300 feet, then traverse north toward Mount Stuart, gaining 300–400 feet to Stuart Pass at the end of the Ingalls Creek valley. Follow the right (south) side of the ridge and ascend the climbers track to a shoulder at the base of the west ridge. Descend 200 feet, traversing the talus field ("rock glacier") and snow below the steep west wall until able to ascend scree 500 feet to Goat Pass (7,650 feet), 2–3 hours from Ingalls Lake.

Route: From Goat Pass, descend 100–200 feet until able to begin a traverse across the Stuart Glacier (steep, to 25–30 degrees) toward the North Ridge. Beware of falling ice or rock. To gain access to the ridge, climb across a steep and exposed

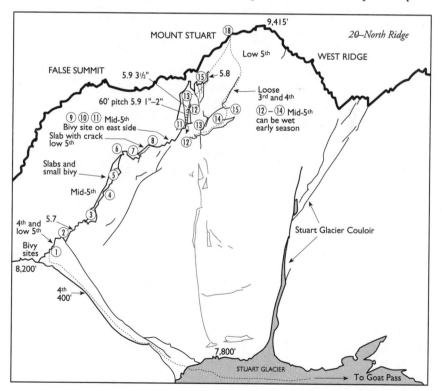

Mark Bunker on a one-day May ascent of Mount Stuart's North Ridge
(Photo by Colin Haley)

snow pitch to a snow-filled gully leading from the glacier at 7,800 feet to the ridge crest. The gully is usually climbed via 4th-class rock on the edge of the gully, reaching the ridge at 8,200 feet and decent bivy sites.

Climbing on or near the ridge crest is recommended (there is also a 4th-class ledge system traversing 100–200 feet below the crest on the right (west) side of the ridge). Climb ten to eleven pitches of 4th- and 5th-class rock climbing, quite exposed in places, to the base of the Great Gendarme. From this point, two routes are possible:

Option 1: Rappel 75 feet off the right (west) side of the ridge, then traverse into and across a gully (melting snow and wet or icy rock until mid-July). Gain and traverse a ledge right (west) to easier though loose climbing leading in another 400–500 feet to the summit.

Option 2: The harder, but better option is to climb the gendarme directly via 5.9 crack climbing. The second pitch on the gendarme (pitch 13) requires a Number 11 hex nut or 3¹/₂-inch cam to protect a short off-width section. Continue up and right another full pitch to a notch beyond the gendarme. A short 5.9 wall is followed by another three pitches of blocky 4th- and 5th-class climbing.

Descent: The Cascadian Couloir is the recommended descent route for the North Ridge when approached from the south (see climb 19, Girth Pillar, Descent).

Climber Andrea Leuschke belays the second pitch of the Great Gendarme, North Ridge of Stuart. (Photo by Tim Matsui)

21 STUART GLACIER COULOIR GRADE IV

A classic mixed route on this outstanding peak presents a host of classic mountaineering problems, including steep rock and snow coupled with changeable conditions. The setting for the climb, on Mount Stuart's steep north and northwest flanks, is wild and alpine.

Although the route involves both rock climbing and snow-and-ice climbing, it is the latter that dictates the character of the climb. The couloir is safest in winter or spring conditions, which means there may be a fair amount of snow on the rock-climbing sections. The upper portion of the couloir holds a fair amount of snow and gets midmorning sun—so be wary of warm temperatures in early season. Like most snow-and-ice climbs, good conditions make all the difference: cold, stable conditions make for pleasant and straightforward climbing, while warmer weather can make the route strenuous, unpleasant, even nerve-wracking.

Slightly unstable spring weather frequently makes the best scenario for climbing the Stuart Glacier Couloir, with cool temperatures and inconsequential snow flurries. More stable weather patterns can also be advantageous, but be wary of unseasonably warm temperatures when the snow does not freeze overnight.

First ascent ▲ Helmy Beckey and Larry Strathdee, June 1944; first winter ascent: Paul Ekman and Joe Weis, 1976

Elevation ▲ 9,415 feet

Difficulty ▲ Grade IV; 80-degree snow and ice, glacier travel

Time ▲ 2–3 days round trip

Equipment ▲ Ice ax, crampons, second ice tool, medium rack rock protection to 3 inches, ice screw

Season ▲ April-May

Approach (Grade III+): Follow the Icicle Creek Road/Mountaineer Creek Trail approach given for climb 18, Ice Cliff Glacier; this enables the climber to depart from a camp at the head of Mountaineer Creek (5,200 feet), and then return via the Sherpa Glacier.

Route: From good campsites at 5,400 feet, just below the Ice Cliff Glacier, follow the crest of the moraine to the base of the North Ridge. Continue up the left (east) side of the Stuart Glacier to the base of the Stuart Glacier Couloir (7,800 feet). Cross the bergschrund and climb the steep (40- to 50-degree) slope for 400–500 feet to where the couloir narrows and finally constricts down, blocked by two very short steps of up to 80-degree ice. Above the steps, the couloir opens onto a large snow slope, still steep (40–50 degrees), that can hold snow after a storm. Beware of snow sloughing off in warm conditions. Climb the snow slope to where it ends on the west ridge. Traverse on the south side of the ridge for one pitch (class 3) to the base of the summit pyramid. Climb a blocky pitch (low 5th class) on the crest, then traverse a ledge leading across the north face, followed by a steep pitch (mid-5th class) with good protection that leads back to the narrow ridge crest at a small notch. Drop down 10 feet and follow a ledge across the south face for a full pitch (class 3). Two more pitches follow a crack system (5.6) on good rock.

Lowell Skoog in Stuart Glacier Couloir, January 1978 (Photo by Jim Nelson)

Descent: Since this route is approached via Icicle Creek Road/Mountaineer Creek Trail, and is usually climbed early in the season (before June 1), it makes sense to descend the Sherpa Glacier (see climb 18, Ice Cliff Glacier, Descent).

COLCHUCK PEAK ━━━━━━━━━━━━━━━━
▲ *Colchuck Glacier* ▲ *North Buttress Couloir*

Colchuck Peak is strategically located in the central Cascades, providing outstanding views and a variety of enjoyable climbing, but without the seriousness of some of the longer neighboring routes, such as those on Dragontail Peak.

The Colchuck Glacier is an interesting and accessible snow-and-ice climb that changes dramatically as the season progresses. The route is particularly enjoyable early in the year, because summer comes to this area a few weeks ahead of climbing areas in the North Cascades. Early in the season, straightforward snow technique is the rule on this route, but by late July a section of hard water ice can develop at the steepest part of the glacier, adding a high degree of interest and a few hundred feet of 40-degree ice climbing. (The glacier also serves as the descent route for this and other climbs on Colchuck Peak; woe to the rock climber who forgets crampons and has to come down the steep section in late August wearing boots or rock shoes.) Crevasse danger is virtually nonexistent on this slow-moving and largely forgiving glacial remnant. The summit of Colchuck is attained by easy scrambling above the glacier.

The North Buttress Couloir on Colchuck is a good route option for those looking for something steeper and a bit more technical, yet not overly committing. From the north end of Colchuck Lake and from points along the Stuart Lake Trail, the upper part of the route (the northwest face) looks awesome, like the classic alpine line it is.

Both routes on Colchuck are particularly recommended as early-season objectives. Although this adds to the approach time due to snow, the opportunity to see the area around Colchuck Lake that time of year is worth the trouble.

The summit of Colchuck Peak is a particularly good vantage point for viewing the face routes on Dragontail Peak, Mount Stuart's Ice Cliff Glacier cirque, and the headwalls forming Mount Stuart's northeast face.

Special Considerations: Permits are required for camping and backcountry travel in the Alpine Lakes Wilderness Area. Colchuck Lake is a popular spot, and the necessary permits to camp there can be hard to come by. Hikers and backpackers on their way to the Enchantments, Boy Scout troops, climbers, and other visitors are drawn to the lake as a destination or an interim camp. Good campsites can be found around the lakeshore, but beware of extremely heavy use, particularly on weekends and holidays. Call the Leavenworth ranger station (509-548-6977) for information. The best advice is to obtain your permits well ahead of time—or take your chances with the low-percentage daily permit "lottery," held summer mornings at 7:45 A.M., in which the few remaining permits are handed out on the spot. Northwest Forest Pass required.

22 COLCHUCK GLACIER GRADE II

On one side of the Colchuck Glacier is Colchuck Peak; on the other is Dragontail Peak. The glacier route ascends alongside the steep and massive granite slabs of Dragontail Peak's northwest face, providing an impressive backdrop for such an easily attained summit. Exposure to rockfall danger is extreme immediately under the steep walls of Dragontail Peak. Keep well away from the face while on the glacier. It is worth noting there was major rockfall on the northwest face of Dragontail in 1991–92; debris traveled as far as the eastern lobe of the Colchuck Glacier. A large white scar marks the location of the rockfall.

First ascent ▲ Elvin and Norma Johnson, William and Kathy Long, August 1948

Elevation ▲ 8,705 feet

Difficulty ▲ Grade II; class 3 rock, snow and ice, steep in places (30–40 degrees)

Time ▲ 1–2 days round trip; 3–6 hours one-way from Colchuck Lake, 1–2 hours one-way from Dragontail-Colchuck col

Equipment ▲ Ice ax, crampons

Season ▲ June-July generally best; year-round for experienced climbers

Approach (Grade II+–IV): The difficulty of this approach varies, depending on snow conditions for March-May trips when parts of the road are closed. From US 2 at the western edge of Leavenworth, turn south onto Icicle Creek Road and drive 9.2 miles to Bridge Creek Campground. (The road is plowed to here in winter. Expect to walk, ski, or snowshoe from this point before about mid-April). Drive south (left) across the bridge onto Mountaineer Creek Road and continue 3.5 miles to the Stuart Lake/Mountaineer Creek trailhead (3,400 feet).

The trail follows the left (east) side of Mountaineer Creek for 2 miles before crossing to the west side. At 3 miles the trail forks. Take the left fork, which crosses Mountaineer Creek again to the east side (4,700 feet). At 5 miles the trail arrives at the north shore of Colchuck Lake (5,600 feet), where good campsites can be found. The trail continues around the south (right) shore of the lake past a small lakelet and

Colchuck Peak and Colchuck Glacier from Colchuck Lake (Photo by Jim Nelson)

onto a talus field below the Colchuck Glacier moraine. Climb talus and scree to the low point in the moraine, where a small stream exits (6,350 feet).

Route: Ascend snow slopes to the left (east) lobe of the lower glacier, keeping well away from the northwest face of Dragontail Peak while on the glacier. Climb the moderate slopes of the glacier to the Dragontail-Colchuck col (8,100 feet).

Scramble 3rd-class sandy ledges, avoiding steep snow slopes, to the summit plateau (8,500 feet); it is a good idea to mark this location with a wand or cairn for an easier return. Climb west and northwest through big boulders to open slopes leading to the summit.

Descent: Descend the climbing route, via the Colchuck Glacier. From the summit, descend east and southeast through big boulders to the summit plateau at 8,500 feet. Expect some slogging and postholing on the summit plateau before about June. Descend 3rd-class sandy ledges to the Dragontail-Colchuck col (8,100 feet), and climb down to the glacier. Crevasse danger is virtually nonexistent on this slow-moving and largely forgiving glacial remnant. The descent is made below the steep and massive granite slabs of Dragontail's northwest face, which provide an impressive backdrop but possible rockfall hazard that can be extreme. **Keep well away from the face while descending the glacier.**

Colchuck Lake

Steve Swope on the Colchuck Glacier
(Photo by John Sharp)

23 NORTH BUTTRESS COULOIR GRADE III

This route is greatly influenced by snow and weather conditions, as well as season. With fresh snow, the risk of snow sloughs or slides goes up. The initial couloir is east facing, so expect sun warming as well. As this climb makes the transition from winter to summer conditions, rockfall becomes a greater concern than the soft snow issues common in early season.

First ascent ▲ Ray Lilleby and Jim Wickwire, July 15, 1962
Elevation ▲ 8,705 feet
Difficulty ▲ Grade III; class 3–4 rock; snow and/or ice, steep in places (30–50 degrees)
Time ▲ 1–2 days round trip; 4–8 hours one-way from lake
Equipment ▲ Ice ax, crampons, small rock rack
Season ▲ June-July generally best; year-round for experienced climbers

Approach (Grade II+–IV): The difficulty of this approach varies, depending on snow conditions for March-May trips when parts of the road are closed. Follow the approach given for climb 22, Colchuck Glacier, to the low point in the Colchuck Glacier moraine (6,350 feet), where a small stream exits.

Colchuck Peak from the northeast, showing the North Buttress Couloir
(Photo by Jim Nelson)

Route: The couloir begins a short way above, below the western glacier and near the western (right) lateral moraine. Enter the gully (approximately 6,800 feet) and climb 40- to 50-degree snow to the top of the couloir at a small notch on the North Buttress (approximately 8,000 feet). The couloir is narrow at a couple of spots in its first half, where moats around rocks become an issue after about early July.

Colchuck Peak from the north, showing the upper portion of the North Buttress Couloir route (Photo by Jim Nelson)

From the notch at the top of the couloir, traverse up and right, moving out onto the northwest face and away from the north ridge. This upper section of the route continues on 40- to 50-degree snow (some exposure) on the west (right) side of the

Climbers in the North Buttress Couloir, Colchuck Peak (Photo by Andreas Schmidt)

Sean Courage and Christine Boskoff on the Colchuck North Buttress Couloir route (Photo by Andreas Schmidt)

ridge crest, avoiding rock climbing for the most part. Depending on the party's comfort level on snow, occasional rock pro is available for much of the climb. A final snow gully joins the summit plateau a few feet from the true summit.

Descent: Descend via the Colchuck Glacier (see climb 22, Colchuck Glacier, Descent).

COLCHUCK BALANCED ROCK ───────────

▲ *West Face*

Colchuck Balanced Rock is located high above Colchuck Lake, with views of Colchuck Peak and the north side of Mount Stuart, which makes the route a special one for those who can manage the technical difficulties. Located above Colchuck Lake east of where the Aasgard Pass Trail begins, the route is approached from low on the Aasgard Pass Trail itself. Clearly visible from the lake, the route faces almost due west and so does not see the sun until mid- to late afternoon, depending on the season. With an altitude of more than 8,000 feet, cool temperatures should be expected most of the year. A fast party starting at midday and returning to a nearby bivouac might be able to climb sun-warmed granite for much of the climb. In late season, water is scarce beyond the lake; the southerly slopes can be comfortably descended in rock shoes, although there is some snow early in the season.

Special Considerations: Permits are required for camping and backcountry travel in the Alpine Lakes Wilderness Area. Colchuck Lake is a popular spot, and the necessary permits to camp there can be hard to come by. Hikers and backpackers on their way to the Enchantments, Boy Scout troops, climbers, and other visitors are drawn to the lake as a destination or an interim camp. Good campsites can be found around the lakeshore, but beware of extremely heavy use, particularly on weekends and holidays. Call the Leavenworth ranger station (509-548-6977) for information. The best advice is to obtain your permits well ahead of time—or take your chances with the low-percentage daily permit "lottery," held summer mornings at 7:45 A.M., in which the few remaining permits are handed out on the spot. Northwest Forest Pass required.

24 WEST FACE GRADE III; 5.11 AND A1, OR 5.12

Here is a route for the modern hard man or woman who is prepared for a five-star crack pitch and its wildly exposed belay—an outstanding, strenuous crack climb on a very steep wall with a well-protected crux that goes free at 5.11. A big corner below the obvious huge roof provides the crux crack climbing, and leads to the spectacularly airy belay.

Colchuck Balanced Rock from the south (Photo by Jim Nelson)

The West Face of Colchuck Balanced Rock (Photo by Jim Nelson)

First ascent ▲ Tomas Boley and Jack Lewis, July 1980; first free ascent: Doug Mercer and Heather Paxson, 1986
Elevation ▲ 8,200 feet
Difficulty ▲ Grade III+; 5.11 and A1, or 5.12
Time ▲ 1–2 days round trip; 6–10 hours one-way from Colchuck Lake
Equipment ▲ Medium to large rack to 3¹/2 inches
Season ▲ June-September

Approach (Grade III+): Follow the approach to Colchuck Lake (5,600 feet) given for climb 22, Colchuck Glacier.

From Colchuck Lake, follow the trail around the southwest side of the lake, catching glimpses of Colchuck Balanced Rock through the trees as you go. The climbing route is approached by ascending the gully directly below Colchuck Balanced Rock, near the eastern shore of the lake. But because where the gully meets the lakeshore is overgrown with slide alder and other vegetation, it is best to ascend the Aasgard Pass Trail to about 300–400 feet above the lake level, traversing over to enter the gully at the base of cliffs forming the right-hand side of the gully. Once in the gully, the routefinding is straightforward; move up the gully into a small basin directly below the start of the climb (7,000 feet; good camping here, but no water after early season).

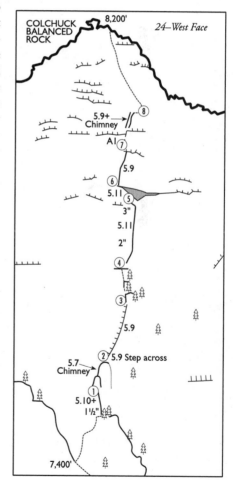

Route: The route begins in the center of the face in a rocky gully. The gully ends on ledges below a short thin crack that goes 5.10+ (**pitch 1**). The **next pitch** ascends easy cracks and ledges into a 5.7 chimney to a ledge on a pedestal. Step across (5.9) to the main face and climb a 5.9 corner (**pitch 3**) to **pitch 4**: ledges below the large corner in the center of the face, capped by a large roof.

The crack up the corner (**pitch 5**) is 1–3 inches and straightforward though strenuous (5.10, rated 5.11 due to its length). The crack ends at a belay under the big roof (a bolt could be added here). A **short pitch** leads left (5.11) to a good stance. **Pitch 7,** another hand crack, follows (5.9), leading

Guy Davis on the seventh pitch of the West Face of Colchuck Balanced Rock
(Photo by Dave Bale)

to a small roof exited left on aid (A1) or 5.12. A difficult chimney follows (**pitch 8**), leading to easier climbing and the summit.

Descent: Descend sand and scree to the south (snow in early season).

DRAGONTAIL PEAK

▲ *Backbone Ridge with Fin Direct* ▲ *Serpentine Ridge* ▲ *Triple Couloirs*

The enormous northwest face of Dragontail Peak is a striking sight when first viewed from Colchuck Lake. A mile wide and almost 3,000 feet high, the face is an impressive conglomeration of steep buttresses, deep couloirs, ridges, and slabs. Its complex architecture harbors both long, hard rock climbs and challenging ice climbs.

All three routes recommended on Dragontail Peak can be called serious, and all are approached via Colchuck Lake. When camping by the lake, it is enjoyable to sit back and watch the dramatic evening light on the big face—followed by brilliant alpenglow, a few streamers of cloud racing across the "dragontail" summit ridge of gendarmes. It is an appropriate setting and prelude to Dragontail Peak's challenging routes. The view from the routes is into the rocky reaches of Colchuck Peak and the Colchuck Glacier.

Special Considerations: Anyone climbing Dragontail Peak by any route should be aware of the potential for rockfall caused by parties above. This is a relatively accessible and popular mountain; scan the face and your proposed route from the base of the climb. If you do not like the location of other climbing parties, abandon the climb or consider climbing something else.

Because Colchuck Lake is a popular spot, the necessary permits to camp there can be hard to come by. Hikers and backpackers on their way to the Enchantments, Boy Scout troops, climbers, and other visitors are drawn to the lake as a destination or an interim camp. Good campsites can be found around the lakeshore, but beware: the area sees heavy use, particularly on weekends and holidays. Permits are required to camp at the lake, but may be unavailable during busy times. Call the Leavenworth ranger station (509-548-6977) for information. Get your permits well ahead of time or take your chances with the low-percentage daily permit "lottery," held summer mornings at 7:45 A.M., in which a small number of permits are handed out on the spot. Northwest Forest Pass required.

25 BACKBONE RIDGE WITH FIN DIRECT GRADE IV+; 5.9

One of the more easily accessible of the long (2,000-foot) alpine rock climbs in the Cascade Range, the Backbone Ridge on Dragontail Peak is easier to get to than it is to climb. A fair amount of 5.8 and 5.9 climbing, combined with a whole lot of 4th-class and low-5th-class climbing, requires that those who choose to do this route have a high standard of free-climbing proficiency and a superior fitness level. Competent route-finding and the ability to travel light and fast are necessary to avoid a bivy on this climb.

First ascent ▲ Mark Weigelt and John Bonneville, August 1970; with Fin Direct: Pat Cruver and Kit Lewis, July 1975

Elevation ▲ 8,840 feet

Difficulty ▲ Grade IV+; 5.9

Time ▲ 1–2 days round trip; 6–10 hours one-way from Colchuck Lake

Equipment ▲ Medium rack to 3 inches, plus several larger pieces (5–6 inches); crampons and/or ice ax

Season ▲ June-September

Dragontail Peak from the northwest, showing Backbone Ridge and Serpentine Ridge routes (Photo by Jim Nelson)

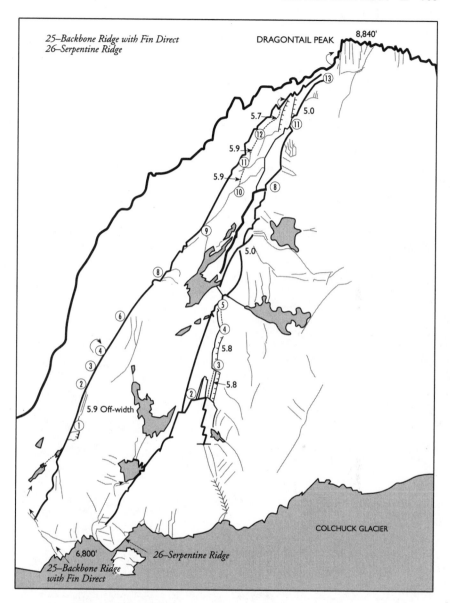

25–Backbone Ridge with Fin Direct
26–Serpentine Ridge

DRAGONTAIL PEAK

8,840'

5.7
5.0

5.9

5.9

5.0

5.8

5.8

5.9 Off-width

6,800'
26–Serpentine Ridge
25–Backbone Ridge
with Fin Direct

COLCHUCK GLACIER

Approach (Grade II+): For all routes recommended on Dragontail Peak, follow the approach to Colchuck Lake (5,600 feet) given for climb 22, Colchuck Glacier.

The trail continues around the south (right) shore of the lake past a small lakelet and onto a talus field below the Colchuck Glacier moraine. Follow the trail around the lake 0.6 mile to the talus below the moraine; leave the trail and climb talus and scree south to the moraine on the east side of the Colchuck Glacier. Ascend to the top of the moraine (approximately 6,800 feet), where the steep western profile of Backbone Ridge can be seen.

Dragontail Peak's northwest face, showing Backbone Ridge and Serpentine Ridge routes (Photo by Jim Nelson)

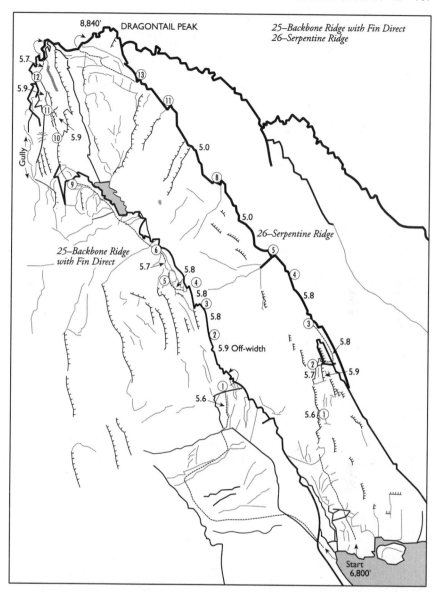

Route: From the top of the moraine on the Colchuck Glacier (approximately 6,800 feet), begin the climb beneath the broad gully and slabs that divide Backbone Ridge from Serpentine Ridge. Traverse east on ledges past the base of the ridge and beyond until able to work back up and right (west) 500 feet on ledges to the base of a corner below the crest. The **first pitch** climbs the corner (5.6) to the crest of the ridge and the start of the real difficulties. **Pitch 2** climbs the 6-inch crack right (west) of the crest (5.9; protectable only with large pieces). **Pitches 3 and 4** continue near the crest (5.8; cracks and steps) to a belay on the narrow crest. **Pitch 5** moves down and left (exposed 5.8) to gain a crack system left (east) of the crest. Follow the crack

Colchuck
Lake

Climber Marshall Balick on the Fin, Backbone Ridge, Dragontail Peak
(Photo by Tim Matsui)

Carl Diedrich on the Fin, Backbone Ridge, Dragontail Peak (Photo by Dave Bale)

system (5.7) for **two pitches** (bypassing a 5.9 off-width crack) up to the crest of the ridge. Continue up big blocks and short steps on or near the crest for another **two or three pitches** (low to mid-5th class) to the end of Backbone Ridge at the base of the Fin, the large white slab.

Low class 5 climbing leads up and across the Fin on the main ledge system. Face climbing followed by twin cracks (5.8–5.9) ends at a belay on the left end of a large ledge in the middle of the Fin. **Pitch 12** climbs a flake, with undercling moves (5.9) up then back left to a belay. **Pitch 13:** Face climbing and small ledges lead right and up to the crest beyond a blocky gendarme (5.7). **Pitch 14:** From the crest, the final pitch leads to easier climbing, which leads to the top of the route just east of the summit.

Descent: Descend 30-degree snow slopes until able to traverse toward Aasgard Pass; descend the Aasgard Pass Trail back to Colchuck Lake.

Route detail for the Fin, Backbone Ridge (Photo by Jim Nelson)

26 SERPENTINE RIDGE GRADE IV; 5.8

The Serpentine Ridge is another long alpine rock climb, but not as long or as serious as its neighbor on Dragontail Peak, the Backbone Ridge. Still, at more than 2,000 feet in length and with considerable routefinding challenges, the Serpentine Ridge is not to be taken lightly.

Pitches of 4th-class and low-5th-class climbing eventually lead to two outstanding pitches of 5.7–5.8 climbing that give the route its strong appeal. Above these two pitches, the character of the climb changes abruptly. Expect tricky routefinding on the upper third of the route, and many pitches of class 3–4 climbing with loose blocks on ledges and danger from party-inflicted rockfall. For a well-coordinated team, the upper pitches are enjoyable roped scrambling and great training for longer alpine excursions. Short spacing on the rope is recommended for this advanced simul-climbing technique.

Routefinding decisions on this long climb can often come down to "left-ledge" system or "right-ledge" system, and it is often possible to examine both options before making a choice.

First ascent ▲ Tom Hargis and Jay Ossiander, July 1973

Elevation ▲ 8,840 feet

Difficulty ▲ Grade IV; 5.8

Time ▲ 1–2 days round trip; 5–10 hours one-way from lake

Equipment ▲ Medium rack to 3 inches; crampons or ice ax

Season ▲ June-September

Climbers on the pitch that adjoins the pillar, Serpentine Ridge, Dragontail Peak (Photo by Mike Gauthier)

Approach (Grade II+): Follow the approach to the moraine on the east side of the Colchuck Glacier (approximately 6,800 feet) given for climb 25, Backbone Ridge with Fin Direct.

Route: From the top of the moraine, climb class 3–4 slabs and steps into the depression between Backbone Ridge and Serpentine Ridge. Several low- to mid-5th-class pitches follow corners to the crest of the Serpentine arête at a large ledge at the base of the prominent pillar, approximately 500 feet above the moraine.

From this ledge on the west (right) side of the pillar, the crack formed by the right-hand side of the pillar can be climbed (5.8–5.9); an easier option is to move right 15 feet to a system of small face cracks that can be followed (5.8) to a ledge. The second pitch above the pillar climbs a shallow dihedral or clean corner system (5.7–5.8). Another short pitch, low 5th class, leads to the crest of Serpentine Ridge. (These may be the most enjoyable pitches on the entire climb.)

From here, follow the crest of Serpentine Ridge (mostly class 4 with short steps of low- to mid-5th-class climbing); it is also possible to climb easier ground on ledge systems to the right of the crest (class 3–4, with rockfall potential from parties above).

Near the summit, climb directly upward (5.7), or traverse east under the summit (class 4) to the south slope and then on to the summit.

Descent: Follow the descent route for climb 25, Backbone Ridge with Fin Direct.

27 TRIPLE COULOIRS GRADE III–IV; 5.8

One of the first of the modern Cascade winter-spring mixed (snow, ice, and rock) climbs, Triple Couloirs, when in condition, is an appealing route providing challenging and enjoyable climbing for the seasoned alpine mountaineer. As with all ice climbs, the quality of the climb varies greatly with conditions, but it is not unusual for moderate sections of firm, stable snow to alternate with 60- to 75-degree sections of water ice, with a few ice-covered rock moves thrown in for good measure.

Triple Couloirs is long and committing, with two crux sections. The first comes at the exit of the first, or "hidden," couloir; the second crux connects the second and third couloirs. Some rock protection can usually be found throughout much of the climb.

First ascent ▲ Bill Joiner, Leslie Nelson, Dave Seman, May 1974; first winter ascent: via First Couloir (Hidden Couloir) to its end (bypassing Second Couloir) and Third Couloir, Cal Folsom and Don Heller, January 1974 (tragically, Don Heller was killed on descent)

Elevation ▲ 8,840 feet

Difficulty ▲ Grade III–IV; 5.8; steep snow and ice

Time ▲ 1–3 days round trip; 5–9 hours one-way from lake

Equipment ▲ Ice ax, crampons, second ice tool, ice screws, pitons

Season ▲ January–May

Approach (Grade II+): Follow the approach to Colchuck Lake (5,600 feet) given for climb 22, Colchuck Glacier.

The trail continues around the south (right) shore of the lake. From the south end of Colchuck Lake, climb to the base of the first couloir, just uphill (east) from the lowest point of the north face of Dragontail Peak (approximately 6,400 feet).

Dragontail's north face, showing Triple Couloirs in winter conditions (Photo by Jim Nelson)

Triple Couloirs route detail for Option 1 (Photo by Jim Nelson)

Route: Find the entrance into the First Couloir (Hidden Couloir) a short distance uphill (to the left/east) of the lowest point of the north face. Straightforward snow-and-ice climbing of 40 to 50 degrees leads up approximately 800 feet until just below steep ice runnels leading into the Second Couloir. From this point, there are three possible options:

Option 1: Climb the steep ice runnels (70–80 degrees) directly for three pitches into the Second Couloir. The difficulty of these pitches varies greatly depending on conditions and the amount of ice formed. This can be hard climbing on thin ice, and the climber should expect three pitches of sustained mixed climbing (70- to 80-degree ice) with only occasional protection (pitons are useful here).

Option 2: Continue up the First Couloir another pitch or so until a

Mark Kroese and Phil Eckes in the Third Couloir of Triple Couloirs
(Photo by Bob Kroese)

small snow couloir leads up and left for two pitches to a good belay on rock, very close to the base of the Second Couloir. Entrance into the Second Couloir is gained by climbing down and across steep rock (5.8) a short distance.

Option 3: Continue up the First Couloir several more rope lengths to the top of the First Couloir. From here it is not feasible to traverse back left into the Second Couloir—several rock ribs block the way. Instead, this option bypasses the Second Couloir completely and climbs 40- to 60-degree snow and ice on the north face up to the Third Couloir. Entrance into the Third Couloir is gained by climbing behind the prominent tower at the top of the Second Couloir. (Because this variation does not ascend the Second Couloir, it is not, strictly speaking, the Triple Couloirs route.)

Assuming the first or second option is taken, climb the Second Couloir for approximately 600–700 feet (40- to 50-degree snow and ice) until it is possible to exit up and right across a rock slab into the Third Couloir. The difficulty of this pitch depends on the conditions, and on how much ice is formed. Rock pitons are useful here as well.

The Third Couloir is straightforward 40- to 50-degree snow and ice leading to the summit ridge a short distance east of the summit.

Climbers exiting the Second Couloir on Triple Couloirs (Photo by Jim Nelson)

Descent: Descend 30-degree snow leading to Aasgard Pass, and descend through the pass back to Colchuck Lake (use caution on the Aasgard Pass Trail, because snow conditions can make for a dangerous descent).

SNOW CREEK WALL

▲ Orbit ▲ Outer Space

One of the best of the Cascade crag-climbing areas, the Snow Creek Wall offers a variety of interesting climbing on sound, clean rock in the heart of the Leavenworth climbing scene. With a relatively easy approach—less than 2 hours from the car—Snow Creek Wall has genuine multipitch climbs of sustained difficulty and a variety of terrain, including crack climbing and face climbing.

The best climbs on the wall are good barometers of rock-climbing skills and make excellent prerequisites for more committing routes such as Dragontail Peak's Backbone Ridge (climb 25), North Ridge of Mount Stuart (climb 20), or Bear Mountain (climb 85). But Orbit and Outer Space are challenging climbs in their own right, and the Snow Creek Wall offers a miniature "big-wall" feel for so accessible an area. From high on the wall, climbers can look downvalley to see the edges of Leavenworth in the Icicle Creek valley. On the summit, there is a fairly healthy population of curious mountain goats to be seen.

Special Considerations: No climbing permit required; Northwest Forest Pass required.

28 ORBIT GRADE III; 5.9

An excellent and by now truly classic climb, Orbit has sustained 5.8 difficulties coming one pitch after the other over a variety of terrain and climbing moves. Highlights include outstanding exposure climbing past a series of small roofs and exposed face climbing on nicely textured granite. Near the top, where the route eases somewhat, there are attention-getting runouts on knobs and chickenheads.

First ascent ▲ Fred Beckey and Dan Davis, 1962; first free ascent: Ron Burgner and John Marts, 1966
Elevation ▲ 3,900 feet
Difficulty ▲ Grade III; 5.9
Time ▲ 4–8 hours one-way, car to summit
Equipment ▲ Medium rack to 2¹/₂ inches with assortment of small sizes
Season ▲ April-October

Approach (Grade II): From US 2 at the western edge of Leavenworth, turn south onto Icicle Creek Road and drive 4.2 miles to the Snow Creek trailhead (1,300 feet).

Snow Creek Trail No. 1553 switchbacks steeply, gaining 1,500 feet in 2 miles before it begins to follow the course of Snow Creek directly beneath the Snow Creek Wall. From this point on the trail, take the small climbers path steeply downhill for 80 feet to Snow Creek and a crossing via a rapidly rotting log. Cross the log, then cross a second channel of Snow Creek (also on a log) and follow the climbers path to the base of the Snow Creek Wall (approximately 3,200 feet).

Route: From the point where the approach trail reaches the base of the wall, Orbit closely follows the left skyline of the wall. Walk along the base of the wall left (south) a couple of hundred feet until able to climb slabs easily to a large ledge

Mike Drake and Andy Dappen on Orbit on Snow Creek Wall (Photo by Jim Nelson)

Orbit Route Line

Orbit route, Snow Creek Wall (Photo by Jim Nelson)

system. Continue left to a gully/corner system below a large tree and the start of the difficulties.

The **second pitch** climbs an awkward chimney (5.8) followed by easier climbing leading to a ramp below a steep wall. The ramp leads left (south) until a suitable belay site is reached. The **third pitch** continues across the ramp until a nice finger crack (5.9) leads to a belay at a bush by a block. (Low-5th-class climbing bypasses the finger crack down and left, then back up to the same bush-belay spot.) The **fourth pitch** ascends via face climbing (5.8) up and right past two small roofs, leading out and right onto the main face. Face climbing (5.7) leads up past a 2-inch crack and a bolt to a small stance with good cracks for anchors. It is also common to continue 40 feet higher to another belay near the start of a left-facing corner near several 1/4-inch bolts. In

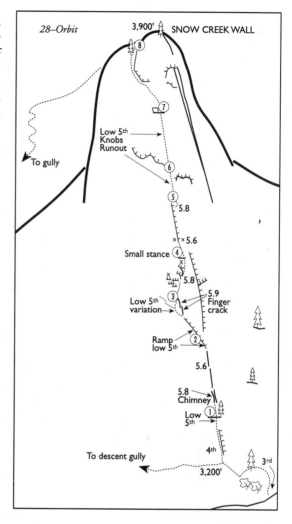

either case, continue up the corner via very nice climbing (mid-5th class) until forced to move right, out of the corner and onto the face (5.8). The face above is highly textured and continues for a **short pitch** to a very large roof. The **seventh pitch** is another long pitch, climbing past the roof (low 5th class), followed by long runouts on knobs (low to mid-5th class) to a large ledge. Climb the short chimney (5.7) to easier climbing past an arête, then up to a steep wall and left again past a wide crack.

Descent: Descend by first traversing south, away from the wall, then descending over a short rock step (class 3). Continue a descending traverse until very close to the stream/gully, then descend slabby terrain 300–400 feet, with party-inflicted rockfall a potential here. Upon reaching the trees, where the gully narrows, find a climbers path traversing left (north) past the Orbit route until able to down-climb (zigzagging) 3rd-class slabs to the base of the wall.

29 OUTER SPACE GRADE III; 5.9

This is a splendid route with magnificent final pitches that are as beautiful to look at as they are to climb. Stim Bullitt, one of the few climbers to have done all of the fifty highest mountains in the Cascades, rates this climb (the crux pitch of which he led at age seventy-three) as one of the best he has ever done. It has got crack climbing, an interesting dihedral, and challenging sideways moves that involve a diagonal crack for hands, smearing for the feet, and awesome exposure.

Outer Space route (alternate start), Snow Creek Wall (Photo by Jim Nelson)

On a climb as popular as this one, it is not unusual to encounter other parties on the route. Be prepared to be slowed by less experienced or slower, more cautious parties. On the other hand, really slow parties should be willing to allow faster parties to pass them. (If you have never been passed on a popular rock climb, you have probably not been climbing very long; everybody gets passed eventually.)

This is not a good climb for inexperienced trad rock climbers; proficiency on two- or three-pitch trad climbs should be considered a prerequisite for Outer Space. It is also recommended that less-experienced parties carry two ropes to facilitate quick, efficient retreat, particularly if rain threatens.

First ascent ▲ Fred Beckey and Ron Niccoli, 1960; first free ascent: Fred Beckey and Steve Marts, 1963

Elevation ▲ 3,900 feet

Difficulty ▲ Grade III; 5.9

Time ▲ 4–8 hours one-way, car to summit

Equipment ▲ Medium rack to 3 1/2 inches

Season ▲ April-October

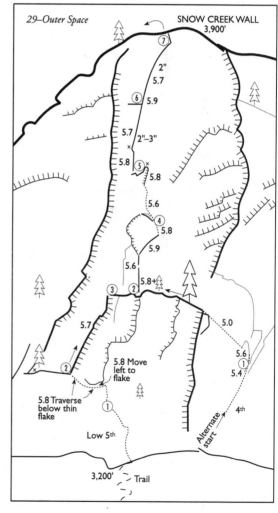

29–Outer Space

Approach (Grade II): Follow the approach to the base of the Snow Creek Wall (approximately 3,200 feet) given for climb 28, Orbit.

Route: The first three pitches of the Remorse route are recommended as a more direct start; this begins where the approach trail meets the face. Climb broken rock (low 5th class) to a convenient belay ledge where the rock steepens. The **second pitch** follows cracks to a committing balanced move left (5.8) to a large, thin flake. Continue left below the flake 40–50 feet to a large ledge (5.8). **Pitch 3** climbs blocks and a chimney (5.7) to gain Two Tree Ledge (one of the big trees may have died).

Option: Another way to begin the climb starts from 200–300 feet to the right of where the approach trail reaches the base of the wall. Climb a broken corner system (low to mid-5th class) until able to traverse left near a small pedestal.

Climber Jeff Friesen, belayed by Andrea Leuschke, begins the final pitch of Outer Space, Snow Creek Wall. (Photo by Tim Matsui)

The second pitch follows small ledges left (4th class), leading onto the large Two Tree Ledge.

From Two Tree Ledge, the **fourth pitch** begins with a difficult move (5.8+) climbing cracks for 50–60 feet until able to begin an exposed traverse right (5.9), then up 15 feet (5.8). **Pitch 5** moves left below the roof until able to climb onto low-angle but exposed face climbing with good holds. Wander up (low 5th class, long runouts) to the base of a right-facing corner (5.8) forming a small pedestal. The **sixth pitch** starts from the left side of the pedestal/ledge: climb the solitary face crack (2–3 inches wide) to a small but good ledge approximately 140 feet above. The **seventh pitch** climbs the final solitary face crack, which begins as a finger crack (5.9), or via a short corner immediately left of the finger crack. The crack (2–3 inches wide) continues for a full 160 feet of mid-5th-class climbing to a stance a short distance from the top.

Descent: Follow the descent route given for climb 28, Orbit.

PRUSIK PEAK

▲ South Face ▲ West Ridge

These are two rock climbs of very different character on a mountain whose shape and locale have made it a symbol for the rugged beauty of the Alpine Lakes Wilderness Area. One is a moderate, appealing ridge route steeped in the lore of Fred Beckey's early forays into this high country, and the other is a sustained 5.9 crack climb that was an impressive achievement when it was put up in the late 1960s. The peak's unique setting above the idyllic Enchantment Lakes basin gives these superior climbs the added appeal of incomparable scenery and ambience. Without question, these routes on Prusik Peak are among the most aesthetic rock climbs in the range.

The often photographed rock peak has become a landmark for the Alpine Lakes Wilderness Area (and specifically the Enchantments), that quintessential Northwest wilderness that, due to its proximity to Seattle, is endangered from overuse. To rock climbers, Prusik Peak is the most famous of the Cashmere Crags, the name that Fred Beckey and his contemporaries applied to the high country between Icicle Creek and Ingalls Creek.

For an alpine region, this area is one of the driest in the state. Not only does the Stuart Range lie east of the Cascades crest, Prusik Peak itself lies farther east still. The fact that Prusik Peak is shielded from storm fronts, coupled with the steepness of its South Face, means that it is frequently the first of the high peaks to come into climbing condition.

Prusik anchors the western end of the complex and jagged Temple Ridge, dotted with numerous, intriguing summits as it stretches eastward. These peaks offer challenging climbing in their own right. From the summit of Prusik Peak, it is possible to traverse this ridge to the Flake, the Monument, and onward to Boxtop and beyond. Monument is particularly appealing and notable for a fine hand crack leading to a flawless summit block required a rope throw and prusik ascent. Boxtop, one of the more distinctive summits on Temple Ridge, is also one of the more challenging.

Special Considerations: This part of the Alpine Lakes Wilderness Area is one of the most popular areas in the Cascades for climbers, backpackers, and hikers. To protect these fragile areas from overuse, the Forest Service requires permits for camping within the Enchantments permit zone and the surrounding wilderness area, as well as day-use permits for some approaches.

Be aware that both Colchuck Lake and the Enchantments Lakes basin are heavily used and can be very crowded. Campsites in the Enchantments are so coveted that permits are often snapped up in the spring for summer months. Plan ahead if you wish to camp at Colchuck Lake or in the Enchantments by visiting or calling the Leavenworth ranger station (509-548-6977). Be prepared to apply for permits months in advance, or take your chances with the daily permit "lottery," in which a drawing is held each summer day at 7:45 A.M. to determine the few lucky persons who receive on-the-spot permits. Northwest Forest Pass required.

30 SOUTH FACE GRADE III; 5.9+

Prusik Peak's South Face is a high, clean rock climb of purity and grace on rock of such quality that it has become the standard by which other Cascade climbs boasting good rock are compared. Pitch after pitch of sustained crack climbing on solid granite puts this route in a class by itself.

First ascent ▲ Ron Burgner and Fred Stanley, June 1968

Elevation ▲ 8,000 feet

Difficulty ▲ Grade III; 5.9+

Time ▲ 2–3 days round trip; 4–8 hours one-way, car to summit

Equipment ▲ Rock protection to 4 inches, including small wires; ice ax in early season for Aasgard Pass

Season ▲ May–October

Approach (Grade III+): Two common approach routes are used to reach the Enchantment Lakes Plateau and Prusik Peak. Debate continues among climbers as to the relative merits of each: The Colchuck Lake/Aasgard Pass route begins higher, but is more strenuous and requires losing hard-won elevation. The Snow Lakes approach

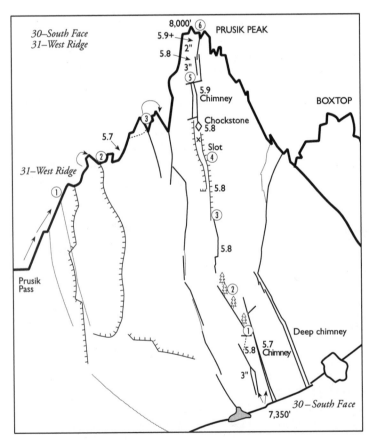

involves more elevation gain but follows a direct route, most of it on good trails. Both approaches are approximately 10 miles.

Via Snow Lakes: Follow the approach to Snow Creek Wall given for climb 28, Orbit, and pass Snow Creek Wall (across the creek) at 2 miles (2,800 feet); continue to Nada Lake at 5.5 miles (5,000 feet) and Snow Lakes at 7 miles (5,415 feet). Campsites can be found at the lakes. From the lakes, cross the dam and proceed around the east side of upper Snow Lakes to where the trail crosses the stream on a bridge. From here the character of the trail changes: it becomes steeper and requires scrambling over rocky benches. Watch for numerous cairns, which mark the trail well. At the first lake, Lake Vivian (6,785 feet), follow a faint path on the rib above the lake right (east) for several hundred feet of elevation gain past a second lake (Temple Lake). Continue up and left (west) to the base of Prusik Peak's South Face (7,350 feet).

South Face of Prusik Peak, with the West Ridge on the left skyline
(Photo by Jim Nelson)

Armand DuBois on the South Face route of Prusik Peak (Photo by Dave Bale)

Via Colchuck Lake/Aasgard Pass: Follow the approach to Colchuck Lake (5,600 feet) given for climb 22, Colchuck Glacier, and proceed toward Aasgard Pass: the trail continues around the south (right) shore of the lake past a small lakelet and onto a talus field below the Colchuck Glacier moraine. Follow cairns through talus to the south end of the lake where the trail steepens. The way becomes loose and rocky as it winds steeply to Aasgard Pass (7,800 feet). Cairns continue to mark the way down through the barren upper basin to Inspiration Lake (7,190 feet). Prusik Peak is clearly visible from the lake; from the east end of the lake, hike up Prusik Pass to the base of the West Ridge, or continue in a northeasterly direction past Gnome Tarn, traversing talus and rock slabs to the base of the South Face (7,350 feet).

Route: The route starts at the left-hand side of two deep chimneys, with two options: climb the chimney (5.7) or the crack (5.8) immediately left of the chimney. Both starts end in a belay below larch trees. The route continues up and slightly left through a second patch of larch trees. The **third pitch** climbs corner systems up and slightly right (5.8) toward a shallow chimney; the **fourth pitch** climbs the chimney (5.8) to a belay below the chockstone. Climb under the large chockstone (5.8), watching for loose blocks, to an awkward 5.9 flaring chimney, protectable with 2- to 3-inch cams or chocks, ending at the west end of the large ledge 150 feet below the summit. The **final pitch** ascends a strenuous crack system from the east end of the ledge (5.9+).

Descent: Descend via three to four single-rope rappels to the north until able to traverse left (west) to Prusik Pass at the base of the West Ridge.

31 WEST RIDGE GRADE II; 5.7

The West Ridge is a fun, not-as-hard-as-it-looks ridge route to the top of this famous peak, whose name derives from the first-ascent climbers' resorting to lassoing the summit and climbing up the rope for the final few feet. No such measures are required on the West Ridge, however, where the routefinding is straightforward and the climbing surprisingly moderate. But the notorious crux moves require a cool head as protection is minimal for this short but exposed section midway on the climb. This now classic route in the heart of the Enchantments, with the good weather typical of the immediate vicinity and the solid rock on Prusik Peak, is hard to beat. The main problem now is getting a permit to get in to the peak.

First ascent ▲ Fred Beckey, John Rupley, Don Gordon, Fred Ayres, May 1957; first winter ascent: Dave Anderson, Cal Folsom, Tom Linder, Jim McCarthy, January 1975

Elevation ▲ 8,000 feet

Difficulty ▲ Grade II; 5.7

Time ▲ 1–2 days round trip; 3–5 hours one-way from the base

Equipment ▲ Small rack to 3 inches; ice ax in early season

Season ▲ June–September

Approach (Grade III+): Follow either of the approaches given for climb 30, South Face. To reach the West Ridge from the base of the South Face, continue moving west around the peak up to Prusik Pass (7,440 feet).

Sean Holling on the crux moves of the West Ridge of Prusik
(Photo by Mark Westman)

Route: From Prusik Pass, hike up the West Ridge until it steepens. Two pitches of low-5th-class climbing on blocky, solid rock takes the climber to the crest of the West Ridge proper below a slab. The third pitch begins with the short but unprotected 5.7 friction slab, followed by easier climbing. Traverse around the prominent horn on the right (south) side to a belay on the ridge. From the belay, traverse ledges left (north) until under the final summit pyramid (class 4). The final pitch begins from the highest easy ledge: lieback up a steep corner (5.6) for 10 feet to a ledge that leads out and right. A short flake leads to another ledge, followed by a chimney (low 5th class) to the top.

Descent: Follow the descent given for climb 30, South Face.

TEMPLE RIDGE

▲ Mount Temple

Mount Temple is a short but aesthetic route to the highest point of Temple Ridge, a complex crest of craggy summits on generally good rock located deep in the heart of the Enchantments. From the high vantage of the summit, the climber has a good look at the neighborhood: McClellan Peak, the Flagpole, Little Annapurna, Witches Tower, Dragontail, and the upper Enchantments, plus a glimpse into the center of what Fred Beckey and his comrades from the '50s called the Cashmere Crags. The Snow Lakes drainage is laid out below.

While the quality of rock is consistently good, some north-facing crags in this area are known for their thick covering of lichen that can be annoying and even somewhat troublesome on infrequently done routes. The nearby Black Pyramid is so named because of its dark covering in this lichen.

The west end of Temple Ridge from the north (Photo by Jim Nelson)

Temple Ridge has numerous quality climbing possibilities, including the route described here, which is located near the center of the ridge. The peaks on the east end of the ridge—the Professor, Meteor, Razorback—are typically approached from the north via Temple Canyon. Those on the western end of the ridge—Boxtop, Monument, even Prusik—are more commonly approached from the south, as described below, from the Temple Lake–Gnome Tarn area.

Special Considerations: This part of the Alpine Lakes Wilderness Area is one of the most popular areas in the Cascades for climbers, backpackers, and hikers. To protect this fragile environment from overuse, the Forest Service requires permits for camping within the Enchantments permit zone and the surrounding wilderness area, as well as day-use permits for some approaches. Even more stringent and controversial restrictions may be applied to this backcountry in the near future.

These regulations mean that campsites within the Enchantments area are so coveted that permits are often snapped up in the spring for summer months. If you wish to camp within the Enchantment Lakes area, plan ahead by visiting or calling the Leavenworth ranger station (509-548-6977). Be prepared to apply for permits months in advance, or take your chances with the daily permit "lottery," in which a drawing is held each summer day at 7:45 A.M. to determine the few lucky persons who receive on-the-spot permits. Northwest Forest Pass required.

Temple Ridge from the north (Photo by Jim Nelson)

32 MOUNT TEMPLE GRADE II+; 5.6

This is a great two-pitch climb in one of the most scenic areas of the Cascades, an exceptionally grand landscape. This route has a high payoff for effort applied, not the least of which is the view. The combination of setting and enjoyable climbing makes for an outstanding experience here in the fabled Enchantments; the area is aptly named—there is something special about this and other climbs on the high plateau that derives from the local ambience.

First ascent ▲ Ken Prestrud, William Herston, Keith Rankin, July 1946
Elevation ▲ 8,292 feet
Difficulty ▲ Grade II+; 5.6
Time ▲ 1–2 days round trip; 2–4 hours one-way from high camp, 4–5 hours from lake
Equipment ▲ Small rack to 3 inches
Season ▲ May-October

Approach (Grade III+): Follow the Snow Lakes approach given for climb 30, South Face, to Nada Lake (5,000 feet; good camping here) at 5.5 miles.

At the midpoint of the lake, a footbridge crosses a stream (sometimes called Nada Creek), which flows from Tamarack Meadows and the high country below the Temple. Shortly after crossing the stream, look for a faint climbers path that leads

Ray Borbone summits the Boxtop on Temple Ridge. (Photo by Jim Nelson)

Climber rappels off the High Priest, Temple Ridge. (Photo by Andreas Schmidt)

right (west) and soon disappears in talus. The talus leads to a cliffy area at approximately 5,500 feet. A short 5th-class section leads to easier ground. Third- and 4th-class scrambling leads to still easier ground. Continue westward, soon entering lower Tamarack Meadows (6,000 feet); more good camping can be found in the upper meadows (approximately 6,500 feet).

Route: Ascend to the upper bench at 7,200 feet. From this perspective, Mount Temple is the left-hand (easterly) of the high summits visible above on Temple Ridge. Climb talus in a southerly direction, leading to a snow gully (steep in places), and climb (4th class) to a notch just west of the summit towers. Climb directly toward the summit tower; the upper part of this pitch ascends a clean rock face (5.6) to ledges. Scramble ledges leftward to the block just below summit. Crack and mantel moves lead to the summit.

Descent: Make a single rappel (a steep, memorable one) to the northwest from fixed anchors and retrace the climbing route.

TUMWATER CANYON

▲ *Drury Falls*

One of the highest waterfalls in the state of Washington, Drury Falls is a spectacular sight when viewed from US 2 (Stevens Pass Highway) as one drives through Tumwater Canyon. Drury Falls is located high above the Wenatchee River, near the eastern end of the highway. The water volume here is low enough that the falls freeze solid for parts of most winters. The result is a fierce-looking frozen-waterfall route of severity and commitment. The lower and main falls together provide more than 500 feet of steep ice climbing. To complicate matters, just crossing the river to reach the falls can be an arduous and even risky undertaking. While the river crossing adds a certain element of adventure to the climb, the degree to which the river is frozen can also serve as a reliable indicator of the condition of the climb. All things considered, Drury Falls is a route for only competent ice climbers.

Waterfall climbing came into vogue with the advent of modern ice tools in the early 1970s, though waterfall climbing in the Cascades remains a problematic proposition. Not every winter brings weather cold enough for the formation of climbable ice. But for those who watch closely, Drury Falls usually comes into shape for at least some portion of the winter.

Special Considerations: None.

33 DRURY FALLS GRADE III; WI 3–5

Once the smaller and more easily accessible Cascade Mountains waterfalls were climbed, Drury Falls became the obvious ice-climbing prize. The steep, five-pitch route in Tumwater Canyon is definitely the granddaddy of waterfall climbs in the Cascades. Early attempts include one in late season led by Kit Lewis, who retreated after one pitch to avoid serious icefall hazard, and another led by Paul Boving, who succeeded in climbing a combination of ice and rock to the left of the main falls. The main falls was eventually climbed in cold conditions in 1978 by Steve Pollack

Kit Lewis on Drury Falls (Photo by Greg Jacobson)

and Bob McDougal. The route is now climbed several times per season by strong ice climbers. Although moderate by current standards, Drury is considered a must-do route for Cascade ice climbers.

First ascent ▲ Steve Pollack and Bob McDougal, February 1978
Elevation ▲ 4,900 feet
Difficulty ▲ Grade III; WI 3–5, depending on conditions; 60- to 90-degree water ice
Time ▲ 1–2 days round trip; 5–8 hours one-way from high bivy sites
Equipment ▲ Rigid crampons, ice tools, ice screws, 2 ropes for double-rope rappels and retreating
Season ▲ December-February

Approach (Grade III+): Drive US 2 to approximately 3 miles east of Tumwater Campground (approximately 6 miles from the western edge of Leavenworth). The falls are located on the south side of the river (across the river from the highway), high in Tumwater Canyon. Two options are suggested for crossing to the opposite bank of the Wenatchee River, neither of them perfectly reliable.

Option 1: Under the right conditions (freeze, thaw, hard-freeze), an ice dam can form immediately downstream from Falls Creek, or at the top of the rapids above Lake Jolanda (the body of water behind the low dam). If the river is frozen solid, walk across; 2-by-6 or 2-by-8 planks have also been used here to bridge suspect areas, but not always with success. In 1987, Doug Klewin became stranded on an ice island while attempting to reach the falls and was marooned until friends and rescue materials were summoned from town by his partners.

Option 2: Consider crossing by boat or raft across Lake Jolanda, or any other suitable spot. Be creative; some success at this technique has been had farther upstream as well.

Once across the Wenatchee River, walk (upstream or down) to Falls Creek at 1,550 feet elevation. The route to the base of the falls is directly up the Falls Creek drainage, but remember that snow conditions must be stable for this route to be safe, as the drainage is a giant

Upper Drury Falls, Tumwater Canyon
(Photo by Kurt Smith)

funnel. Beware of avalanche danger. Turn back if conditions indicate avalanche potential in the Falls Creek drainage.

At approximately 2,800 feet, the approach follows the left (south) side of the stream; at 3,800 feet, there is a suitable bivy spot and also several attractive two-pitch ice climbs. Drury Falls itself is a short distance above at approximately 4,200 feet.

Route: Lower Drury Falls is approximately 200 feet high; it is usually climbed in two pitches, the ice approaching 80 degrees near the top.

The upper or main falls is several hundred feet above the lower, reached by a pitch of 30-degree snow. The main falls is climbed in a series of vertical steps (three–four pitches, depending on belays), totaling approximately 400 feet. The climb finishes on a vertical pillar on the left (south) side of the falls. The falls face east-southeast and so get midmorning sun.

Descent: Walk south below the falls until able to rappel from tree anchors.

MOUNT INDEX, NORTH PEAK ──────────────
▲ *North Face*

The Mount Index peaks, easily visible from the highway, look so steep, so rugged, and so intriguing that they seem surely to rival the Dru or Mount Whitney as climbs. Unfortunately, Mount Index's appealing visage is an illusion. The low elevation—barely 5,000 feet—combined with brittle rock and thick vegetation have conspired to make for difficult and somewhat unappealing climbing typical of lower-elevation peaks on the west slope of the Cascades.

The friable rock is hard to protect and, except for the steepest sections of rock, the entire massif is covered with dense foliage. Although usually recommended as a winter climb, this route is also recommended as a 1-day outing in summer months. Expect some bushes and trees throughout the climb, as well as some enjoyable rock climbing on the upper section of the north rib.

While the climb is irresistible in any season, it is as a winter climb that Index deserves special attention. In winter, when the vegetation is covered by snow, Mount Index becomes a different sort of climb. Set so far west, the mountain catches the brunt of wet winter storms off Puget Sound. The low elevation actually helps, as the flanks of Mount Index frequently warm up, then freeze over, a situation that makes for good icing conditions. Cold arctic highs provide superb conditions for winter climbing. Lastly, Mount Index's proximity to US 2 (Stevens Pass Highway) makes it quite accessible, a rare attribute for a good winter climb in the Cascades. Taken together, these factors can result in outstanding climbing conditions on Mount Index.

The fact that the peak is now a magnet for climbers who enjoy difficult mixed alpine climbing owes to a great tradition of hard winter ascents on the peak. In 1963, Pat Callis and Dan Davis completed the first winter ascent of the classic North Face route on the North Peak after 3 days of hard climbing. The feat marked the beginning of great alpine climbs on Mount Index. In 1977, Steve Swenson, Todd Bibler, Gary Frederickson, and Reese Martin completed the first winter traverse (north to south) of the three Mount Index peaks. Bill Sumner and Fred Dunham climbed the

Index Peaks from the north, showing the North Face routes on the North and Middle Peaks: A. North Face, Middle Peak (McNerthney-Klewin); B. North Face, North Peak (Photo by Jim Nelson)

northeast face of the Main Peak in 1984, and Doug Klewin and Dan McNerthney climbed the elegant line on the north face of the Middle Peak in 1978. In 1988, Jim Nelson and Mark Bebie completed the first ascent of the Eve Dearborn Memorial Route on the North Peak. The fact that so many strong Cascade climbers have been drawn to Mount Index in winter underscores its appeal when under ice and snow.

Special Considerations: Northwest Forest Pass required.

34 NORTH FACE GRADE III+–V; 5.7

This route on Index's North Peak is a spectacular winter climb that can vary tremendously in difficulty, depending on conditions. Cold temperatures are absolutely imperative for this and other winter climbs on Mount Index. With part of the route following drainages, the importance of below-freezing temperatures cannot be over-emphasized. Even with cold weather, the climbing can change radically. On key pitches climbing out of the North Face bowl—class 4 ground in summer—the climbing can take hours when the rock is covered in new snow. Conversely, when ice has formed, the climber can dash up these same pitches. Surprisingly good mid-5th-class rock is found on the upper ridge.

First winter ascent ▲ Patrick Callis and Dan Davis, January 1963

Elevation ▲ 5,353 feet

Difficulty ▲ Grade III+ (summer)–V (winter); 5.7; steep mixed ground

Time ▲ 2–3 days round trip in winter; 8–10 hours one-way, car to summit, in summer

Equipment ▲ Ice ax, crampons, medium rack to 3 inches, pitons, 2 ropes for descent

Season ▲ December-March; July-September

Approach (Grade II): Drive US 2 to where the highway crosses the Skykomish River on the Skykomish River Bridge 0.5 mile west of the Index town exit, and turn south on the Mount Index Road. Drive the Mount Index Road for 0.3 mile, take the

Climbing out of the bowl toward the north rib on Index, North Face, North Peak (Photo by Joe Catellani)

first right, and walk or drive the very rough road approximately 1.5 miles to where a trail traverses a brushy slope toward Bridal Veil Falls (approximately 1,500 feet).

Below the falls, in heavy timber, take the trail as it switchbacks steeply uphill. Beware: this is no ordinary trail. In places it climbs through short rock bands (class 3–4) with tree roots for holds. The trail reaches Lake Serene (2,509 feet) in 1 steep mile from the end of the rough road. From the far right (northwest) side of the lake, climb to the shoulder where the North Face and the east face of the mountain meet. The climbing begins on or near the crest of a low-angled rib.

Route: The first two pitches climb on or near the crest of the low-angled rib; these pitches (4th-class climbing in summer) may have some difficult climbing in winter (snow or, much worse, rock thinly covered in snow), leading to a belay below a very steep wall. This wall is bypassed by moving left (east) and then traversing up into a shallow gully.

Take precautions, as in winter this gully can be exposed to icefall caused by morning sun, due to the eastern exposure.

From here the route traverses back right on a hidden ledge leading to an exposed slab (low 5th class in summer). Easier climbing to the right leads to a steep alder patch (vertical bushwhacking here), continuing up to a ramp leading right and onto the North Face bowl. Climb the bowl (40- to 50-degree snow or ice) to its upper right side. Two difficult pitches climb out of the bowl (again, ice- or snow-covered), up and right and onto the crest of the north ridge and possible bivy sites. These mixed-climbing pitches are difficult to protect and are easiest when thickly iced.

Once on the ridge, the rock is good; two and a half pitches follow on and just right of the crest. The climbing here is mid-5th class, but the rock is solid and good anchors are available. Exposed snow slopes lead through trees and then up to the false summit. An exposed ridge and snow slope are traversed west to the true summit.

Descent: From the summit, traverse the exposed ridge east to the false summit. From the false summit, descend snow slopes down, trending northeast, through trees to the top of the north rib. Make two double-rope rappels and a third short rappel down the rock rib to a snow shoulder, then two more double-rope rappels from the trees into the North Face bowl. Make one double-rope rappel down and across the bowl to its eastern edge; continue rappeling down and east out of the bowl—a long rappel through thick trees followed by a traversing rappel east on snow ledges. Make one long rappel over a steep wall, and two final rappels to slopes above Lake Serene.

INDEX TOWN WALL
▲ Centerfold ▲ Town Crier ▲ Godzilla–Slow Children and City Park

Nestled up against the western edge of the Cascades in the Skykomish Valley near the town of Index is a place with more exposed granite than almost anywhere else in the range. Only an hour from Seattle, this tremendous expanse of rock—found on both the lower and upper walls as well as other, smaller outcroppings—has drawn climbers in great numbers and made Index a true center for Northwest rock climbing.

Discovered by climbers in the 1960s, the routes at Index followed the usual progression: First to be climbed were the cracks—on aid. Next the cracks were gradually climbed free by a generation of improving climbers, creating some routes of tremendous difficulty. These days, a very high level of climbing skill is necessary for the hardest routes at Index, which see visits from both sport climbers doing free routes as well as the occasional big-wall climber doing the aid climbs, some of which still take more than 1 day.

True to the modern trend, new face routes have been developed or engineered at Index following sport-climbing techniques: fixed bolts for protection to be used with quickdraws. With easy accessibility (including new trails built by Cal Folsom, climber and trails advocate) and proximity to the population centers of western Washington, Index continues to be a popular spot for climbers, and a focus for high-standard rock climbing.

Although there are numerous cliffs and crags in the neighborhood, the climbs

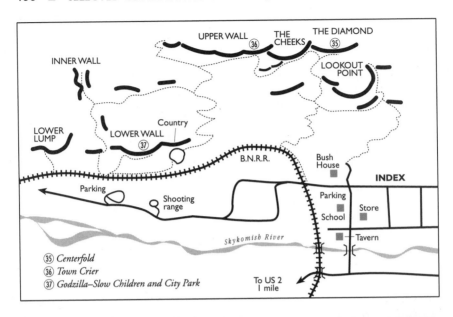

Index Town Wall, Upper Wall, the Cheeks, and the Diamond. Index townsite is in the foreground. (Photo by Jim Nelson)

recommended here—on the main Lower Wall (west of town, along the railroad tracks), the main Upper Wall, and the Diamond—are representative of the quality of routes that can be found at Index.

Special Considerations: None.

35 CENTERFOLD GRADE III; 5.11

Centerfold is a good example of a climb that was discovered from above on rappel as opposed to the more traditional bottom-up technique. Emphasizing the quality of climbing, and safety, this practical approach to new route establishment is generally considered standard by most climbers.

But do not assume that all of the adventure has been removed—on Centerfold, bolt-protected face climbing connects beautiful crack climbing in which the leader will have to judge when and where to place protection. With wonderful exposure on the cleaned (extensively gardened) rock, the four-pitch Centerfold is one of the most enjoyable rock climbs in the Cascades.

Tom Hargis on Centerfold (Photo by Larry Kemp)

First ascent ▲ Cal Folsom and
Andy Tuthill, 1988
Elevation ▲ 2,200 feet
Difficulty ▲ Grade III; 5.11
Time ▲ 3–5 hours one-way from the base
Equipment ▲ Medium rack to 2 inches,
quickdraws, 2 ropes
Season ▲ Year-round

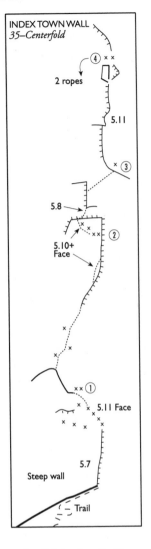

INDEX TOWN WALL
35–Centerfold

2 ropes

5.11

5.8

5.10+
Face

5.11 Face

5.7

Steep wall

Trail

Approach (Grade I+): Drive US 2 to the Index turn-off and exit north, toward town. From Index, reach the Diamond by walking from town along the railroad tracks just beyond the Bush House to a trail that begins as wood planks across the ditch (see map of Index).

Route: From where the trail reaches the Diamond, follow along its base right (east) to a left-facing corner. **Pitch 1** climbs the left-facing corner (5.7) leading to 5.11 face climbing. **Pitch 2** begins by moving left on easy ground followed by face climbing into a left-facing corner. The **third pitch** begins with 5.10+ face climbing until able to climb through the roof (5.8) up and right to the belay (short pitch). **Pitch 4** climbs a spectacular crack system (5.11) to a belay with rappel anchors.

Descent: Descend via double-rope rappels from the top of pitch 4.

36 TOWN CRIER
GRADE IV; 5.8 AND A2

The second route done on the Index Town Wall, Town Crier has become a classic aid-climbing experience with genuine big-wall ambience—and problems. The climbing is on good rock, and the route is at low-enough elevation that it affords a season much longer than other "alpine" walls. Town Crier is traditionally done with a combination of free climbing and aid.

First ascent ▲ Fred Beckey and Dave Beckstead, March 1966
Elevation ▲ 2,400 feet
Difficulty ▲ Grade IV; 5.8 and A2
Time ▲ 1–2 days round trip
Equipment ▲ Large rack to 3 inches
Season ▲ Year-round

Approach (Grade I+): Drive US 2 to the Index turnoff and exit north, toward town. Drive west along the road beside the Skykomish River to a small parking area below the Lower Wall.

Chuck Hampson on the fourth pitch of Town Crier (Photo by Dave Bale)

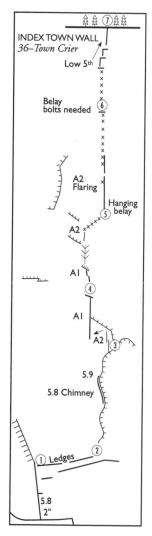

INDEX TOWN WALL
36–Town Crier

Hike the trail that begins near the right-hand (eastern) end of the Lower Wall climbing areas; continue up via a good trail through the trees to the base of the Upper Wall.

Route: Begin the climb 50 yards left (south) of the spring waterfall at the spot where the original Upper Wall trail reaches the wall. The **first pitch** climbs an awkward (5.8) hand crack 30 feet to easier climbing that leads to a good ledge at 75 feet off the ground. **Pitch 2** involves moving the belay right across the ledge to the base of a flared chimney. **Pitch 3** climbs the chimney (5.8) 40 feet to a difficult exit move (5.9) leading to mid-5th-class climbing and a good belay on "Smoke Out Ledge" above the larger "Big Honker Ledge." **Pitch 4**, the first aid pitch on the route, ascends face cracks up to a large roof; tension (A2) left to a straightforward face crack (A1) leading to a small ledge just above. **Pitch 5** starts off on blocky A1, then moves left under a small roof to a shallow open book. The wall above overhangs (A2); above this bulge, move right to a bolt ladder leading to a hanging belay. **Pitch 6** ascends awkward, flaring cracks (A2) with occasional bolts, followed by more aid on bolts. This pitch can be concluded with a hanging belay at approximately 100 feet, or at a nice stance at 150 feet where a new bolt makes a safe belay. **Pitch 7** ascends a final bolt ladder that leads to a small ledge. Mid-5th-class climbing leads up and left past an alcove, followed by a dirty crack to the top.

Descent: A single 150-foot rappel can be made from the south end of the Upper Wall, past a gully, from slings around a large tree.

37 GODZILLA–SLOW CHILDREN AND CITY PARK
GRADE I–II; 5.9+–5.14 OR A1

An outstanding three-pitch climb on the Lower Wall, this classic route is identified by individual pitches: the first is Godzilla, the second is called the Second Pitch, the third is Slow Children.

City Park, the thin, steep face crack 15 feet left of Godzilla on the Lower Wall, can be used as a direct start to Godzilla–Slow Children, as it leads to the same belay ledge at 120 feet. City Park takes wired nuts very well (A1), so pitons are neither necessary nor recommended. One of the early routes put up on the Lower Wall, this route is an excellent place to practice aid climbing on a steep and relatively safe wall, as well as a nice top-roped problem for 5.14 climbers.

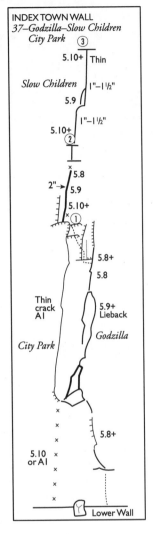

First ascent ▲ John Carpenter, Pat NcNerthney, John Nelson, Terry Lien, date unknown

Elevation ▲ 850 feet

Difficulty ▲ Grade I–II; Godzilla, 5.9+; Second Pitch, 5.10+; Slow Children, 5.10+; City Park, 5.14 or A1

Time ▲ 1–3 hours one-way from the base

Equipment ▲ Medium rack to 3 inches, including small wires (and small cams for Slow Children); 2 ropes

Season ▲ Year-round

Approach (Grade I): Follow the approach to the parking area below the Lower Wall given for climb 36, Town Crier. Take the trail straight ahead to the Lower Wall.

Route: **Pitch 1,** Godzilla, is located on the right side of the main Lower Wall, left of Narrow Arrow overhang (a large roof at 120 feet). A direct start can be made via the City Park bolt ladder, which goes free at 5.10. The bolt ladder leads to the start of the crack at 30 feet off the ground. The crack takes wired nuts well. For an alternate route to bypass City Park's 5.10 bolt ladder, move 20 feet to the right and climb a mantel and corner (5.8+) on small protection.

At 40 feet a strenuous lieback flake (5.9+) leads to 5.8 climbing in a corner, reaching a point under a small roof. Move left and mantel onto a small ledge (5.8+). From the small ledge, a final bit of 5.8+ moves up and left to the belay ledge.

The **Second Pitch** begins with a difficult stem-and-mantel (5.10+). A nice hand crack (5.9) follows, leading to an exposed move (5.8) at an old bolt. Mid-5th-class climbing leads to the belay.

Chuck Gerson on Slow Children, Lower Wall (Photo by Jim Nelson)

Pitch 3, Slow Children, begins with a steep corner, with a fixed angle pin (5.10+, originally rated 5.11), which leads to a belay above a difficult flared thin crack at 80 feet.

Descent: Rappel the climbing route via fixed anchors using two ropes to make double-line rappels.

BIG FOUR MOUNTAIN

▲ *North Face—Carlstad-Folsom Route*

Along with neighboring peaks in the Monte Cristo vicinity, Big Four Mountain stands well west of the Cascades crest. Despite its relatively low elevation, the mountain has become one of the most popular attractions in the Mount Baker–Snoqualmie National Forest—not because of its climbing routes, but because of the Big Four ice caves, which see thousands of visitors each year. The ice caves are less than a mile from the Mountain Loop Highway, at the base of the mountain in one of the lowest glacial remnants in the range.

The North Face of Big Four in winter. From left to right, climbing routes are:
A. Martin-Pratt; B. Catellani-Adams; C. Cordery-Cotter descent; D. Cordery-Cotter
ascent; E. Carlstad-Folsom; F. Paull-Littauer. (Photo by Jim Nelson)

For climbers, the appeal of Big Four is its North Face, one of the most massive nonvolcanic north faces in the range. At more than 4,000 vertical feet from base to summit, the North Face of Big Four is impressive by any measure. In summer, the face is covered by loose rock and vegetation typical of lower-elevation western Washington peaks. But in winter, the snow-covered face can become an attractive alpine objective. A series of steep couloirs and ridges are the defining features of several obvious lines.

In terms of accessibility, position, sheer size, and the quality of climbing, the North Face is an attractive, if serious, winter destination. When in good condition, these routes are composed of ice or compact snow, making for rewarding climbing. On the other hand, the routes can be long and demanding, and retreat may be difficult. The North Face is a venue best suited to experienced alpine climbers.

A real danger is that the North Face of Big Four is one of the most avalanche-prone faces in the range. The forest at the base of the face is continuously pummeled by frequent slides of ice and snow. Avalanche danger and route conditions should be skillfully scrutinized by any party preparing to attempt a route. The descent can be problematic as well. Dan Cauthorn, who climbed the North Face in 1985 and bivied on top, says, "The descent down the west ridge back to the car the next day was the crux of the climb. Steep trees, hidden cliffs, tangling rappel ropes, etc."

As for climbing conditions, apply the basic rules of the complex science of snow conditions. Aspect, sun, wind, rain, gravity, temperature, and time are some of the factors to consider. Still, there is nothing like recent, firsthand field observations when considering conditions for a climb as serious as the North Face of Big Four Mountain.

Big Four was first climbed in 1931 by Forest Farr and Art Winder. The first recorded North Face ascent was done via the north rib by Montgomery Johnson, Ken Prestrud, and Charles Welch in 1942. Confusion prevails regarding new routes on the North Face because, as Cauthorn explains, "There are three or four couloirs that parallel each other, separated by ribs, and they can all seem quite similar. Distinguishing between them in casual conversation is not always easy."

The broad face has seen many routes. What follows are some that the authors have been able to confirm, although there may well have been others: In February 1982 Joe Catellani and Gordon Adams climbed the central rib of the North Face. Debbie Martin and Bruce Pratt climbed a rib to the left (east) of the central rib in 1980s. Also in the '80s, Greg Child and Steve Swensen climbed a North Face route, as did Dan Cauthorn and Steve Mascioli, both parties ascending near the orginal Carlstad-Folsom route. In 1994 Alan Kearney and Greg Cronn ascended a route west of the central rib.

The North Face has seen some memorable solo climbs as well. In December 1988, Robert Cordery-Cotter soloed a more direct route to the east of the original line, and descended a parallel line east of his ascent route (near the Kearney-Cronn line). In the 1990s, Jim Dockery soloed both the Carlstad-Folsom route and the Cordery-Cotter descent route. Bart Paull reports doing an ascent in 1996 up a steep, attractive line to the west of the Carlstad-Folsom line. He calls his route Spindrift Couloir, which was climbed with partner Doug Littauer.

Special Considerations: Climbing permits are not required at present. For more information and up-to-date regulations, call the Verlot ranger station (360-691-7791). Northwest Forest Pass or Sno-Park permit required.

38 NORTH FACE—CARLSTAD-FOLSOM ROUTE
GRADE V; WI 4

Partly through an interest in local mining history, Rich Carlstad was spending a lot of time in the area when he began to realize the potential for a winter climb on Big Four's North Face. Conditions were superb that December 1974 when he and Cal Folsom quickly made plans for a light and fast attempt. Leaving at midnight from their camp below the face, the pair was able to climb mostly unbelayed, arriving at the summit ridge by midafternoon. Following the spectacular summit ridge over several lower subsummits put them on top late in the day. The evening light on snow shapes along the ridge was spectacular. They began the long and unknown descent just minutes before sunset. Partly due to favorable snow conditions, Carlstad and Folsom were able to make a very quick descent of the west ridge to a snow gully leading back toward their camp.

Temperatures on their climb were estimated to be in the 0- to 15-degree-Fahrenheit range. Both climbers wore leather single boots, and Carlstad suffered frostbite on his

Climber Kristie Arend enjoys the Carlstad-Folsom route on the North Face of Big Four Mountain. (Photo by Tim Matsui)

toes (partially due to the snug fit that he preferred for improving rock climbing performance). Modern ice climbing equipment was scarce in the '70s, and particularly for young climbers. They customized $15 ice axes from REI by heating the picks, bending them, tempering them, and then filing the teeth. Cal was able to braze front points onto his 10-point Salewa crampons, and continued using them for years.

First ascent ▲ Rich Carlstad and Cal Folsom, December 1974

Elevation ▲ 6,135 feet

Difficulty ▲ Grade V; WI 4; ice to 85 degrees, expect some 5th-class rock climbing if conditions are thin

Time ▲ 1–2 days round trip; 8–20 hours one-way, car to summit

Equipment ▲ Ice screws of varying lengths, small rock rack, 2–3 pickets or deadmen

Season ▲ Late December–March

Approach (Grade I): From US 2 east of Everett, drive north on State Highway 9; then take State Highway 92 northeast to the town of Granite Falls. At the east end of town, turn left and pass the high school; the street becomes Mountain Loop Highway in a few blocks. Drive 24 miles and park at the Big Four Mountain scenic area (1,700 feet) if possible.

In the winter the road is normally closed at Deer Creek, 2 miles before the parking area; if this is the case, park near the turnaround by the road closure (1,575 feet). Hike the 2 miles along the road to the Big Four scenic area; the going is usually easy due to high snowmobile and cross-country ski traffic.

At the Big Four scenic area, search for the beginning of the ice caves trail, near the outhouses. Hike 1 mile along the winding ice caves trail, crossing three foot-bridges and gaining about 200 feet in elevation; this trail may be difficult to follow in the snow and in the dark, but often there are footprints left by the hikers and snowshoers who frequently travel to the ice caves, ignoring the warning signs that there is extreme avalanche hazard all winter long. The trail trends left as it approaches the mountain, and ends in the open area below the North Face of Big Four, which is usually covered with avalanche debris.

Route: Depending on how much avalanche debris has accumulated, it may be possible to ascend an avalanche cone right up the middle of the slabby cliff bands that lie to the right of the main lower rocky headwall (these cliff bands lie directly below the couloir itself), and then link snow-covered ledges rightward and up through a small thicket of trees to the bottom of the North Face bowl. The orginal (Carlstad-Folsom) ascent climbed ice smears through the lower cliff bands. However, conditions may or may not permit this direct start option.

Once in the North Face bowl, ascend the 25- to 35-degree snowfield up to the bottom of the technical part of the route at roughly 3,800 feet. For direction, if cloud cover allows, it is possible to use the notch between the two rightmost peaks of the mountain as a "sight."

Sean Courage on the Carlstad-Folsom route on the North Face of Big Four Mountain (Photo by Andreas Schmidt)

The technical part of the couloir starts with 50-degree ice or compact snow, with occasional small bumps or steps of up to 70 degrees. When conditions are cold enough, the angle is steep enough here to allow new snow not to accumulate but to slough off as spindrift (hence the name of the route); in snowy weather the couloir sloughs continuously. Pickets or screws can be regularly used for protection. The couloir gradually steepens until it reaches a steep ice or mixed headwall at approximately 5,000 feet.

The headwall is usually 120 feet of nearly vertical ice (WI 4), depending on conditions. It is possible to bypass the steepest part by climbing mixed terrain to the left of the headwall (WI 3) for 300 feet before veering back right to rejoin the main couloir. This is not necessarily less difficult, but an interesting variation, of which there are many on this route.

Above the headwall, the angle slacks off. Climb approximately 1,000 more feet of mostly 60-degree ice and snow toward the ridge crest. There may be occasional sections of exposed rock that afford little in the way of protection, and the summit ridge may be barricaded by soft flutings or large cornices, depending on conditions. Atop the summit ridge, the climber is still a long way from the summit; as much as 1 to 3 hours of climbing along the ridge may be required (depending on conditions).

Descent: Big Four is a complex mountain, with multiple routes and changeable conditions. All these factors are important considerations in choosing the best descent route. All four of the following options have been used by climbers ascending the North Face.

Note: The routes on the western side of the face are a long way from the summit and involve exposed climbing along the ridge.

Option 1/Northeast descent route: From the summit, descend to the east, aiming for a large northeast-facing gully. Descend the gully, then traverse north across a basin above cliff bands until a ramp leads down to the lower basin, and down to the road near the Big Four picnic area.

Option 2/West ridge: Follow a descending traverse around the southwest side of the mountain and link snowfields down and toward the northwest ridge between clumps of trees until it becomes too steep. Rappel off trees, still trending around toward the northwest ridge. Three 50-meter rappels and some down-climbing are probably necessary to gain the large treed saddle between Big Four and neighboring Hall Peak. Beware of large cornices on the northwest ridge. Traverse the saddle between large trees to just where it begins to rise to Hall Peak, and then descend the obvious long diagonal northeast gully back down to the North Face bowl (a single rappel may be required at the top of the gully). Find the ascent tracks, and follow them the rest of the way down. Rappels may be required to get past the cliff bands at the bottom of the face, depending on conditions.

Option 3: With ideal snow conditions, the orginal ascent party was able to descend the west ridge. Depending on conditions, this may be a good option. One rappel was made from the ridge crest into a snow gully that lies east of the long diagonal gully described in option 2 above. It may be difficult to locate the key snow gully, as it is not obvious in the accompanying photograph.

Option 4: Descend the chosen climbing route.

GREEN GIANT BUTTRESS

▲ *Dreamer and Giants Tears*

Located on the edge of the Boulder River Wilderness, Green Giant Buttress has a remote and out-of-the way feel to it. Situated well west of the Cascades crest, its proximity to Seattle is somewhat offset by a long drive in on a deteriorating logging road. Still, Dreamer—and other worthwhile routes in the Darrington area—will attract growing numbers of climbers. Located in an area notorious for being wet and brushy, the buttress, while low in elevation, is a very impressive wall and a surprisingly brush-free climb. The old jungle-hell stories are passé.

Special Considerations: Northwest Forest Pass required.

Three Fingers Mountain looms behind the exposed rock of Green Giant Buttress.
(Photo by Jim Nelson)

Martin Volken on Dreamer's Blue Crack, Green Giant Buttress
(Photo by Jim Nelson)

39 DREAMER AND GIANTS TEARS
GRADE IV; 5.9–5.11 OR A0

Dreamer is a ten-pitch climb on superb rock with a variety of challenges: the lower section features slab and friction climbing, while the upper half offers crack climbing and steep face climbing. Unlike earlier routes on this crag—climbs such as Botany 101 that followed obvious, wet drainages—this south-facing route climbs clean slabs. Giants Tears is a variation that offers a harder start to the route, ascending left of Dreamer and eventually joining Dreamer at the top of its fourth pitch.

First ascent ▲ Duane Constantino and Chris Greyell, 1979

Elevation ▲ 3,084 feet

Difficulty ▲ Grade IV; Dreamer, 5.9; Giants Tears, 5-11 or A0

Time ▲ 1–2 days round trip; 5–10 hours one-way from the base

Equipment ▲ Medium rack to 3¹/₂ inches

Season ▲ May-October

Approach (Grade II+): From Interstate 5 near Arlington, exit onto State Highway 530 and drive 32 miles east to Darrington. From Darrington, turn right on the Mountain Loop Highway and drive 2.9 miles to Forest Road 2060, directly across from the Clear Creek Campground. Turn right on FR 2060 and continue—the road is potholed but otherwise drivable; there is a view of Three O'Clock Rock at 5 miles. At the intersection at 5.5 miles, keep right. At 6.1 miles pass Squire Creek trailhead; continue into Copper Creek valley and park at approximately 7.8 miles from the Mountain Loop Highway, with views of Green Giant Buttress (1,865 feet; camping possible here).

Hike the rest of the road, which soon becomes a trail through timber. Emerge from the timber in approximately 1 mile at a brushy area near a small stream; cross the creek and try to find a path through the brush until able to traverse left (west) through a boulder field toward Copper Creek. Follow the climbers path along the right (north) bank of Copper Creek a short distance to the base of a series of waterfalls and granite slabs. Find and ascend a dry creekbed leading north through a brushy section to the base of Green Giant Buttress (2,900 feet).

Route: At the base of the buttress, climb several hundred feet of class 3 slabs. The **first pitch** of Dreamer starts at the base of a prominent, brushy dihedral (the Botany 101 route) near the center of the face. Angle left and up on small ledges and cracks to a belay below a prominent crack. The **second pitch** climbs the crack (5.7) to a belay. **Pitch 3** ascends slabby friction slabs (5.8), with bolts for protection, to a

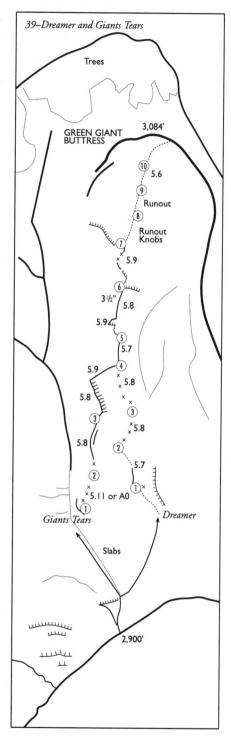

39–Dreamer and Giants Tears

belay at the base of a small corner. For **pitch 4,** climb up the corner to a bolt and continue left and up across more 5.8 slabby friction climbing (bolts) to a belay below a small roof.

The **fifth pitch** climbs small cracks (5.7) left of the roof. **Pitch 6** follows cracks up to a bigger, more prominent roof (5.8), and underclings left (5.9) out under the roof (possible rope drag here); then move right into a long, clean crack (a feature called the Blue Crack because the film that Duane and Chris used rendered a bluish color). This long, clean crack widens to 3½ inches (5.8) to a belay. The **seventh pitch** climbs left of a small overlap (off-route bolts visible above) past a bolt, then left under a roof (more possible rope drag) onto bolt-protected 5.9 face climbing above. **Pitch 8** climbs knobs (5.4) to the right of a brushy corner, with 5.8 moves near the top of the pitch (some long runouts on this pitch). **Pitch 9** is similar, 5.8 at mid-pitch, also long runouts. The **final pitch** (5.6) leads to the ridge. (Many climbers rope off from the top of the seventh pitch.)

Giants Tears direct variation: Giants Tears is a direct start variation to Dreamer that begins at the large gully/corner located left of Dreamer. Scramble several hundred feet of class 3 slabs to where the wall steepens at the base of the gully/corner, an even larger brushy gully system (the Avoidance route) than Botany 101. Giants Tears begins at the gully system (see climbers topo).

Pitch 1 begins with tricky 5.7 face climbing to a belay stance in the corner. **Pitch 2** climbs a bolt ladder (5.11 or A0) leading to 5.10 friction climbing. Bolts are ¼ inch and could be replaced with larger ones. **Pitch 3** climbs past 5.8 cracks and a 5.6 flake. On the **fourth pitch,** a left-facing corner leads to 5.9 friction moves right to join Dreamer for pitches 5–10.

Descent: Descend by walking off and right down a brushy gully and slabs, or by rappelling the climbing route.

GLACIER PEAK ———————————————————————
▲ *Sitkum Glacier*

This is a straightforward glacier route in a very scenic area guarded by an exceptionally long approach for a Cascade volcano. In fact, Glacier Peak holds the distinction of being the Cascades' only true wilderness volcano. Whereas Mounts Rainier, Baker, and Hood all have roads high on their flanks, Glacier Peak is situated in isolated splendor, surrounded by the Glacier Peak and Henry M. Jackson Wilderness Areas. Not only are there no visitors centers on this mountain, it is a long walk in from any direction. This backcountry setting, when combined with the peak's altitude and central location—creating an exceptional summit panorama over much of the range—make Glacier Peak an appealing if somewhat time-consuming summit.

The route recommended here presents few technical difficulties but, like any other route on a Cascade volcano, harbors the usual potential for rapidly changing weather and deteriorating visibility. Bad weather and whiteout, combined with altitude and the inherent dangers of glacier travel, can create a deadly mix. Any climber contemplating a route on Glacier Peak or other volcanoes should be aware of the

Labels on image: Sitkum Spire, Saddle, Sitkum Glacier

Glacier Peak, the Sitkum Glacier (Photo by Austin Post, USGS)

dangers and be prepared to handle them. Crevasse-rescue capability, map-and-compass skills, and good judgment are the minimum requirements for even a moderate route such as this one.

Special Considerations: At present, permits are not required to climb or camp in the Glacier Peak Wilderness, part of the Mount Baker Snoqualmie National Forest. For information and up-to-date regulations, contact the Darrington ranger station (360-436-1155). Northwest Forest Pass required.

40 SITKUM GLACIER GRADE III

The nontechnical nature of the Sitkum route has made it popular not only with climbers and skiers, but with a growing coterie of alpine snowboarders. If the hike in—almost 10 miles—seems like a long way to carry skis or a snowboard, the other side of the equation is that a long and largely uncrevassed wilderness run is worth the trouble.

Despite the long approach, the climb is frequently done in 2 days from the car, but many climbers spend 2 nights at high camp (Boulder Basin or at the intersection of the Pacific Crest Trail and the Sitkum Ridge climbers path) to better savor the mountain's wilderness feel.

First ascent ▲ Unknown
Elevation ▲ 10,541 feet
Difficulty ▲ Grade III; 30-degree snow, glacier travel, altitude
Time ▲ 2–3 days round trip; 4–7 hours one-way from Boulder Basin
Equipment ▲ Ice ax, crampons, wands
Season ▲ May–October

Approach (Grade III+): From Interstate 5 near Arlington, exit onto State Highway 530 and drive 32 miles east to Darrington. From Darrington, turn right on the Mountain Loop Highway and drive 10.5 miles to the White Chuck River Road. Turn left and follow the White Chuck River Road for 11 miles to the campground and trailhead at the end of the road (2,300 feet).

Skier on Sitkum Glacier, Glacier Peak, with the White Chuck Valley in the distance (Photo by Gordy Skoog)

Spring conditions on the Sitkum Glacier on Glacier Peak (Photo by Mark Kroese)

Hike the White Chuck River Trail 5.5 miles to Kennedy Hot Springs and campsites (3,300 feet)—have a soak if you are so inclined, or save this luxury for the trip out. Hike another 1.5 miles to Sitkum Creek and the junction with the Pacific Crest Trail (3,850 feet), approximately 7 miles from the road. Follow the Pacific Crest Trail 0.5 mile north to 4,100 feet and the start of a climbers path to Sitkum Ridge (sometimes called Glacier Trail or Boulder Basin Trail). Follow the path steeply along the ridge (south of Sitkum Creek) to timberline and Boulder Basin (5,500 feet) and good camping. This area is the usual high camp for an ascent of Glacier Peak via the Sitkum Glacier.

Route: From Boulder Basin, climb southeast out of the basin toward the lower lobe of the Sitkum Glacier. Climb slightly rightward (south) to the narrow corridor just left (north) of the cleaver that divides the glacier's lower lobe. Continue up the glacier in a northeasterly direction toward the saddle in the western summit ridge (9,500 feet), just east of the obvious Sitkum Spire. Then climb toward the summit by turning right and following Sitkum Ridge (loose pumice). Bear right (east) several hundred yards (keeping right, or east, of the summit, and just below it) to the snow chute that leads to the summit area. (**Note:** Near the end of the above-mentioned eastern traverse, take necessary precautions when crossing a short—approximately 15-foot—but very steep south-facing chute, the site of at least one fatal accident in recent years.)

Descent: Descend the climbing route.

DOME PEAK

▲ *Dome Glacier and Southwest Summit*

Dome Peak marks the end (or beginning) of the world-famous Ptarmigan Traverse, the chain of mountains first climbed in 1938 by a loose association of hard men who called themselves the Ptarmigan Climbing Club. The long journey into Dome Peak is strenuous, well traveled, and quite scenic: 6 miles of valley bottom through now rare old-growth forest, rising through gentle parkland to a ridge crossing, a small alpine lake, and more classic Northwest meadows of huckleberries, wildflowers, streams, and parkland, and finally on to the talus, snowfields, and glacier of the climbing route described here.

From Itswoot Ridge, the last barrier to the mountain, Dome Peak (showing both its Main and Southwest Summits) stands big and close, with the Dome Glacier and climbing route clearly visible. The higher Main Summit is by far the easier and more popular climb. However, the more technical Southwest Summit is equally recommended: a short, steep snow-and-ice face leads to a pitch and a half of outstanding rock climbing, low-5th-class, to a tiny summit.

Dome Peak and the Dome Glacier routes (Photo by Austin Post, USGS)

North
Gunsight Peak

Sinister
Peak

Chickamin
Glacier

Climbers near the summit on Dome Peak (Photo by Mark Kroese)

Ironically, massive and remote Dome Peak may be viewed from the easily accessible peaks of the North Cascades Highway's Washington Pass area. That view shows Dome Peak's neighboring Chickamin Glacier, one of the biggest in the range, to its best advantage.

Special Considerations: At present, permits are not required to climb or camp in this area. For information and up-to-date regulations, contact the Darrington ranger station (360-436-1155). Northwest Forest Pass required.

41 DOME GLACIER AND SOUTHWEST SUMMIT GRADE II+

A technically easy climb with straightforward routefinding to a high, massive, and prominent summit, this recommended route and its optional side trip to the Southwest Summit features the same long approach through varied and classic Cascades mountain backcountry. The whole package makes for a strenuous but rewarding outing over hill and dale, with the added allure of a big and still-remote mountain with historical importance.

First ascent ▲ George Freed and Erick Larson, August 1936; Southwest
Summit: Don Blair, Forest Farr, Norval Grigg, July 1936
Elevation ▲ 8,920 feet
Difficulty ▲ Grade II+; Dome Glacier, class 4 glacier travel; Southwest
Summit, low 5th class, glacier travel
Time ▲ 2–3 days round trip; 6–9 hours one-way from Itswoot Ridge
Equipment ▲ Ice ax, crampons
Season ▲ May-October

Main Summit
of Dome

Carl Skoog approaching the Southwest Summit of Dome Peak, with the Main Summit beyond (Photo by Gordy Skoog)

Approach (Grade III+): From Interstate 5 near Arlington, exit onto State Highway 530 and drive east through Darrington. North of Darrington, turn off Highway 530 onto the Suiattle River Road (Forest Road 26) and drive approximately 19.5 miles east to the Downey Creek campground and trailhead (1,450 feet).

Follow the Downey Creek Trail for 6.5 miles through old-growth forest beside the creek to Six Mile Camp at Bachelor Creek (2,420 feet). Locate and follow the trail east along the north side of Bachelor Creek. At 9.5 miles, the trail crosses Bachelor Creek (3,750 feet) and leads into a brushy area where it turns sharply left (east) and continues up the valley near the stream. (Many people have gotten lost here and report horrendous bushwhacking; if you find yourself bushwhacking, you are off route—stop, take off your pack, retrace your steps,

In the brush at 3,800 feet on the Bachelor Creek Trail (Photo by Jim Nelson)

and locate the trail where you lost it.) The trail enters timber and climbs steeply up switchbacks before entering a grassy side valley beside a year-round stream at 11 miles. Good camping can be found here. The trail crosses a pass (6,000 feet) in another 1.5 miles before dropping quickly down to Cub Lake (5,338 feet) at 14 miles. Some climbers camp here, but another option is to make the final steep climb northeast to Itswoot Ridge (6,200 feet) and a few campsites with good views of Dome and Glacier Peaks.

Route: From Itswoot Ridge, the approach follows a long traverse east across snow and talus, eventually climbing to the Dome Glacier at 7,600 feet. Ascend the Dome Glacier, traversing southward, to a flat area on the glacier (8,000 feet).

From the flats, climb the snow slope (20–30 degrees) east, leading to a gully (snow in early season, scree by midseason) to the Dome Glacier–Chickamin Glacier col (8,450 feet). Follow the snow ridge southeast to sand and heather benches and the final, exposed rock section—50 feet of class 3–4 climbing.

Southwest Summit variation: From the flat section of upper Dome Glacier (8,000 feet), cross the bergschrund and climb a steep snow-and-ice face (to 40 degrees) for approximately 300 feet to the ridge crest between the Main and Southwest Summits. Climb a pitch and a half of low-5th-class climbing on high-quality rock to finish the route.

A traverse to the Main Summit can be made by climbing east, mostly along the south side of the crest (low 5th class), finishing near the ridge crest with a 5.5 crack pitch.

Descent: Descend via the Dome Glacier climbing route.

GUNSIGHT PEAK, NORTH PEAK ────────

▲ *West Face*

Climbers have been aware of the superb rock on both of Gunsight's peaks—the main and the north—since 1940 when Fred Beckey, Robert Craig, and Will Thompson first climbed the peak, but the long approach, the necessity for heavy rock-climbing equipment, and the relatively moderate elevation have for some reason discouraged many potential climbers. This steep and direct rock climb on some of the best rock in the range takes the climber up a dramatic alpine face hidden away in a remote and icy corner of one of the Cascades' biggest glaciers. Note that a major rockfall has recently occurred on Gunsight Peak, which may have affected the Skoog/Brill route on the east face of the main peak (described in *Selected Climbs in the Cascades, Volume II*).

Gunsight Peak from the north, showing neighboring peaks around the Chickamin Glacier (Photo by Jim Nelson)

Special Considerations: At present, permits are not required to climb or camp in the Glacier Peak Wilderness. For information and up-to-date regulations, contact the Darrington ranger station (360-436-1155). Northwest Forest Pass required.

42 WEST FACE GRADE III+; 5.10 AND A1

The whole package here is stupendous—the setting, the line, the 500–600 feet of hard climbing—but it is the quality of the rock that stays with you. Hard crack climbing (with some lovely face climbing on small knobs and chickenheads) makes this a challenging route in a powerfully scenic area.

First ascent ▲ Carl Diedrich and Jim Nelson, August 1986

Elevation ▲ 8,190 feet

Difficulty ▲ Grade III+; 5.10 and A1

Time ▲ 3–5 days round trip; 6–9 hours one-way from high camps

Equipment ▲ Medium rack to 4 inches (at least 1 big cam or hex), ice ax, crampons, bolt kit recommended

Season ▲ July-September

Approach (Grade IV+): Follow the approach to Itswoot Ridge (6,200 feet) given for climb 41, Dome Glacier and Southwest Summit. From Itswoot Ridge, follow the Dome Glacier climbing route nearly to the top (8,750 feet), to sand and heather benches and good campsites. (Besides being much closer to the route, these are high, spectacular bivy sites that add greatly to the climb.)

From the high campsites, backtrack the Dome Glacier climbing route on the ridge northwest to the Dome Glacier–Chickamin Glacier col (8,450 feet). From the col, find a route through large crevasses at the top of the Chickamin Glacier. Descend the Chickamin Glacier to the southeast toward the gentle upper Chickamin Glacier valley directly below the west faces of the Gunsight North and Main Peaks (7,150 feet). An easy snow slope leads to the base of the rock climbing.

Route: Access to the center of the face is gained by walking right (south) across a large ledge. The route climbs

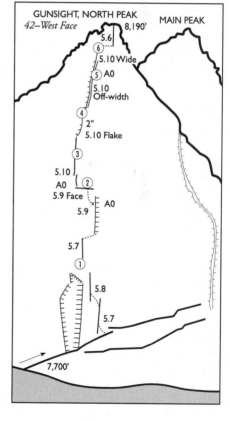

cracks for **one pitch** toward the base of a large white dihedral. On the **second pitch,** climb into the dihedral and when the crack ends, climb face holds (5.9) up and left

Carl Diedrich on Gunsight Peak's North Peak, West Face (Photo by Jim Nelson)

past a bolt to a ledge and belay. (A bolt or two is needed at this belay.) The **third pitch** climbs difficult thin cracks and face holds (5.10) up to a belay below a flake and hand crack. Undercling the flake and climb the hand crack to an exposed belay (5.10; short pitch). Two pitches in a difficult off-width crack follow (5.10), until the climber can traverse right to easier climbing and the summit.

Descent: Descend to the northeast (via down-climbing and/or rappelling) until able to cross the ridge back to the west side and down to Dome Glacier.

Sentinel Peak Bonanza Peak Mutchler Peak Mount Buckindy Glac Peak

Climber Julie Vithoulkas near the summit of Snowking, with Mutchler and Glacier Peaks in the distance (Photo by Andreas Schmidt)

SNOWKING MOUNTAIN

▲ *East Ridge/Snowking Glacier*

The approach to Snowking Mountain is not unlike the route into Snowfield or Eldorado: steep, dry, and long. (In warm weather, a very early start is helpful.) But the setting, in a somewhat out-of-the-way part of the North Cascades, is well worth the trouble and suffering. Snowking is not a particularly high peak, but it is distinctive and prominent in its own way: it is the big snowy peak to the southwest that you see from many of the popular peaks in the Cascade Pass area. The approach and route take the climber past some beautiful lakes, including two turquoise mountain gems tinged by glacier silt. The glacier itself looks imposing on the approach, but can be almost completely bypassed by climbing the ridge route.

The views are another good reason to come to Snowking, as in all directions the rugged peaks of the North Cascades are visible from this vantage: Eldorado, Boston, Sahale, Forbidden, and Johannesberg. Even though Snowking is outside North Cascades National Park, some park rangers secretly list this among their favorite places, saying that some of the best things about the climb are the view and, if you have a few days, access into the little-known and seldom visited Chaval-Mutchler-Buckindy area.

But getting there is not easy. Snowking is approached from a road that is rapidly deteriorating, so it is safe to assume that the walking distance is going to get longer as the road gets more difficult to drive. It is a rough road already, so climbers will find a beefy, high-clearance vehicle helpful.

Early Morning Spire — Dorado Needle — Eldorado Peak — Mount Torment — Forbidden Peak — Mount Logan — Boston Peak — Sahale Peak

Point 5791

Found Lake

Cyclone Lake

Climber Julie Vithoulkas near the summit of Snowking on the Snowking Glacier
(Photo by Andreas Schmidt)

Although Snowking counts as its neighbors some of the most appealing peaks in North Cascades National Park, Snowking itself lies outside the park boundary despite the fact that some references erroneously place the peak within the park. Snowking instead is part of the Glacier Peak Wilderness of the Mount Baker–Snoqualmie National Forest.

Special Considerations: Even though Snowking is outside the national park and therefore not subject to park regulations, some climbers do use the Park Service climbing register. And the park rangers at Marblemount may have the best information on current conditions. At present, permits are not required for this area, and currently no Northwest Forest Pass is required for parking on Forest Road 1170, but that could change. For information and current park regulations, call the North Cascades National Park ranger station in Marblemount, officially known as the Wilderness Information Center (360-873-4500); the National Park Service/U.S. Forest Service ranger station in Sedro Woolley, officially known as the North Cascades National Park Headquarters/U.S. Forest Service Mount Baker Ranger District (360-856-5700); or the Darrington ranger station (360-436-1155).

43 EAST RIDGE/SNOWKING GLACIER GRADE II

For those with aspirations to climb in the North Cascades, but without experience there, this route on Snowking is one to consider. It is a classic North Cascades climb, with all the usual ingredients: the predictably strenuous approach, much like the other notorious valley bottom–to–ridge top approaches common in this part of the range, killer views in one of the most scenic mountain areas of the Lower 48, and extreme alpine ambience. The East Ridge on Snowking is a nontechnical route, a gentle peak comparatively speaking, and it requires no glacier travel. The route is a good one for those who are up to the strenuous physical demands of the approach but without a lot of alpine climbing experience.

First ascent ▲ Albert Heath and Hermann F. Ulrichs, September 1938
Elevation ▲ 7,433 feet
Difficulty ▲ Grade II; class 3; moderate snow/glacier slopes
Time ▲ 1–2 days round trip; 1–2 hours one-way from lakes
Equipment ▲ Ice ax, crampons in early season
Season ▲ April-October; trail not snow free until mid-July or later

Approach (Grade IV+): From Interstate 5 near Burlington, take the Cook Road exit (exit 232) east approximately 5 miles to where it joins State Highway 20 (North Cascades Highway) in Sedro Woolley. Drive 47 miles from I-5 to Marblemount, turning onto the Cascade River Road; drive 14.5 miles to Kindy Creek Road (Forest Road 1570). FR 1570 descends several hundred feet and crosses the Cascade River (1,150 feet). From the river, the increasingly rough road switchbacks up the northeast-facing hillside; the road continues to deteriorate, but with a high-clearance vehicle, one can drive to the end of the road (just over 2,400 feet). Since this road is

Snowking from Point 5791 (Photo by Jim Nelson)

not maintained, in the future it may not be possible to drive it as far as described here. But whether you are driving or walking to the road end, from the west edge of an old clear-cut at 2,400 feet, be sure to find the footpath.

The steep path climbs up into the hemlock old growth. After about 1.5 hours, the angle of ascent lessens somewhat. Soon a boggy area is reached, with a tent spot nearby (approximately 4,800 feet), where the trail fades. The climbers track ascends from behind some boulders and proceeds steeply upward to the southwest. There may be a trail junction at approximately 5,200 feet; the fishermans trail descends to the west toward Found Lake; the climbing path continues up (south) to Point 5791, with views of Snowking and the glacier-tinged water of Found Lake. This trail has no water.

Follow the ridge south-southwest; a short way past the viewpoint, the trail descends steeply through some rock cliffs and is difficult to find and follow. After about 100 feet of elevation loss, the climbers track becomes more distinct and continues in a southwesterly direction, passing several minor points, to Cyclone Lakes, where campsites can be found around the benches and lakes (5,400 feet). Small parties can find a low-impact flat rock site on the north side of Lake 5442, just above the outlet, with great views.

Route: From the east end of Cyclone Lakes, the way follows the rocky ridge to the west. The route to the summit generally follows this ridge, with some minor scrambling detours, easily navigated by dropping off the ridge crest on one side or the other. The ridge affords a route to the top that avoids glacier travel. An alternate route is to move out to the right (north) and ascend snowfields, then the glacier, to just below the summit. Scramble rocks to the summit.

Descent: Descend the climbing route.

ELDORADO PEAK
▲ *Eldorado Glacier/East Ridge*

A big mountain perched on the edge of an expansive ice sheet, Eldorado Peak's dramatic summit—a Himalayan-like knife-edge of snow—makes an alluring destination for alpine climbers. The route recommended here is a relatively straightforward glacier climb reached by steep, strenuous approaches.

The approach is more than a passing matter, because in many ways it symbolizes the wildness of the North Cascades and the manner in which many appealing climbs are "protected" by unsavory obstacles. In this case, one approach goes straight up from the road and gains 5,500 feet of elevation before high camp is reached; the other follows a sinewy ridge that leaves the climber far from the mountain. Newcomers to the range may find these approaches unreasonable if not brutal, but climbing Eldorado is a good barometer of one's fitness level and routefinding skills.

Special Considerations: Permits are required to camp in North Cascades National Park, anytime, anywhere, but at present there is no fee. For information and current park regulations, call the North Cascades National Park ranger station in Marblemount, officially known as the Wilderness Information Center (360-873-4500), or the National

Eldorado Peak and Eldorado Glacier above the Roush Creek drainage
(Photo by Austin Post, USGS)

Park Service/U.S. Forest Service ranger station in Sedro Woolley, officially known as the North Cascades National Park Headquarters/U.S. Forest Service Mount Baker Ranger District (360-856-5700). Northwest Forest Pass required.

44 ELDORADO GLACIER/EAST RIDGE GRADE II

This is a technically easy climb with a grand finish along an exposed snow crest with arguably the best view in North Cascades National Park. Most agree that Eldorado Peak has it all. The approach, though strenuous, is well worth the effort. The second day of this ascent is as scenic a climb as any in the range, with views to Marble Creek, Dorado Needle, Early Morning Spire, and the vast expanse of the Eldorado, Klawatti, and Inspiration Glaciers. To the east lie Forbidden Peak, Mount Buckner, and Sahale Peak; to the south, one can see the peaks of the Ptarmigan Traverse.

First ascent ▲ Donald Blair, Norval Grigg, Arthur Wilson, Art Winder, August 1933

Elevation ▲ 8,868 feet

Difficulty ▲ Grade II; glacier travel, steep and exposed snow to 35 degrees

Time ▲ 1–3 days round trip; 6–10 hours one-way from edge of glacier

Equipment ▲ Crampons, ice ax, snow anchors (picket or deadman)

Season ▲ April-October

Approach (Grade IV): Two approaches can be used to climb either route on Eldorado Peak. The Eldorado Creek route is probably better—it starts lower and has

Climbers on Eldorado's distinctive summit ridge (Photo by Cliff Leight)

some bushwhacking, but it is more direct. The Sibley Creek Pass route starts higher, but is longer and more technical.

Via Eldorado Creek: From Interstate 5 near Burlington, take the Cook Road exit (exit 232) east approximately 5 miles to where it joins State Highway 20 (North Cascades Highway) in Sedro Woolley. Drive 47 miles from I-5 to Marblemount, turning onto the Cascade River Road; drive 19 miles to a large parking lot on the right side of the road (2,160 feet).

To cross the Cascade River, walk downstream along the road for approximately 300 feet until an obvious path leads down to the river. Cross on the log or, when water level is low, ford the river to its north side. Continue into the woods a short distance until a path leads back upstream for approximately 0.2 mile, then turns left (north) uphill before reaching Eldorado Creek.

The climbers path, located on the west side of Eldorado Creek, climbs steeply through old-growth forest (no water) to a small talus field at 4,000 feet. Climb to the top of the talus field, exiting on a steep path through slide alder to a second, and much larger, talus field (snow in early season). Make an ascending traverse up and right (east), locating a climbers path along the right (east) edge of the talus. The approach is much easier when paths are followed, so when this path fades near large boulders, look for another path continuing up along the left (west) side of the talus. Traverse right (east) across talus to a stream at the base of small waterfalls (5,000 feet); cross the creek at the large cairn and begin following a switchbacking tread through the last trees and subalpine meadow to an open basin (5,400 feet; campsites here). The Park Service has made a significant effort in recent years to rehabilitate the old, eroded, muddy route in this section, and in fact has "disappeared" the route so it can recover while climbers use the newer trail, which is much drier.

Continue up on heather and rock slabs until able to climb up to the adjoining ridge crest to the left (west) at just above 6,000 feet. Where the ridge steepens (6,150 feet), descend a class 3 gully 150 feet left (west) into the Roush Creek basin (the correct gully can be identified as the one with a large boulder in it just below the ridge crest).

Once in the Roush Creek drainage, traverse right (north) over talus, then ascend slabs and moraine toward the southeast edge of the Eldorado Glacier. Snow slopes (20–30 degrees) lead to the large, flat area of the glacier at 7,500 feet and good bivy sites. A rock island at the base of Eldorado Peak's East Ridge (7,800 feet) is a small bivy site. Additional bivy sites can be found several hundred feet higher.

Via Sibley Creek Pass: From I-5 near Burlington, take the Cook Road exit (exit 232) east approximately 5 miles to where it joins Highway 20 (North Cascades Highway) in Sedro Woolley. Drive 47 miles from I-5 to Marblemount, turning onto the Cascade River Road; drive 1.5 miles past the Marble Creek bridge (approximately 9.5 miles from Marblemount) to Sibley Creek Road (Forest Road 2503) and turn left. Drive the rough road 4.2 miles to the end and the Hidden Lakes Peak trailhead (3,400 feet).

Follow Trail No. 745 through timber, crossing Sibley Creek and switchbacking up the slope to 5,300 feet, where the trail begins a long traverse to the southwest. Leave the trail at the beginning of this traverse, and ascend directly up heather slopes to Sibley Creek Pass (6,100 feet). Continue north and east along the crest of the ridge (climbers path), passing several possible campsites (5,400 feet) within the first mile. Just before the point where the ridge is blocked by the western base of the Triad, descend a steep, class 3 gully down and south onto snow slopes. (There are several possible gullies, some steep and dangerous; take time to find the correct, easternmost gully leading onto the snow slopes below.)

Descend approximately 300 feet until able to traverse east (at approximately 6,700 feet) before ascending snow slopes to the ridge crest (7,100 feet). From the ridge crest, traverse scree and snow northeast to the southwest edge of Eldorado Glacier (7,600 feet; good bivy sites). Another mile across the gentle Eldorado Glacier leads to campsites at a rock island at the base of Eldorado's East Ridge (7,800 feet).

Route: From the base of Eldorado's East Ridge (7,800 feet), climb the East Ridge/shoulder of Eldorado, beginning on snow on the right (north) side. Talus, then scree (snow in early season) leads to the final snow slope at 8,400 feet. Climb to the narrow and very exposed snow arête and follow it to the summit rocks. Inexperienced climbers can stop short of the exposed ridge, enjoying the view to the south and east from 400 feet below the summit.

Descent: Descend the climbing route.

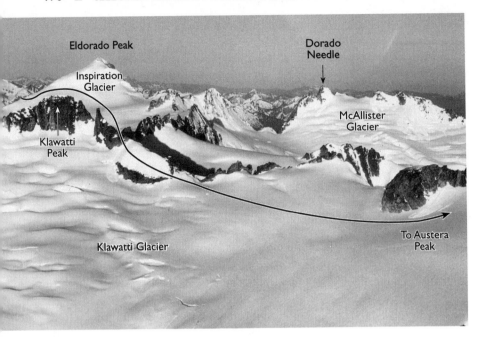

Route from Eldorado Peak to Austera Peak (Photo by Jim Nelson)

AUSTERA PEAK ▬▬▬▬▬▬▬▬▬▬▬▬▬▬▬▬▬▬▬
▲ *Inspiration-McAllister-Klawatti Ice Cap*

More of a glacier excursion than a traditional ascent—the highest summit itself is not recommended—this grand journey across the expansive sheets of ice that form the Inspiration, Klawatti, and McAllister Glaciers offers an experience that is unique in the Cascades. The view from this high plateau of ice is one reason to come. Its unusual location affords unique perspectives on Forbidden Peak and Mount Buckner, with a whole platoon of peaks to the south: Formidable, Dome Peak, Glacier Peak, Sloan, and Mount Rainier. Once on the rocky summit pinnacle of Austera Peak, views north across the Skagit River reveal the Pickets, Mount Baker, Mount Shuksan, the Chilliwack peaks, and the Backbone Ridge peaks above the McAllister cirque. But it is the view into the heart of the McAllister cirque itself that stays with you, those twin icefalls tumbling into that pristine wilderness valley, as wild as any place in the range.

Special Considerations: Permits are required to camp in North Cascades National Park, anytime, anywhere, but at present there is no fee. For information and current park regulations, call the North Cascades National Park ranger station in Marblemount, officially known as the Wilderness Information Center (360-873-4500), or the National Park Service/U.S. Forest Service ranger station in Sedro Woolley, officially known as the North Cascades National Park Headquarters/U.S. Forest Service Mount Baker Ranger District (360-856-5700). Northwest Forest Pass required.

45 INSPIRATION-MCALLISTER-KLAWATTI ICE CAP
GRADE II

Most of the necessary elevation is gained upon reaching the base of Eldorado Peak (climb 44), the starting point for this high glacial traverse. Traversing eastward past an array of crevasses, moats, and rock spires, the route crosses a series of glaciers that form this small ice cap. The place is remote, really the middle of nowhere. Numerous summits and geographic features await exploration along the way to the Austera Towers, of which Austera Peak is the highest and most accessible. Good camping can be found at Klawatti Col, near Austera Towers, and at other places along the route.

First ascent ▲ Joan and Joe Firey, Irene and John Meulemans, Anthony Hovey, September 1965

Elevation ▲ 8,334 feet

Difficulty ▲ Grade II; class 4 climbing, glacier travel

Time ▲ 2–3 days round trip; 2–3 hours one-way from bivy sites at 7,600 feet

Equipment ▲ Ice ax, crampons

Season ▲ May-October

Approach (Grade IV): Follow either of the two approaches to the base of Eldorado Peak's East Ridge (7,800 feet) given for climb 44; this is the starting point for the traverse to Austera Peak. The Eldorado Creek approach is probably better—it starts lower and requires some bushwhacking, but it is more direct. The Sibley Creek Pass approach starts higher, but is longer and more technical.

Heather Paxson on the traverse to Austera Peak (Photo by Jim Nelson)

Route: From the base of Eldorado's East Ridge (7,800 feet), where the ice sheets of the Eldorado and Inspiration Glaciers meet, begin traversing east, maintaining elevation and contouring around Eldorado Glacier and onto the main body of Inspiration Glacier. There are two routes from this point to Klawatti Col at the base of Klawatti Peak at the eastern end of Inspiration Glacier.

Crevasse rescue training on the Inspiration Glacier (Photo by Carl Skoog)

Option 1: The quickest route to Klawatti Col requires traversing the Inspiration Glacier at 7,800 feet (with minor deviations for crevasse avoidance). It is helpful to pick a route through the crevasses well before this point, in fact as early as the traverse near Eldorado Glacier. The distance to Klawatti Col at the eastern end of Inspiration Glacier is approximately 1.5 miles from the base of Eldorado Glacier, requiring 1.5–2.5 hours, depending on snow conditions.

Option 2: A second, more scenic route is to ascend to the top of Inspiration Glacier to a pass (8,200 feet) that leads to the McAllister Glacier. Deans Spire, the first in a series of small rocky summits, marks the way toward the pass. From the pass, continue the traverse along the base of the jagged Tepeh Towers to Klawatti Col. This higher traverse is slightly longer, at 3–4 hours.

From Klawatti Col, continue east along the north side of Klawatti Peak on the McAllister Glacier. A short (150-foot) descent from the col begins the moderately steep (30-degree) traverse to a small notch (7,900 feet) at the base of Klawatti Peak's north ridge. By midseason a short rappel is usually necessary to reach the Klawatti Glacier from the col.

Once on the Klawatti Glacier, traverse beyond the rocky summit (Point 8200) and begin an ascending traverse to the top of the glacier approximately 200 feet below the rocky subsummit (8,300 feet) of Austera. It is a short scramble to the subsummit and best viewpoint, just short of the main summit. The true summit (8,334 feet) is 15 minutes to the north over loose and unpleasant going. It is not recommended. This is an outing where getting there is not just an end in itself, but the whole point.

Descent: Descend the climbing route.

EARLY MORNING SPIRE
▲ *Southwest Face*

Located in the Marble Creek cirque, Early Morning Spire is easily viewed from the North Cascades Highway (State Highway 20) from just east of the town of Rockport. Getting there is another matter; as with so many routes in the North Cascades, the approach is not easy. While the climb is a mere 3 miles from the Cascade River Road, there is no trail or established route in the Marble Creek valley, only a tangle of devils club, slide alder, and other typical vegetation. A mile a day is good time in that stuff. The approach to the base of the Southwest Face, therefore, involves a long and circuitous route. There are two possibilities, but whatever you do, do not try to force a route up Marble Creek.

Special Considerations: Permits are required to camp in North Cascades National Park, anytime, anywhere, but at present there is no fee. For information and current park regulations, call the North Cascades National Park ranger station in Marblemount, officially known as the Wilderness Information Center (360-873-4500), or the National Park Service/U.S. Forest Service ranger station in Sedro Woolley, officially known as the North Cascades National Park Headquarters/U.S. Forest Service Mount Baker Ranger District (360-856-5700). Northwest Forest Pass required.

Early Morning Spire   Dorado Needle

Early Morning Spire and Dorado Needle from the southwest (Photo by Jim Nelson)

46 SOUTHWEST FACE GRADE III+; 5.9

This route on Early Morning Spire is one of the best technical rock climbs in the Cascade Pass region: eleven pitches of sustained, mid-5th-class rock climbing on clean, reasonably sound rock. In an area known more for snow-and-ice climbs than rock climbs—notorious, in fact, for poor rock—Early Morning Spire's Southwest Face is remarkable for its soundness and quality. The rock is wet through much of the summer, until a snow patch higher up melts away completely. The central crack system is a drainage, and the climb is much more enjoyable when dry. Go late most years.

> **First ascent** ▲ First five pitches: Tom Hornbein and Richard Emerson, September 1971; upper half of route: Gary Brill, Lowell Skoog, Mark Bebie, August 1981
>
> **Elevation** ▲ 8,200 feet
>
> **Difficulty** ▲ Grade III+; 5.9
>
> **Time** ▲ 2–3 days round trip; 8–10 hours one-way from Marble Creek cirque
>
> **Equipment** ▲ Ice ax, crampons, medium rack to 2¹/₂ inches
>
> **Season** ▲ August–September

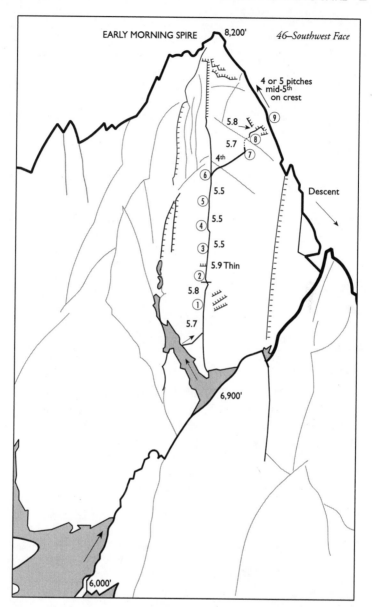

EARLY MORNING SPIRE   8,200'   *46–Southwest Face*

4 or 5 pitches
mid-5th
on crest

5.8   9
     8
5.7   7
4th

6   5.5

Descent

5   5.5

4   5.5

3   5.5

2   5.9 Thin

5.8
1

5.7

6,900'

6,000'

Approach (Grade IV): Two approaches can be used to climb the Southwest Face. The Eldorado Creek approach is probably better—it starts lower and has some bushwhacking, but it is more direct. The Sibley Creek Pass approach starts higher, but is longer and more technical.

Via Eldorado Creek: Follow the approach to the base of Eldorado Peak's East Ridge (7,800 feet) given for climb 44. Begin traversing north, contouring around Eldorado Peak and onto the main body of the Inspiration Glacier. Deans Spire, the first in a series of small rock summits encountered along the way, marks the route

Dan Cauthorn on Early Morning Spire (Photo by Mark Kroese)

toward a glacier pass (8,200 feet) and descent into Marble Creek cirque from the col (7,600 feet) below Dorado Needle. Descend to 6,000 feet to skirt the steep rock buttress, and climb into the snow gully (30–40 degrees) leading to the start of the rock climbing (6,900 feet).

Via Sibley Creek Pass: Follow the approach via Sibley Creek to the Eldorado Glacier given for climb 44. From the southeast edge of the Eldorado Glacier (7,580 feet), make a descending traverse to the west until able to climb 3rd- and 4th-class rock up to the Triad-Eldorado col (6,750 feet). This col provides access to the Triad Glacier; descend the Triad Glacier into the Marble Creek cirque. Begin traversing north at 5,600 feet and then beyond the west face and west arête of Eldorado; continue across the cirque, traversing scree, talus, and snow, and then beyond the steep rock buttress (6,000 feet) and into the snow gully (30–40 degrees) leading to the start of the rock climbing (6,900 feet).

Route: Start just left of the prominent crack system going up the middle of the Southwest Face. **Pitch 1** climbs a ramp (5.7) to the main crack system. The **second pitch** follows a slot (5.8) in the main system to a large ledge. The **third pitch** starts out as a dihedral blocked by a small roof, passed on the right (5.9; small protection). The **next three pitches** (mid-5th class) continue up the crack system (the last pitch is another short one). **Pitch 7** moves right, out of the crack system on low-angled slabs (class 4). **Pitch 8** is a short 5.7 pitch (short, steep crack and mantel). **Pitch 9** is a hand-and-fingertip traverse above a steep, awkward slab (5.8) out to the ridge crest. **Four to five pitches** follow of mid-5th-class climbing along the ridge to the summit. Stay on the crest of the ridge, avoiding gullies to the right.

Descent: Follow easy down-climbing north and then east until able to descend a glacial remnant back into Marble Creek cirque.

SAHALE PEAK

▲ *Quien Sabe Glacier*

Sahale Peak from the Quien Sabe Glacier side is a particularly varied climb with a genuine wilderness feel, more alpine than the route up Sahale Arm from Cascade Pass. One of the best reasons for coming to Sahale Peak is to enjoy the scenery of Boston Basin: Boston Peak, Sharkfin Tower, and the imposing north face of Johannesberg Mountain with its dramatic hanging glaciers. Camps here—particularly high camps—are something to savor. Near the summit, the whole panorama of Cascade Pass peaks are at hand, from Mount Baker to Glacier Peak, including flattering views of nearby Forbidden Peak and Mount Buckner.

Special Considerations: Permits are required to camp in North Cascades National Park, anytime, anywhere, but at present there is no fee. For information and current park regulations, call the North Cascades National Park ranger station in Marblemount, officially known as the Wilderness Information Center (360-873-4500), or the National Park Service/U.S. Forest Service ranger station in Sedro Woolley, officially known as the North Cascades National Park Headquarters/U.S. Forest Service Mount Baker Ranger District (360-856-5700). Northwest Forest Pass required.

Labels on image:
Boston Peak
Sahale Peak
Sharkfin Tower
Quien Sabé Glacier
Boston Basin Camp

Sahale from the southwest, showing the Quien Sabe Glacier (Photo by Jim Nelson)

47 QUIEN SABE GLACIER GRADE II

This is a moderate and very appealing mixed climb in one of the most scenic areas of the Cascades. The route follows a pure, aesthetic line on a small but steep glacier rising out of Boston Basin in North Cascades National Park. The route traverses up under the shadow of Sharkfin Tower before climbing steeply to the Boston-Sahale col and onto the orange rocks of the summit ridge.

First ascent ▲ Unknown

Elevation ▲ 8,680 feet

Difficulty ▲ Grade II; class 3–4 rock; steep glacier, exposed snow

Time ▲ 1–2 days round trip; 4–7 hours one-way from Boston Basin, 1–2 hours one-way from Boston-Sahale col

Equipment ▲ Crampons, ice ax, snow picket

Season ▲ June-September; glacier can be icy in late season

Approach (Grade III): From Interstate 5 near Burlington, take the Cook Road exit (exit 232) east approximately 5 miles to where it joins State Highway 20 (North

Cascades Highway) in Sedro Woolley. Drive 47 miles from I-5 to Marblemount, turning onto the Cascade River Road; drive 21.7 miles and park at the small pullout area (3,200 feet) directly opposite the spectacular northeast face of Johannesberg Mountain.

Follow the abandoned road 0.75 mile, until beyond the mine site, then climb steeply uphill through the open slopes. The trail is badly eroded here. (In early season, when the trail is under snow, it is best to ascend directly up to Boston Basin.) The trail continues through heavy timber for several hundred yards before traversing west to cross four streams in 0.5 mile. Expect some brush and possibly troublesome stream crossings in warm weather. (Spring 2002 saw tremendous avalanches in this area from high on Sahale. These avalanches seem to occur every decade or so, and while they have complicated the approach, they have not changed it. Rangers recommend that climbers hold their elevation while scrambling through the areas of avalanche debris

Rope teams work up through crevasses on the Quien Sabe Glacier toward the ridge that leads to the summit of Sahale. (Photo by Jim Nelson)

and look for the trail on the other side.) Switchback uphill on a good trail through the trees to reach Boston Basin (5,700 feet).

From where the trail enters Boston Basin, designated campsites and composting toilets (only excrement, nothing else, should go in these black boxes) are located behind the small moraine to the east at 5,800 feet. In addition to the campsites in lower Boston Basin, consider these options: From where the trail enters Boston Basin at 5,700 feet, follow the trail north (difficult stream crossings) to the grassy moraine; at 6,300 feet, leave the grassy moraine and traverse left (west) to upper campsites and composting toilets (6,400 feet). Or climb onto the lower slopes of the Quien Sabe Glacier and ascend to the flat bench below Sharkfin Tower (7,500 feet).

Route: From where the trail enters Boston Basin (5,700 feet), follow the trail north (difficult stream crossings) toward the grassy moraine. Follow the moraine crest until the moraine ends at 6,900 feet. Cross the crest of the moraine and ascend to the western edge of the Quien Sabe Glacier (7,500 feet). Ascend the glacier (past the base of Sharkfin Tower) as it curves to the right (east and south) below Boston Peak. The final steep portion (25–35 degrees) of glacier can present crevasse problems, and the route changes from season to season. Climb through crevasses to the Boston-Sahale col. From the col, climb the exposed rock and snow ridge to the summit. Be aware that cornices form to the east, and remain through midseason.

Descent: Descend the climbing route.

MOUNT TORMENT– FORBIDDEN PEAK TRAVERSE
▲ *Torment-Forbidden Traverse*

Just about any climb in this Cascade Pass/Eldorado region has a lot going for it in terms of sheer alpine ambience and atmosphere. When the route is a long ridge of mostly sound rock—with the variety of snow and ice climbing in some sections— that connects a renowned objective such as Forbidden with one of the lesser-known peaks in the area, you know it is hard to go wrong. The Torment-Forbidden Traverse is a route that has gone from curiosity to classic in recent years, and for all the right reasons: challenging, interesting climbing in one of the most scenic areas of the North Cascades.

Torment, of course, is neither the highest nor most well-known peak in the Cascade Pass area. In fact, with so many attractive objectives in the area, it is easy to overlook the peak. But Torment offers much of the same appeal as its far more popular neighbor to the east, Forbidden: reasonable rock and unsurpassed alpine flavor. So it is easy to understand how combining the two peaks—along with the long connecting ridge between—into a single route can be considered one of the finest climbs in the range.

The first ascent party made the traverse in fine style, using no bivy gear at all. Ed Cooper, who made a number of quality first ascents in the North Cascades, including the North Ridge of Mount Terror, calls this route one of his favorites in a region famous for being rich in quality climbs.

Forbidden
Peak

Mount
Torment

Forbidden
Glacier

Torment-Forbidden Traverse from the northwest (Photo by Jim Nelson)

"I thought it would be a great mountaineering adventure, and it was," Cooper says forty-three years after the first ascent. "I had seen this long ridge in three previous trips to Cascade Pass that same year [1958]. Our gear was primitive; we did not take sleeping bags, to save weight. We knew that we would spend the night up there, and actually looked forward to the experience. Despite a cold night it was a splendid trip. It would provide a total North Cascade experience to anyone doing the traverse. We experienced on that route some of the best scenery and alpine climbing to be had in the North Cascades."

The scenery along the route is among the most stunning in the range. Besides the expected views of the Ptarmigan Traverse peaks to the south, such as Johannesberg, Formidable, and Dome, and the ice-mantled slopes of Glacier, the northern views are more intimate: Spectacular glacial lakes, such as Moraine Lake, lie just below, with the Klawatti Lakes set against the Klawatti Glacier. Remote trail-less valleys such as the West Fork Thunder Creek, to the northeast, are iconic symbols of this part of the range, lush and choked with vegetation, perhaps even harboring elusive grizzly bears. The West Fork alone drains the Inspiration, Forbidden, and Klawatti Glaciers.

Forbidden Peak

Mount
Torment

From
Torment Basin

Torment-Forbidden Traverse from the southwest (Photo by Jim Martin)

Special Considerations: Permits are required to camp in North Cascades National Park, anytime, anywhere, but at present there is no fee. Permits for Boston Basin can be hard to come by in season, so try to plan ahead; even with permits, camping is permitted only on snow, rock, or bare ground. For information and current park regulations, call the North Cascades National Park ranger station in Marblemount, officially known as the Wilderness Information Center (360-873-4500), or the National Park Service/U.S. Forest Service ranger station in Sedro Woolley, officially known as the North Cascades National Park Headquarters/U.S. Forest Service Mount Baker Ranger District (360-856-5700). Northwest Forest Pass required.

48 TORMENT-FORBIDDEN TRAVERSE GRADE IV–V; 5.6

Although this spectacular ridge route is not technically difficult, it is long, in places it is quite exposed, and it does therefore call for a wide range of alpine climbing skills. Its length means that the climb is physically demanding, and on an alpine traverse this long, routefinding difficulties are to be expected—here, those routefinding problems are found on the first half of the route. And finally, this is a committing climb: descent from anyplace along this ridge in case of emergency would be very difficult.

Tim Bonnet on the Torment-Forbidden Traverse (Photo by Jim Nelson)

Torment-Forbidden Traverse from the southeast (Photo by Jim Nelson)

The various components of the route quickly add up to make for a very appealing package: moderate technical difficulty, some routefinding challenges, dramatic exposure, great views, a high commitment factor, generally sound rock, and an aggressively scenic bivy spot for those who want one. (With increasing frequency, climbers are now doing this route without a bivy, and rapid ascents are now commonplace; Mark Kroese and Sean Courage completed the route in just 9.5 hours, car to car, in 2001.)

First ascent ▲ Ed Cooper and Walter Sellers, via Torment's south ridge, July 1958

Elevation ▲ Forbidden, 8,815 feet; Torment, 8,120 feet

Difficulty ▲ Grade IV–V; 5.6 rock climbing; steep snow

Time ▲ 1–2 days round trip

Equipment ▲ Crampons, ice ax

Season ▲ July-September

Approach: The Torment-Forbidden Traverse begins at Mount Torment, and since there are a half dozen worthy routes on Mount Torment, several approaches are possible. The shortest itinerary would be to approach via Boston Basin and climb Torment's southeast face or south ridge. Two approach options are described here. The first option is via Boston Basin, but bear this in mind: the permit you need for the traverse on this approach is a Boston Basin permit, and that can be hard to come by in season (see Special Considerations, above). The second option is via Torment Basin;

though longer, this option provides a nice traverse loop, with the opportunity to experience quite a bit of this spectacular region of the North Cascades. Park rangers advise that it is easier to get camping (or bivy) permits for Torment Basin, as opposed to Boston Basin.

Via Boston Basin (Grade III): Follow the approach to Boston Basin given for climb 47, Quien Sabe Glacier. From the upper Boston Basin campsites (6,400 feet), continue traversing left (west) to the base of a waterfall coming off the eastern portion of the Taboo Glacier (after passing below the spur ridge separating Boston Basin from Taboo Basin). Scramble alongside the waterfall (class 3–4) to gentle slabs below the glacier. Walk across slabs to the west, and then ascend the Taboo Glacier, aiming for a gully leading to the narrow notch below a steep step in the south ridge of Torment (7,440 feet).

Via Torment Basin (Grade IV): This option is steep and strenuous, although there is a fairly well-traveled path most of the way. Expect the initial 3,000 feet above the road to be dry, without water.

Tim Bonnet avoids the steep snow on the Torment-Forbidden Traverse. (Photo by Jim Nelson)

From Interstate 5 near Burlington, take the Cook Road exit (exit 232) east approximately 5 miles to where it joins State Highway 20 (North Cascades Highway) in Sedro Woolley. Drive 47 miles from I-5 to Marblemount, turning onto the Cascade River Road; drive approximately 20 miles and park near a bridge where the road crosses the Cascade River. This is approximately 1 mile beyond the parking area for the Eldorado Creek approach given for climb 44, Eldorado Glacier/East Ridge. The start of the faint trail is unmarked, but begins within 50 feet upstream of the bridge (at approximately 2,300 feet).

A small path climbs steeply through forest, until reaching a small talus field. After breaking into the open near a second talus field, and below cliffs, the path traverses left (west). The traverse left includes slide alder and some brushy sections, but is necessary to skirt more cliff bands. Where the trees end, and the way ahead is straightforward, continue up to the small snowfield/glacier below Torment's south face. Aim for the narrow notch below a steep step in the south ridge (7,440 feet).

Route: From the notch in the south ridge of Torment at 7,440 feet, ascend via 4th-class rock up 20 feet, then follow ledges down and left into a rubble-filled alcove. A steep gully/chimney is on the right and a big gray dihedral leads up left.

Sean Courage approaches Forbidden Peak near the end of the Torment-Forbidden Traverse. (Photo by Mark Kroese)

Follow the dihedral, not the chimney. Go left up the left wall of the dihredal to its top (80 feet of low-5th-class climbing). Climb up steep blocks, then follow a groove up and right past rappel slings, and past a short jam crack to a nice ledge with more slings below a gray wall with quartz intrusions. Climb up and left, around a corner into a dirty gully. A short, steep wall leads to another belay at rappel slings. Keep traversing up and left another full pitch (200 feet of 4th class) to a large ledge that leads to a notch in the south ridge below the summit. From the notch, a grassy ledge cuts across the southeast face. Follow the grassy ledge. Halfway across is a good place to leave your packs and head for the summit, approximately 250 feet above, class 3 and 4.

From the summit, return to your packs. Continue down and across the southeast face of Torment toward a notch and access to a small glacier on the north side of the ridge. Bypass a narrow section (with gendarmes) of ridge on the north until able to get back onto the rock heading for the top of the first major high point on the ridge (4th and 5th class). A good bivy is located a little to the north. The ridge crest can be bypassed on the next section by traversing 50-degree snow/ice (very exposed) for several hundred feet before regaining the ridge crest. This middle section of ridge is straightforward, and numerous bivy options are available. The routefinding problems and challenges are found in the first half of the traverse, and problems can be expected. The second half of the traverse is characterized by a long narrow section with great exposure leading to the couloir that marks the start of the West Ridge of Forbidden.

Climb the exposed West Ridge, much of the time on or near the crest (see climb 52, West Ridge), sometimes venturing to the left (north) side of the crest for two or three pitches of low-5th-class climbing on good rock. At the point where the ridge crest steepens at an obvious step, climb past the fixed pin (5.6) to a comfortable belay on top of the step. Continue climbing on the crest or just left of the crest, bearing left (north) around the west summit (5.6) to the notch below the true (east) summit. Scramble to the top.

Descent: There are multiple descent options for Forbidden, but in keeping with the spirit of the traverse theme, climbers may choose to use one of the descents given for climb 52, West Ridge. However the descent is made, the fact is that there is no easy way off Forbidden; it is one of the more difficult descents in the range. The climber's options are to descend the West Ridge (three variations) or take the so-called "East Ridge" descent route (it is more accurately the northeast face ledges). When there are parties on the West Ridge, the East Ridge descent route may be the best way down.

Regardless of which descent route is used, from the small unnamed glacier below Forbidden's south face, continue to the foot of the glacier, down some slabs and past the upper Boston Basin campsites (6,400 feet). Here the route traverses left (east) across Boston Basin for about 0.5 mile before descending the grassy moraine trail, leading to stream crossings (difficult in high water) and into the forest following the well-traveled trail back to the Cascade River Road approximately 2 miles from the Torment Basin route/trail.

The Buckner North Face routes above the Boston Glacier: A. North Face Couloir (climb 50); B. North Face (climb 49) (Photo by Jim Nelson)

MOUNT BUCKNER

▲ North Face ▲ North Face Couloir

Two classic north-face snow-and-ice routes are recommended on North Cascades National Park's Mount Buckner, one of the elusive Cascades Range "nine-thousanders." The volcanoes have longer routes, but none have the alpine flavor of Mount Buckner. There are great views to Forbidden Peak, the Eldorado ice cap, and the whole stunning panorama of Cascade Pass and Park Creek Pass peaks.

The North Face of Mount Buckner ranks with Mount Shuksan and a few others as one of an elite group of snow-and-ice climbs in the range. With two routes on one of the highest peaks in the Cascade Pass area, this face boasts great scenery, moderate climbing, and an unparalleled alpine ambience. There is a genuine feeling of remoteness and discovery as the climber trudges across the Boston Glacier to the start of the North Face routes.

Feeding one of the largest glaciers in the range—the Boston—the North Face ice sheet is divided into two sections by a rock buttress. The choice of which route to take can be made at the base of the mountain, depending on conditions. The routes are much the same, and offer similar though subtly different challenges. Other than crevasses on the Boston Glacier, the bergschrund poses the only real routefinding obstacle and may be a factor as to which of the two climbing routes are chosen. Both routes on this remote alpine face are catching on. Because of a short climbing season for this face, the final choice of route may come down to the one that does not have a party already on it.

Special Considerations: Permits are required to camp in North Cascades National Park, anytime, anywhere, but at present there is no fee. For information and current park regulations, call the North Cascades National Park ranger station in Marblemount, officially known as the Wilderness Information Center (360-873-4500), or the National Park Service/U.S. Forest Service ranger station in Sedro Woolley, officially known as the North Cascades National Park Headquarters/U.S. Forest Service Mount Baker Ranger District (360-856-5700). Northwest Forest Pass required.

49 NORTH FACE GRADE III

Both routes on the North Face are approximately 1,300 feet of 40- to 50-degree snow and ice. The face (right-hand) route has a shorter season than the couloir route (climb 50).

First ascent ▲ Calder Bressler, Ralph Clough, Bill Cox, Tom Myers, June 1938
Elevation ▲ 9,080 feet
Difficulty ▲ Grade III; 40- to 50-degree snow and ice, glacier travel
Time ▲ 2–3 days round trip; strenuous
Equipment ▲ Ice ax, crampons, second ice tool, ice screws
Season ▲ July-September

Approach: There are two approach starts and two route options to get to Mount Buckner's North Face, and all add a certain appeal to climbing the route. Since the best descent route from the face returns to Sahale Arm, both of the Boston Basin approach options involve a carryover and bivouac, but the Cascade Pass approach leaves from and returns to a camp high on Sahale Arm.

Via Boston Basin (Grade IV): Follow the approach to Boston Basin (5,700 feet) given for climb 47, Quien Sabe Glacier. From Boston Basin, there are three options for reaching the North Face, and each has merit.

Option 1/Boston Peak: From Boston Basin, follow the Quien Sabe Glacier climbing route (climb 47) to the Boston-Sahale col (8,500 feet). From the col, the traverse around Boston Peak appears improbable, but once located leads easily to the Boston Glacier not far from the North Face. From the col, on the ridge between Sahale and Boston Peaks, climb several hundred feet of 3rd-class loose rock east toward Boston Peak. At a point 200 feet below the summit of Boston Peak, traverse right (east) 100 feet (3rd class) to the Boston Glacier. The base of the North Face of Mount Buckner is about 1 hour across the glacier from here.

Option 2/Sharkfin Col: From Boston Basin, follow the Quien Sabe Glacier climbing route (climb 47) up to the western edge of the Quien Sabe Glacier (7,500 feet). From the western edge of the glacier, gain Sharkfin Col, the low point in the ridge, by climbing 10 feet of difficult (5.8) rock climbing into a 200-foot gully of loose rock (3rd class). From the col, rappel to the Boston Glacier (7,640 feet). Once on the glacier, routefinding is dictated by crevasses, with 2 hours being a reasonable average time to the base of Buckner's North Face.

Pat McNerthney approaches the summit of Buckner via the North Face Couloir.
(Photo by Jim Nelson)

Option 3: From Boston Basin, follow the Quien Sabe Glacier climbing route (climb 47) up to the western edge of the Quien Sabe Glacier (7,500 feet). From there, at a point directly below Sharkfin Col, a gully leads up and right to the ridge. Climb this gully approximately halfway until able to scramble left leading to a ridge crossing (just east of Sharkfin Col) and descent to the Boston Glacier. A short rappel may or may not be necessary. Once on the glacier, routefinding is dictated by crevasses, with 2 hours being a reasonable average time to the base of Buckner's North Face.

Via Cascade Pass (Grade III+): From Interstate 5 near Burlington, take the Cook Road exit (exit 232) east approximately 5 miles to where it joins State Highway 20 (North Cascades Highway) in Sedro Woolley. Drive 47 miles from I-5 to Marblemount, turning onto the Cascade River Road; drive 22.9 miles to the Cascade Pass parking area and trailhead (3,600 feet).

Hike 5.5 miles to campsites on Sahale Arm, below Sahale Glacier (7,500 feet).

From camp high on Sahale Arm, climb over the summit of Sahale Peak and continue on to the Boston-Sahale col and the traverse around Boston Peak, described above in Via Boston Basin, Option 1/Boston Peak.

Route: The North Face—right-hand (west)—route starts on the right side of the face and climbs up and slightly left (east) as the climber follows the obvious line of ascent. When the face begins to melt out a little by midseason, rock outcrops are passed on the way to the summit.

Descent: From the summit, descend to the southwest via gullies and scree into Horseshoe Basin. Once off the mountain, begin traversing west past a mine and onto a wide ledge system at about 6,400 feet, below the Davenport Glacier. Skirt cliffs, looking for a short gully (at approximately 6,400 feet) and scramble (3rd and 4th class) 600 feet to Sahale Arm. From here, retrace the route to Sahale Arm given above (see Via Cascade Pass).

50 NORTH FACE COULOIR
GRADE III

The couloir route is slightly steeper and somewhat more direct than the face route (climb 49). The couloir (left-hand) route tends to hold snow throughout the season.

First ascent ▲ John Holland, Walt Gove, three others, 1976
Elevation ▲ 9,080 feet
Difficulty ▲ Grade III; 40- to 50-degree snow and ice, glacier travel
Time ▲ 2–3 days round trip; strenuous
Equipment ▲ Ice ax, crampons, second ice tool, ice screws
Season ▲ July-October

Approach (Grade IV): Follow one of the approaches given for climb 49, North Face.

Route: Once beyond the Boston Glacier bergschrund, the North Couloir—left-hand (east)—route climbs up and into a narrow couloir. The route follows the couloir directly up to the summit ridge a short distance from the true (southwest) summit.

Descent: Follow the descent given for climb 49, North Face.

Pat McNerthney on the North Face Couloir of Mount Buckner
(Photo by Jim Nelson)

SHARKFIN TOWER ───────────────────

▲ *Southeast Ridge and Southeast Face*

Sharkfin Tower may not be the highest peak in Boston Basin—it is in fact significantly lower than Boston, Sahale, and Forbidden Peaks—but it is a gas to climb, with good rock, great exposure, and a delightful setting. This small crag set among a lot of big alpine climbs is very satisfying and well worth the long approach. Sharkfin Tower's summit offers unusual midheight views into some impressive North Cascades peaks, including Forbidden Peak, Boston Peak, Mount Buckner, Sahale Peak, and Johannesberg Mountain.

Special Considerations: Permits are required to camp in North Cascades National Park, anytime, anywhere, but at present there is no fee. Permits for Boston Basin can be hard to come by in season, so try to plan ahead; even with permits, camping is permitted only on snow, rock, or bare ground. For information and current park regulations, call the North Cascades National Park ranger station in Marblemount, officially known as the Wilderness Information Center (360-873-4500), or the National Park Service/U.S. Forest Service ranger station in Sedro Woolley, officially known as the North Cascades National Park Headquarters/U.S. Forest Service Mount Baker Ranger District (360-856-5700). Northwest Forest Pass required.

51 SOUTHEAST RIDGE AND SOUTHEAST FACE
GRADE II; 5.0–5.10

Two outstanding climbs of radically different difficulty ratings are located on the solid rock of this neat little summit set in the alpine grandeur of Boston Basin. The modern face variation—which requires climbing and then rappelling off the ridge route—is a unique climbing experience for those who are in the mood for a short alpine "sport climb" of high quality.

First ascent ▲ Wesley Grande, Jay Todd, Joseph Vance, August 1947; Southeast Face: Jim Nelson, Jim Martin, Kit Lewis, Bill Liddell, Dave Bale, September 1990

Elevation ▲ 8,120 feet

Difficulty ▲ Grade II; Southeast Ridge, 5.0; Southeast Face, 5.10; 30-degree snow, glacier travel

Time ▲ 1–2 days round trip; 2–5 hours one-way from Boston Basin

Equipment ▲ Ice ax, small rack to 2½ inches

Season ▲ June-September

Approach (Grade III): Follow the approach to upper Boston Basin (6,400 feet) given for climb 47, Quien Sabe Glacier.

Route: From upper Boston Basin, ascend to the western edge of the Quien Sabe Glacier (7,500 feet). From directly below Sharkfin Tower, ascend a snow gully (30–40 degrees) through the steep rock band leading to a snow patch (30 degrees) at the base of the tower. Climb a short gully to a notch at the base of the Southeast Ridge.

From this notch, traverse out across the right-hand (east) side of the ridge (low 5th class), then back to the ridge crest at a large ledge. The next pitch, an exceptional

Climbers on the Southeast Ridge of Sharkfin Tower (Photo by Jim Nelson)

one, climbs the Southeast Ridge (5.0), or an easier gully just left of the ridge crest, to a small notch in the ridge. The final pitch (5.0) climbs the right-hand (east) side of the ridge to the summit.

Southeast Face variation: A steep, very clean face on the right side of the ridge crest is visible from the start of the ridge route; the face route is approached via rappels off the ridge route, and is set up as two 75-foot pitches, thus permitting an ascent with one rope and a small rack. The route is reached by climbing the first two pitches of the Southeast Ridge route (above) to the small notch at the base of the final pitch.

Sharkfin Tower (Photo by Jim Nelson)

From this small notch, make a 75-foot rappel to a belay ledge with fixed pro, and from there make another 75-foot rappel to a lower belay ledge with fixed pro, and the start of this climb. The lower pitch climbs a face crack leading from the top of a block (5.8–5.9) followed by 5.10 face moves to the belay; the second pitch (5.9) follows face holds with fixed pro and small cracks for protection back to the small notch on the Southeast Ridge route.

Descent: Descend the Southeast Ridge climbing route via rappels and down-climbing to the snow patch above the cliff band. Retrace steps down the 30- to 40-degree snow gully (early season), or (mid- to late season) find rappel anchors just west of the gully and make a series of single-rope rappels back to the Quien Sabe Glacier.

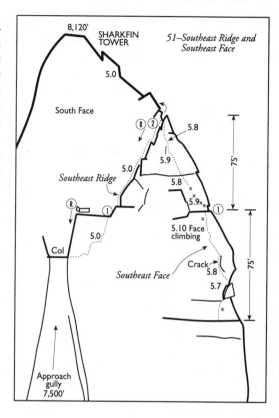

Climbing Ranger Kelly Bush starts the snow gully leading to Sharkfin Tower. (Photo by Bruce Carter)

Forbidden Peak from the south: A. West Ridge route (climb 52); B. East Ridge Direct route (climb 54) (Photo by Austin Post, USGS)

FORBIDDEN PEAK
▲ West Ridge ▲ North Ridge ▲ East Ridge Direct

Forbidden Peak is impressive, standing high above Boston Basin, its three perfect ridges radiating outward from its jagged summit. Climbers frequently rate the routes on Forbidden Peak among the best they have done, and with good reasons: interesting climbing, good-quality rock, and extraordinary views. All three routes recommended here are airy ridge climbs in a North Cascades sea of rock and ice: impressive, wild, alpine, and very scenic. From the summit, the climber looks out to the huge bulk of Johannesberg Mountain, south to the Ptarmigan Traverse peaks, across Thunder Creek to Mount Logan, and down to icy Moraine Lake. The combination of the moderate climbing, wild exposure, and unmatched alpine ambience makes this an aesthetic and scenic peak to climb by any of the three recommended routes. All three recommended routes are approached from Boston Basin.

There is no easy way off Forbidden Peak; it is one of the most difficult descents in the range. The climber's options are to descend the West Ridge or take the so-called "East Ridge descent route" (it is more accurately the northeast face). Descending the West Ridge has its advantages: if you are climbing that route, mountain boots can be left behind and rock shoes worn coming and going, and you do not have to deal with an unknown descent route. When there are other parties on the West Ridge, however, the East Ridge descent route may be the best way down. Beware that this 3rd- and 4th-class descent route is loose and stressful, and routefinding can be a problem.

Special Considerations: Permits are required to camp in North Cascades National Park, anytime, anywhere, but at present there is no fee. Permits for Boston Basin can be hard to come by in season, so try to plan ahead; even with permits, camping is permitted only on snow, rock, or bare ground. For information and current park regulations, call the North Cascades National Park ranger station in Marblemount, officially known as the Wilderness Information Center (360-873-4500), or the National Park Service/U.S. Forest Service ranger station in Sedro Woolley, officially known as the North Cascades National Park Headquarters/U.S. Forest Service Mount Baker Ranger District (360-856-5700). Northwest Forest Pass required.

52 WEST RIDGE GRADE II–III; 5.6

A graceful, unforgettable ridge route of moderate difficulty but supreme alpine grandeur, the West Ridge, a true classic, was the first route pioneered on this attractive peak. A small glacier, a 40- to 50-degree snow couloir to the ridge, then eight pitches of enjoyable rock climbing on or near the exposed ridge crest take the climber to the summit of Forbidden Peak. The rock is sound, with good cracks for anchors and belays (although the route is sometimes climbed unroped).

First ascent ▲ Lloyd Anderson, Fred and Helmy Beckey, Jim Crooks, Dave Lind, June 1940; first winter ascent: Alex Bertulis, Bill Sumner, Pete Williamson, February 1969

Elevation ▲ 8,815 feet

Difficulty ▲ Grade II–III; 5.6; 50-degree snow, glacier travel, bergschrund

Time ▲ 1–2 days round trip; 6–8 hours one-way from Boston Basin

Equipment ▲ Ice ax, crampons, small rack to 2½ inches, 2 ropes

Season ▲ June-September

Approach (Grade III): Follow the approach to upper Boston Basin (6,400 feet) given for climb 47, Quien Sabe Glacier.

Route: From Boston Basin, ascend the unnamed glacier to the base of the West Ridge couloir. Climb 35- to 45-degree snow or ice (possible bergschrund problems by midseason) for 300–400 feet until the couloir peters out under steep chimneys. Move out to the left (south) over class 4 rock into a low-angle gully; scramble up the gully for approximately 150 feet to the ridge crest. Climb the exposed ridge, much of the time on or near the crest, sometimes venturing to the left (north) side of the crest for two or three pitches of low-5th-class climbing on good rock. At the point where the ridge crest steepens at an obvious step, climb on the left (north) side of the ridge past the fixed pin (5.6) to a comfortable belay on top of the step. Continue

Jon Corriveau on the summit of Forbidden Peak in March 1981
(Photo by Joe Catellani)

climbing on the crest or just left of the crest, bearing left (north) around the west summit (5.6) to the notch below the true (east) summit. Scramble to the top.

Descent: *East Ridge descent route:* (Be aware that some climbers find this 3rd- and 4th-class descent route to be loose and stressful, and complicated by problematic routefinding.) From a horn on the summit, make the first of five to six single-rope rappels (approximately 400 feet total) straight down the northeast face to a series of ledges, which are followed east. These ledges are 3rd class, except for short sections of 4th class encountered at several rock-rib crossings. Traverse at this level, staying well below the ridge crest, crossing five ribs before climbing the gully back to the ridge crest at the solitary gendarme. Descend in an easterly direction down snow and scree, toward a rocky ridge leading to a short snow gully, which leads to the small unnamed glacier below Forbidden's south face.

West Ridge descent route: There are several options for this descent. **Option 1:** Descend the West Ridge climbing route (described above) using a combination of belayed down-climbing and a short rappel or two. Once back to the West Ridge couloir, down-climb the couloir, depending on snow conditions (self-arrest is not an option here). **Option 2:** Descend in the same manner to the West Ridge couloir and rappel the entire couloir to the glacier (two ropes work well for this option). **Option 3:** Descend the West Ridge climbing route (described above) but continue down the initial gully rather than moving over into the West Ridge couloir; descend the initial gully via 3rd-class rock and scree leading to a rappel point and a series of four to six single-rope rappels to the glacier.

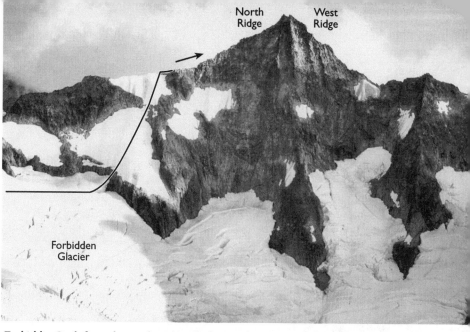

North Ridge

West Ridge

Forbidden Glacier

Forbidden Peak from the northwest, with the North Ridge on the left, West Ridge on the right (Photo by Jim Nelson)

53 NORTH RIDGE GRADE IV; 5.0

Do not be fooled: while rated just 5.0 with some 40-degree snow, the North Ridge on this impressive peak is nonetheless a major undertaking, requiring a wide range of mountaineering skills (but not necessarily a high technical proficiency). The climb comes with a genuine sense of remoteness, as the climber must cross over into the fringes of the wild Thunder Creek valley. The long and serious approach involves crossing a rotten ridge on 5th-class moves, then traversing a large and crevassed glacier and climbing a long, steep snow slope, all of which adds to the sense of commitment entailed by this unusual climb. Weather concerns coupled with the slow and problematic descent are the final components in a complex equation. All these factors combine for an outstanding but strenuous experience in a classic North Cascades setting.

First ascent ▲ Fred Beckey, Jack Schwabland, Don Wilde, June 1952
Elevation ▲ 8,815 feet
Difficulty ▲ Grade IV; low 5th class (5.7 moves over Sharkfin Col on approach); steep snow to 40 degrees, glacier travel
Time ▲ 1–2 days round trip; 8–12 hours one-way from Boston Basin
Equipment ▲ Ice ax (second tool optional), crampons, small rack to 2 inches
Season ▲ June-September

Approach (Grade III): Follow the approach through Boston Basin via Sharkfin Col given for Mount Buckner (climb 49, North Face), and proceed to Boston Glacier (7,640 feet).

Route: From Boston Glacier, routefinding is dictated by crevasses. Begin a descending traverse through crevasses to the left (north) to 7,000 feet, beyond the rock

Climbing on the North Ridge of Forbidden Peak (Photo by Jim Nelson)

buttress. Continue north on a rising traverse to the north end of the Boston Glacier (7,600 feet; bivy sites in the rocks of the lower ridge).

Skirt the base of the ridge, or make a rappel down to the Forbidden Glacier near the base of the snow face (7,600 feet). Climb the steep (30- to 40-degree) snow face for 500–600 feet to the crest of the upper North Ridge (8,300 feet). Follow the snow crest toward the summit, ascending the final 600 feet of low-5th-class climbing on solid rock to the east summit.

Descent: Descend the East Ridge descent route or West Ridge descent route given for climb 52, West Ridge.

54 EAST RIDGE DIRECT GRADE II; 5.8

The Cascade Pass area of the North Cascades offers perhaps the densest concentration of good mixed climbs and unsurpassed alpine ambience in the range. The area has become increasingly popular during the last decade, largely due to the widespread

Bob Kroese on Forbidden Peak's East Ridge Direct route (Photo by Mark Kroese)

Forbidden Peak's East Ridge descent route (Photo by Jim Nelson)

publicity in books and magazines afforded Forbidden Peak's airy West Ridge. While climbers literally queue up to do that popular route, fewer look to the other side of the mountain. Those who do find an unsurpassed route to the summit, a little harder and almost certainly less crowded than the better-known West Ridge.

The East Ridge Direct climbing route should not be confused with the "East Ridge descent route"; the former follows the true crest of the ridge beginning at the base of the solitary gendarme, while the latter traverses ledges across the somewhat unappealing northeast face, well below the crest of the ridge.

Beginning at the prominent gendarme, the route simply follows the crest of the East Ridge, or very near it. Towers on the ridge are bypassed on the north or south side, giving great exposure above the Boston Glacier. The rock is typical of Forbidden Peak—good, but not as good as that on nearby Sharkfin Tower. The route involves six pitches of low- to mid-5th-class climbing with one short stretch of 5.8. The most notable feature of the East Ridge Direct is the unrelenting exposure. As the climber stays very close to the ridge crest, the mountain falls away steeply on both sides to silhouette one's partners against the expansive ice of the Boston Glacier.

First ascent ▲ Fred Beckey, Ed Cooper, Donald Gordon, Joe Heib, May 25, 1958

Elevation ▲ 8,815 feet

Difficulty ▲ Grade II; 5.8

Time ▲ 1–2 days round trip; 6–8 hours one-way from Boston Basin

Equipment ▲ Crampons, ice ax, rock protection to 2 inches

Season ▲ June-October

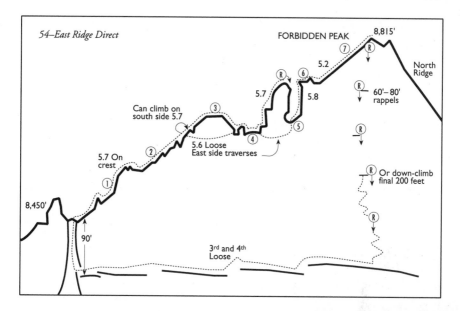

54–East Ridge Direct

FORBIDDEN PEAK 8,815'

North Ridge

8,450'

90'

Can climb on south side 5.7

5.7 On crest

5.6 Loose East side traverses

5.7

5.8

5.2

60'–80' rappels

Or down-climb final 200 feet

3rd and 4th Loose

Approach (Grade III): Follow the approach to upper Boston Basin (6,400 feet) given for climb 47, Quien Sabe Glacier.

Route: From upper Boston Basin, climb slabs (snow in early season) to the unnamed glacier below the south face, then climb the obvious snow couloir (east) to a shoulder. Continue climbing toward the East Ridge, eventually bearing left toward a prominent solitary gendarme. Leave crampons and axes here, and take a quick look down the gully on the north side of the ridge, west of the gendarme. This is the gully used on the descent route to regain the crest of the ridge.

Routefinding from the gendarme is straightforward: follow the ridge crest. The **first two pitches** climb the crest or slightly right (north). The **third pitch** climbs just left (south) of the crest; **pitch 4** continues on or near the crest. **Pitch 5** climbs a tower directly (5.7) or bypasses the tower on the right (east) (low-5th-class). The **sixth pitch** climbs a short but steep step (5.8) with good protection. The **final two pitches** continue on the crest to the summit. Except for the short step, the climbing is low to mid-5th class.

Descent: Follow the East Ridge descent route given for climb 52, West Ridge.

Matt Lambert on the East Ridge of Forbidden Peak (Photo by Matt Fioretti)

MOUNT GOODE

▲ *Northeast Buttress*

While the climb of Mount Goode's Northeast Buttress really cannot be considered a high-quality alpine rock route—such as climbs on Bear Mountain or Prusik Peak— Goode is so high, wild, and remote that it is hard to resist. The mountain (which cannot be viewed from any road), located in North Cascades National Park, is spectacularly situated in a neighborhood of unusually high peaks, with views into Dome Peak and Bonanza Peak, nearby Mounts Logan, Buckner, and Booker, and the peaks around Boston Basin and Cascade Pass.

Special Considerations: Permits are required to camp in North Cascades National Park, anytime, anywhere, but at present there is no fee. For information and current park regulations, call the North Cascades National Park ranger station in Marblemount, officially known as the Wilderness Information Center (360-873-4500); the National Park Service/U.S. Forest Service ranger station in Sedro Woolley, officially known as the North Cascades National Park Headquarters/U.S. Forest Service Mount Baker Ranger District (360-856-5700); or the Chelan Ranger District office in Chelan (509-682-2549). Check in at the Stehekin ranger station (no phone) if approaching the mountain via Lake Chelan.

Backcountry permits for camping in the Bridge Creek area can be obtained at the Marblemount, Chelan, or Stehekin ranger station on the way in to the peak. With the proper backcountry permit, climbers can camp in Bridge Creek valley or on the Park Creek Pass Trail on the way out, if exiting via Park Creek.

For floatplane service from Seattle to Chelan or Stehekin, call Kenmore Air (206-486-8400) or Chrysler Air (206-329-9638). For floatplane service from Chelan to Stehekin, check with Chelan Airways (509-682-5555). A commercial tour boat, the *Lady of the Lake* (509-682-2224), makes the voyage from Chelen to Stehekin and back daily; catch the boat at Chelan in the morning, or at Twenty-five Mile Creek at midmorning, to reach Stehekin around noon. The choice between boat or floatplane makes a difference, because it determines your arrival time at Stehekin. The North Cascades National Park operates a shuttle service from Stehekin to most trailheads, but if you miss the shuttle, you may have to spend the night in Stehekin. It is best to reserve the shuttle in advance by calling the Sedro Woolley ranger station (360-856-5700, ext 340); the call will be forwarded to Stehekin. Call the North Cascades National Park Service/Chelan Ranger District office (509-682-2549) to confirm shuttle times.

Northwest Forest Pass required for North Fork Bridge Creek trailhead on the North Cascades Highway.

55 NORTHEAST BUTTRESS GRADE III+; 5.5

A striking line on a steep, fierce-looking "nine-thousander," the Northeast Buttress is a formidable objective: a long, committing climb on a big and remote mountain. The relief itself is impressive: 6,000 feet from the floor of the Bridge Creek valley to the summit. While the rock is of decent quality and the climbing on the buttress

Mount Goode from the north, showing the approach via Bridge Creek
(Photo by Jim Nelson)

mostly moderate, the route's length, remoteness, and logistical problems combine to make the climb a major undertaking.

Getting off Mount Goode is another matter. An unsavory and potentially dangerous descent dulls some of the climb's appeal, as there is loose rock in the gullies that make up the descent route. But it is really not that bad, at least when compared with the challenge and enjoyment of this big mountain.

First ascent ▲ Fred Beckey and Tom Stewart, August 1966; first winter ascent: Bill Pilling and Steve Masciole, February 1985

Elevation ▲ 9,200 feet

Difficulty ▲ Grade III+; 5.5

Time ▲ 2–4 days round trip

Equipment ▲ Ice ax, crampons, medium rack of small to medium-size protection (including small wired nuts), 1–2 pitons

Season ▲ June-September

Approach: There are at least two feasible strategies: approach via the North Fork Bridge Creek drainage, and either return to that camp via the Mount Goode–Storm King col or, alternatively, return via the Park Creek drainage and the National Park Service shuttle. In addition to these options, the North Fork Bridge Creek valley can be reached by two routes.

Mount Goode from the north, showing the Northeast Buttress (Photo by Jim Nelson)

Note: There are good campsites at 3,800 feet in the North Fork Bridge Creek valley. Check with rangers to obtain the designated camp permits for trail camps at Walker Park or Grizzly Creek in the North Fork, or obtain the Goode Cross Country Zone permit if you intend to leave the trail, cross the creek, and camp under or on the glacier or on Goode itself.

Via State Highway 20 (North Cascades Highway) and North Fork Bridge Creek (Grade III+): This approach is the cheapest (no airplane or boat fares) and easiest logistically, although it involves a longer approach hike. From Interstate 5 near Burlington, take the Cook Road exit (exit 232) east approximately 5 miles to where it joins Highway 20 in Sedro Woolley. Drive 98.3 miles to Rainy Pass, and continue approximately 2 miles east to the large parking lot at the bottom of the hill. Find the trailhead on the south side of the highway (4,400 feet).

Hike south on the Pacific Crest Trail No. 2000 approximately 4 miles to where the trail turns right (west) above Bridge Creek. At approximately 10 miles (2,560 feet), the North Fork Bridge Creek Trail leads right (north) approximately 5 miles until it brings the climber under the northeast face of Mount Goode at 3,800 feet.

Via Lake Chelan/Stehekin (Grade III): Either drive US 2 and US 97 to the town of Chelan at the southern end of Lake Chelan, or take a floatplane from Seattle to Chelan or directly to Stehekin. From Chelan, take the boat or a floatplane to the hamlet of Stehekin at the north end of the lake. From Stehekin, take the National Park Service shuttle to the Bridge Creek trailhead (2,200 feet).

Hike the Pacific Crest Trail No. 2000 for 2.7 miles to the North Fork Bridge Creek Trail, turn left (west), and hike upvalley approximately 5 miles on the trail until it brings you under the northeast face of Mount Goode at 3,800 feet.

Mount
Logan

*Sean Courage and Andreas Schmidt carry over on Goode's Northeast Buttress on a
3-day traverse of Buckner, Logan, and Goode* (Photo by Mark Kroese)

Regardless of which option is chosen to reach the North Fork Bridge Creek valley, from the valley floor, ford the North Fork Bridge Creek and ascend into timber, traversing right (west) across talus below a cliff band. A stream is reached and can be followed along its right side (steep going, with some slide alder and brush), eventually reaching alp slopes below the Mount Goode Glacier. From the stream, it is also possible to ascend up and right across slabs and slide alder, and then more slabs, eventually reaching a gully that leads to alp slopes below the glacier.

Route: Once on the Mount Goode Glacier, traverse left (east) below and past the toe of the obvious Northeast Buttress. Find a safe place to cross the moat where low-5th-class climbing on slabby rock leads onto the buttress crest. The climbing along the broad and blocky crest of the buttress is mostly pitch after pitch of class 4 climbing, and not particularly distinguished from other features on the big face. At approximately midheight, the buttress fades into the face for a section before becoming well defined again to provide a stretch of exposed, mid-5th-class climbing. More class 4 climbing on blocky ground leads to the summit.

Descent: The southwest couloir has become the preferred descent route off Goode. From the summit, descend two long pitches toward the Northeast Buttress route. (Basically, reverse the last two pitches of the climb.) This puts you even with the Black Notch, which is easy (4th class) to get to. Once at the notch, descend about 100 feet of 4th class to an obvious boulder with slings. (You can actually see it from the summit). Rap off (angling left as you face the rock) toward the southwest couloir about 70 feet, landing on a sloping ledge with another rap station of slings around a suspect boulder, not visible from above. Rap again about 70 feet to gain the couloir. Once off the peak, find the climbers trail into the Park Creek valley (see Approach via Lake Chelan/Stehekin for climb 56, Fremont Glacier).

Or, if headed to North Fork Bridge Creek, cross through the Goode–Storm King col northwest of the peak, rappel from the col onto the Mount Goode Glacier, and descend into the North Fork Bridge Creek valley.

MOUNT LOGAN
▲ *Fremont Glacier*

Mount Logan is a remote and spectacularly situated summit in North Cascades National Park that calls for commitment and energy to reach but with few technical difficulties on the climb. At more than 9,000 feet, Mount Logan is one of the highest nonvolcanic peaks in the Cascades. Lying north of Park Creek Pass above Thunder, Bridge, and Fischer Creeks, the mountain is strategically located to afford a vantage point unmatched in the range: a 360-degree panorama from its summit includes Mount Buckner, Sahale Peak, Boston Peak, Forbidden Peak, Eldorado Peak, Klawatti Peak, Austera Peak, Mount Baker, Primus Peak, Tricouni Peak, Mount Triumph, Mount Shuksan, Snowfield Peak, the Southern Pickets, Mount Spickard, Golden Horn, Silver Star Mountain, Mount Goode, Seven Fingered Jack, Bonanza Peak, Gunsight Peaks, Sinister Peak, Dome Peak, Elephant Head, Glacier Peak, Sloan

Peak, and others, plus Lake Diablo and the vast expanse of the Boston Glacier. Mount Logan is an awesome viewpoint, and going for a look around is reason enough to climb the mountain.

Special Considerations: Permits are required to camp in North Cascades National Park, anytime, anywhere, but at present there is no fee. For information and current park regulations, call the North Cascades National Park ranger station in Marblemount, officially known as the Wilderness Information Center (360-873-4500); the National Park Service/U.S. Forest Service ranger station in Sedro Woolley, officially known as the North Cascades National Park Headquarters/U.S. Forest Service Mount Baker Ranger District (360-856-5700); or the Chelan Ranger District office in Chelan (509-682-2549). Check in at the Stehekin ranger station if approaching the mountain via Lake Chelan.

Backcountry permits for the Park Creek Pass area can be obtained at the Marblemount, Chelan, or Stehekin ranger station on the way in to the peak. With the proper cross-country permit, climbers can camp near Park Creek Pass (on the Park Creek side or Thunder Creek side). Good camps can be found, but be sure to follow all national park backcountry camping regulations, particularly those regarding minimum distance from the trail and prohibiting camps on fragile vegetation. Northwest Forest Pass required for the Thunder Creek trailhead on North Cascades Highway.

56 FREMONT GLACIER GRADE II

The climb includes short stretches of exposed class 4 rock climbing, but getting to the mountain is by far the greater challenge to the climber. Mount Logan can be approached from opposite directions; both routes are long but interesting. One approach starts from the tiny village of Stehekin on the north shore of Lake Chelan and requires arriving by boat or floatplane and then catching a ride on the North Cascades National Park shuttle to the Park Creek trailhead. The other starts from Lake Diablo on the North Cascades Highway and requires hiking in from the north along Thunder Creek. Either way, it is at least a day in and a day out. But hurrying is not the point on this climb; savor every minute spent in this wild, beautiful country and on this big, friendly mountain.

First ascent ▲ Lage Wernstedt and companion (possibly Whitey Shull), summer 1926

Elevation ▲ 9,087 feet

Difficulty ▲ Grade II; class 4 rock climbing; glacier travel

Time ▲ 3–4 days round trip; 4–7 hours one-way from Park Creek Pass

Equipment ▲ Crampons, ice ax

Season ▲ June–October

Approach (Grade III): Logan can be approached by two routes; starting from Chelan is probably more interesting than starting from Diablo Lake, although the time required is roughly equal for either route. Both approaches are recommended, Lake Chelan/Stehekin for its variety, Diablo Lake/Thunder Creek for its rare old-growth forests (it is one of the last pristine valleys in the Cascades).

Sean Courage and Andreas Schmidt on the Fremont Glacier of Mount Logan
(Photo by Mark Kroese)

Via Lake Chelan/Stehekin: Follow the approach to Stehekin given for climb 55, Northeast Buttress of Mount Goode. From Stehekin, take the National Park Service shuttle to the Park Creek trailhead (2,300 feet).

The Park Creek Trail switchbacks steeply up the hillside, gaining 1,100 feet in just more than 2 miles; the first campsites are found here. The trail crosses to the east side of the creek and continues up the valley another 2.5 miles to good campsites at Five Mile Camp (4,000 feet), with good views of Mount Buckner. These campsites also mark the beginning of the climbers track to Mount Goode (see climb 55, Northeast Buttress). Above Five Mile Camp, the trail begins a steep climb to tree line and the entrance to the upper valley at 4,800 feet. The way opens up, and by 5,700 feet, parklands rise in benches toward Park Creek Pass. These fragile meadows harbor magnificent views into Mount Booker and Mount Buckner.

Via Diablo Lake/Thunder Creek: From Interstate 5 near Burlington, take the Cook Road exit (exit 232) east approximately 5 miles to where it joins State Highway 20 (North Cascades Highway) in Sedro Woolley. Drive approximately 70 miles to Colonial Creek Campground on Lake Diablo. Find the Thunder Creek trailhead in the campground (1,200 feet).

Follow the Thunder Creek Trail for 18 miles through magnificent stands of old-growth timber, passing the confluence with Fisher Creek. Climb almost to Park Creek Pass, where good camps are available in Thunder Basin (4,300 feet), or south across Park Creek Pass (6,040 feet) in the Park Creek drainage.

Mount Logan from the southwest (Photo by Jim Nelson)

Route: From Park Creek Pass, or just below it, the summit of Mount Logan is not visible, but a large, sharp, rocky peak (7,760+ feet) clearly marks the end of the long traverse across the alp slopes above Thunder Creek. From the pass, descend the Thunder Creek Trail north for approximately 0.4 mile to a rocky flat with a small stream. Look for a climbers track leading out of the flat.

Traverse northeast, crossing a broad, sandy gully at 6,900 feet approximately 1 mile from the pass. Continue traversing northeast toward the sharp, rocky point at 7,760+ feet. Turn right, uphill, before reaching this peak. Ascend talus or snow to the Fremont Glacier (8,000 feet), approximately 2 miles from Park Creek Pass.

Ascend the glacier northeasterly to its highest point, where a gully leads up and left (north) to a low point in the ridge 200 feet above. Once on the ridge, watch for a system of ledges that traverses the east flank of the summit pyramid across exposed rock. The climbing here is mostly 3rd class with some 4th-class moves. Easy scrambling leads to a notch below the summit and one more short stretch of exposed class 4 rock climbing.

Descent: Descend the climbing route.

SOUTH EARLY WINTERS SPIRE ⎯⎯⎯⎯⎯⎯
▲ *Southwest Couloir* ▲ *South Arête* ▲ *Direct East Buttress*

The highest peak in the Liberty Bell group and therefore the best viewpoint, South Early Winters Spire combines ease of approach, a long season, and a variety of interesting climbing. The routes recommended here include a real mixed bag: a snow couloir and two solid and enjoyable rock climbs—an easy "ridge" route and a longer, more challenging route on a steep buttress. The quality of these climbs on the spire is quite high, typical of the outstanding climbing to be found around Washington Pass.

South Early
Winters
Spire

North Early
Winters
Spire

Lexington
Tower

Concord
Tower

Liberty Bell

Minuteman
Tower

Liberty Bell group from the east, showing the hairpin turn of State Highway 20, the North Cascades Highway (Photo by Jim Nelson)

Special Considerations: Permits are not at present required for climbing at Washington Pass, which is in the Okanogan National Forest; camping is prohibited at the pass itself, but bivouacking at the base of some routes is permitted. For information and up-to-date regulations, call the Methow Valley Ranger District, which recently moved from Twisp to Winthrop (509-996-2266). Northwest Forest Pass required at Blue Lake trailhead, but not when parking on the shoulder of State Highway 20 (North Cascades Highway).

57 SOUTHWEST COULOIR GRADE I

This is a broad, gentle snow gully that grows narrower as it steepens, giving the feeling of bigger alpine climbs—such as Triple Couloirs on Dragontail (climb 27)—but without the commitment. Summit views feature the Rainy Pass peaks—Black Peak, Whistler Peak, and Cutthroat Peak; east to Silver Star Mountain and the Wine Spires; west to Bonanza, Dome Peak, the massive Chickamin Glacier, and the north side of Mount Goode.

Often overlooked among the good rock climbs on South Early Winters Spire, the Southwest Couloir is, for a few months in winter and early spring, a route of distinction. The climb provides the aspiring alpinist a chance to acquire basic skills—such as tackling short rock pitches in crampons—while experienced climbers will find it a quick, direct, and enjoyable route to the summit.

With the North Cascades Highway opening typically in April, climbers arriving from western Washington have a one-month window or so to do this climb. Hardier souls willing to approach the mountain on skis in winter will have this route to themselves.

The route follows the obvious snow gully that begins below the South Arête (climb 58). Broad and gentle lower down, the couloir grows steeper and narrower as the climb progresses. Its relatively short length and easy access make this a good route to learn about changing snow conditions and how they affect the climbing. In the Southwest Couloir, snow conditions can com-

Near the top of the Southwest Couloir (Photo by Jim Nelson)

pletely alter the nature of the route. In heavy snow years, there is less scraping on rock; with cold, hard snow, front points hold well; in warmer weather, crampons can ball up with snow. The changeable nature of this route challenges the climber to deal with these different conditions.

First ascent ▲ Kenneth Adam, Raffi Bedayn, W. Kenneth Davis, July 1937

Elevation ▲ 7,807 feet

Difficulty ▲ Grade I; moderate (30- to 50-degree) snow, some rock

Time ▲ 5–8 hours round trip

Equipment ▲ Ice ax, crampons, rock protection to 2 inches, snow picket; skis or snowshoes for winter ascent

Season ▲ December–April or May

South Early
Winters Spire

Climbers approach the Southwest Couloir on South Early Winters Spire.
(Photo by Jim Nelson)

Approach (Grade II): Drive State Highway 20 to 1 mile west of Washington Pass and park at a small plowed area at 5,200 feet on the south side of the highway near the Blue Lake trailhead. (Additional parking is located several hundred yards west on the north side of the highway below Cutthroat Peak.)

Head south into the woods, uphill and slightly right (west); break out of the trees at 5,900 feet and into a large avalanche path coming down from the Early Winters Spires. Head directly up this path to the base of the Southwest Couloir below the South Arête.

Route: Start the climb at the base of the couloir, about 100 feet below the crest of the South Arête. The first 250 feet of the climb is 25- to 30-degree snow except for a short step around the giant chockstone low in the couloir. The chockstone may be completely snow-covered in a heavy-snow year. At half height, the couloir forms two branches. The right-hand branch leads to within 50 feet of the summit. It is 40- to 50-degree snow or ice, depending on conditions. (The left-hand couloir is probably unclimbed, and leads up and under two large chockstones in the couloir.) From the top of the right-hand couloir, a giant snow mushroom overhangs the east wall to the highway below. From this point a short rock move (5.3) on crumbly rock leads left and up to the summit.

Descent: Descend the couloir by a combination of down-climbing and rappelling, determined by snow conditions. If icy, rappel from anchors placed in the rock bordering the couloir; if snow conditions permit, down-climb.

214

58 SOUTH ARÊTE GRADE II; 5.4

A moderate but interesting climb with short steps of 4th- and 5th-class climbing interspersed with 3rd-class scrambling, the South Arête is an appealing route on good rock with plentiful belay points and anchors. The route has two crux sections, including one right off the ground that starts with the hardest moves on the climb.

Although not technically demanding, the South Arête is so enjoyable that it is hard to think of a better climb within its difficulty rating. The route's appeal lies in the Washington Pass ambience, views to Mount Goode and Dome Peak, and nice exposure at the top with views down to the hairpin turn in the highway. The arête makes a particularly good first climb for those new to the Washington Pass area.

First ascent ▲ Fred and Helmy Beckey, June 1942
Elevation ▲ 7,807 feet
Difficulty ▲ Grade II; 5.4
Time ▲ 2–6 hours round trip; 1–3 hours one-way from the base
Equipment ▲ Small rack to 2½ inches
Season ▲ May–October

Approach (Grade II): Drive State Highway 20 to 1 mile west of Washington Pass and park at the Blue Lake trailhead (5,200 feet).

South Early Winters Spire from the south, showing the South Arête route
(Photo by Jim Nelson)

Chimney

Hike the trail 1.5 miles into an open area beneath slabs directly below Liberty Bell. Find the climbers path on the left (north) side of slabs, and ascend until able to traverse right (south) across slabs to open benches. Continue upward, taking the right-hand (south) branch of the climbers trail 1 mile to Early Winters Spires.

Route: The beginning of the route is somewhat nondescript and hard to find. Look for the 15-foot crack behind a flake. Climb the crack rightward, then onto ledges via 5th-class friction moves. (The first pitch is quite short but holds the hardest move on the route.) Scramble easier ground on ledges just right of the crest of the arête into a gully. Climb into the gully that leads into a chimney blocked by a chockstone. Climb around the chockstone via 5th-class climbing and out of the chimney. Sandy gullies and ledges and easy broken rock lead to the broad crest of the South Arête near the summit. Make an unprotected move (5.2) around (or over) the exposed slab at the crest of the ridge, then traverse left

Peter Avolio on the South Arête, South Early Winters Spire (Photo by Jim Nelson)

(north) across the top of the Southwest Couloir (class 3) to a belay on the crest, with views down to the highway. Fourth-class climbing leads to the summit.

Descent: Descend the climbing route via down-climbing and rappels.

59 DIRECT EAST BUTTRESS
GRADE III+; 5.9 AND A1, OR 5.11

One of the most attractive and most direct climbing lines in the entire Washington Pass group, this invigorating route on the steep, narrow East Buttress combines visual aesthetics with quality climbing. While other routes following long natural crack systems and weaknesses in the spire have been established, it is the buttress crest that has fascinated climbers. It is here on the crest that the rock is cleanest and most solid, and the exposure unmatched. The adjoining southeast face is home to several free climbs, including at least one of the "alpine sport" variety.

The first-ascent party spent almost 3 days on the route, mostly due to the time-consuming necessity of constructing two separate bolt ladders connecting the crack systems. Modern climbers ascend the ten pitches of this climb in a day, with the second bolt ladder providing a difficult free-climbing crux at 5.10+. With the exception of the bolt ladders, the climbing is mostly in the 5.8–5.9 range.

Lowell Skoog on the East Buttress of South Early Winters Spire
(Photo by Gordy Skoog)

First ascent ▲ Fred Beckey and Doug Leen, July 1968
Elevation ▲ 7,807 feet
Difficulty ▲ Grade III+; 5.9 and A1, or 5.11
Time ▲ 7–10 hours one-way, car to summit
Equipment ▲ Medium rack to 3 inches
Season ▲ May-October

Approach (Grade II): Drive State Highway 20 to Washington Pass and park at the hairpin turn 0.5 mile east of the pass. The East Buttress is obvious and close.

Climb loose, steep slopes to the base of the buttress, approximately 1 hour from the road.

South Early Winters Spire from the east, showing Direct East Buttress route (Photo by Jim Nelson)

Route: Begin the climb just left (south) of the East Buttress crest. **Two pitches** of mid-5th-class climbing lead to a left-facing corner situated left (south) of the crest. The **next two pitches** ascend this corner via 5.9+ crack climbing to a large ledge.

The **fifth pitch** follows a long bolt ladder right and onto the buttress crest via aid or difficult face climbing (5.10+). Above the bolt ladder a short flake leads to more bolts, followed by a thin crack (5.9) to a small ledge and belay. From the belay, a **short pitch** moves up and right. The **seventh pitch** ascends the bolt ladder (aid or free 5.11) past a rotten arch, with more bolts ending with a difficult mantel (5.10). **Pitch 8** (5.6) climbs to a good ledge. **Pitch 9** continues up via low-5th-class climbing a full rope length. The **final pitch** climbs up, then left to an exposed step-around to the left, then a scramble to the summit. (*Note:* The route could use a new bolt or two, particularly on pitch 7.)

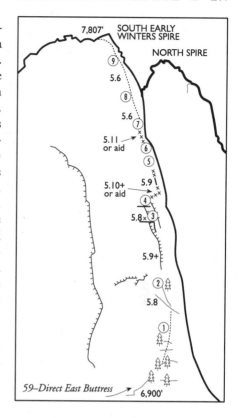

7,807' SOUTH EARLY WINTERS SPIRE

NORTH SPIRE

⑨ 5.6

⑧

5.6 ⑦

5.11 or aid ⑥

⑤

5.10+ or aid 5.9 ④

5.8 ③

5.9+

②

5.8

①

59–*Direct East Buttress*

6,900'

Descent: Descend via the South Arête (climb 58); from there, either descend steep scree and talus directly to the Highway 20 hairpin, or descend west via the longer but more gentle route leading to the Blue Lake trailhead (reaching the road 1 mile west of Washington Pass) and return to the car via hitchhiking or (perish the thought) hiking.

NORTH EARLY WINTERS SPIRE
▲ *Northwest Corner* ▲ *West Face*

These two very fine rock climbs on excellent rock have the delightfully short approaches typical of climbs in the Washington Pass area. At five to six pitches, both recommended routes on North Early Winters Spire are fairly short but, with superb challenges and solid rock, among the best in the area.

Both climbs should be particularly appealing for the strong rock climber without a lot of alpine experience—the way in is not long, and there is no snow or other approach problems. In fact, with a common first pitch, both these climbs are almost like a roadside crag climb. The choice is yours: 5.9 or 5.11.

Special Considerations: Permits are not at present required for climbing at Washington Pass, which is in the Okanogan National Forest; camping is prohibited at the pass itself, but bivouacking at the base of some routes is permitted. For information and up-to-date regulations, call the Methow Valley Ranger District, which recently moved from Twisp to Winthrop (509-996-2266). Northwest Forest Pass required.

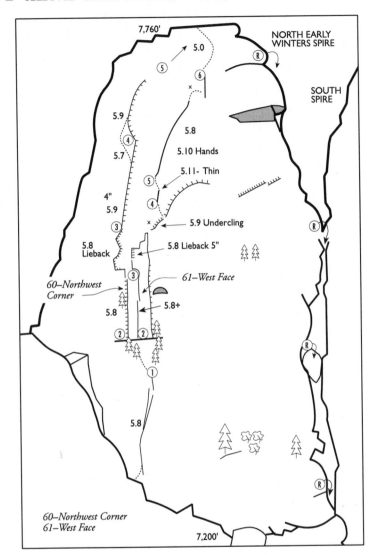

60–Northwest Corner
61–West Face

60 NORTHWEST CORNER GRADE III; 5.9

This route is basically a crack climb on a small, compact dome. With hard crack climbing along with a little friction, here is a climb to be done for the sheer quality of the rock climbing.

    First ascent ▲ Paul Boving and Steve Pollock, September 1976

    Elevation ▲ 7,760 feet

    Difficulty ▲ Grade III; 5.9

    Time ▲ 4–7 hours one-way, car to summit

    Equipment ▲ Medium rack to 4 inches

    Season ▲ June-October

North Early Winters Spire from the west (Photo by Jim Nelson)

Approach *(Grade II)*: Drive State Highway 20 (North Cascades Highway) to 1 mile west of Washington Pass and park at the Blue Lake trailhead (5,200 feet).

Hike the trail 1.5 miles into an open area beneath slabs directly below Liberty Bell. Find the climbers path on the left (north) side of slabs, and ascend until able to traverse right (south) across slabs to open benches. Continue upward, taking the right-hand (south) branch of the climbers trail to North Early Winters Spire. From the left (north) side of the West Face, the climb begins at a chimney of friable rock leading to ledges and trees.

Climbers on the Northwest Corner of North Early Winters Spire
(Photo by Mark Westman)

Route: From the northwest corner of the spire, the **first pitch** climbs a slightly rotten crack system leading to a chimney ending in trees. A **very short pitch** climbs left through the trees and around a corner to the base of a dihedral below an ominous-looking roof. **Pitch 3** climbs the dihedral (5.8) past a tree until under the big roof. Face-climb left (this section can be protected with large protection) to a small stance. Continue up flakes (5.8) to a belay at the base of the left-facing 4-inch crack. The **fourth pitch** ascends via off-width crack climbing (5.9) until the going eases with the appearance of face holds and finally a belay at 80 feet. The **fifth pitch** ascends via friction climbing left (5.7) back into the crack, then over a small roof (5.9) to a belay. **Pitch 6** climbs via low-5th-class ground to the summit.

Descent: Descend via rappels to the notch and gully to the south; begin the rappels approximately 80–100 feet below the top to the west. Two ropes make for a quicker descent, although the descent is reasonable via single-rope rappels.

61 WEST FACE GRADE III; 5.11-

A harder crack climb on sound rock can be found just to the right of the preceding route (climb 60, Northwest Corner). A difficult "adventure" climb very close to the road, the West Face has the makings of a classic. At 5.11, it sounds more intimidating than it really is—with a little aid, it goes at 5.9.

First ascent ▲ Fred Beckey and Dave Beckstad, June 1965; first free ascent: Steve Risse and Dave Tower, July 1985

Elevation ▲ 7,760 feet

Difficulty ▲ Grade III; 5.11-

Time ▲ 4–7 hours one-way, car to summit

Equipment ▲ Medium rack to 3 inches

Season ▲ June-October

Approach (Grade II): Follow the approach given for climb 60, Northwest Corner.

Route: From the Northwest Corner of the spire, the **first pitch** climbs a slightly rotten crack system leading to a 5.8 chimney ending in trees. A short 3rd-class **pitch** (this basically involves moving the belay higher) climbs up through the trees to a large ledge at the base of a large corner with roofs visible above. The **third pitch** climbs cracks on the left wall of the corner (5.8+) to the first good belay (short pitch, 50 feet). The **fourth pitch** continues up the corner (5.7), then liebacks up the edge of a wide crack (5.8; poor protection) followed by a flake/horn to a bolt above a small roof. Undercling right (5.9), then up to a small ledge at the base of a thin, steep crack. **Pitch 5** climbs the thin crack (5.11-) 15 feet until the climber is able to face-climb left (5.10) to a small stance at the base of another crack (short pitch). The **sixth pitch** begins with a hard finger crack, easing into a 2-inch crack (5.10) that eases (to 5.8) below a bolt move to the right (5.7) to an easier crack and a belay. The **seventh pitch** ascends via low-5th-class climbing to the top.

Descent: Descend via rappels to the notch and gully to the south; begin the rappels approximately 80–100 feet below the top to the west. Two ropes make for a quicker descent, although the descent is reasonable via single-rope rappels.

Bill Serontoni on the crux 5.11- crack, North Early Winters Spire, West Face
(Photo by Jim Nelson)

LEXINGTON TOWER ────────────

▲ *East Face* ▲ *Tooth and Claw*

A strenuous and appealing crack climb and a hard face climb on delicate moves—all this exists on one clean, exposed face in the unmatched milieu of Washington Pass.

Viewed from the east, Lexington Tower is overshadowed by its neighbors: the great east face of Liberty Bell and the spectacular twin buttresses of the Early Winters Spires. Despite this unprepossessing appearance, Lexington Tower's East Face boasts two outstanding rock climbs of distinctly different character.

The East Face, first climbed in 1966, has gained a reputation among climbers in the know as an excellent, fun route on solid rock, despite its difficulties. Tooth and Claw, put up in 1990, was a bold and even visionary undertaking. A difficult and committing climb, the route involves thin face climbing to the right of the original route.

Special Considerations: Permits are not at present required for climbing at Washington Pass, which is in the Okanogan National Forest; camping is prohibited at the pass itself, but bivouacking at the base of some routes is permitted. For information and up-to-date regulations, call the Methow Valley Ranger District, which recently moved from Twisp to Winthrop (509-996-2266). Since parking for this route is on the highway, the Northwest Forest Pass is not required.

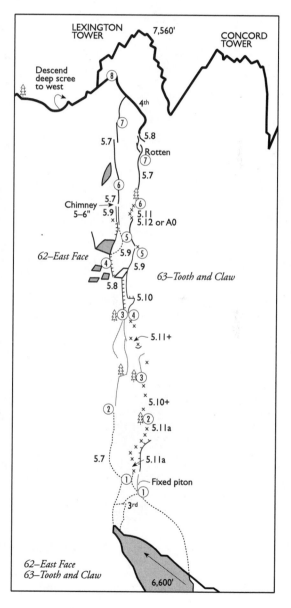

62–East Face
63–Tooth and Claw

The East Faces of Lexington Tower, Concord Tower, and Liberty Bell, with Minuteman Tower in the foreground (Photo by Jim Nelson)

62 EAST FACE GRADE III+; 5.9

The climb begins in a snow-filled gully steep enough to warrant an ice ax or crampons; some rock climbers have been known to use chock picks and sharp rocks in lieu of an ice ax, which would only get in the way once on the rock. The route follows a steep crack system in mid-face, with a particularly airy section that skirts an immense roof at two-thirds height. A strenuous and intimidating off-width crack follows.

First ascent ▲ Steve Marts and Don McPherson, June 1966
Elevation ▲ 7,560 feet
Difficulty ▲ Grade III+; 5.9
Time ▲ 6–8 hours one-way, car to summit
Equipment ▲ Medium rack to 3 inches, with 1–2 pieces of 5–6 inches
Season ▲ June-October

Approach (Grade I+): Drive State Highway 20 (North Cascades Highway) to 0.2 mile east of Washington Pass and park (5,400 feet).

From a small pond, several paths climb through woods leading to talus (snow in early season) below the east wall of Liberty Bell.

Gary Brill on the fifth pitch of the East Face of Lexington Tower
(Photo by Jim Nelson)

Route: The climb begins in the gully on the left (south) side of Lexington Tower, although it is also possible to climb the rock directly, bypassing the gully. In either case, **pitch 2** of the route involves tricky routefinding on slabby rock, past small overlaps (5.7).

On **pitch 3,** the climbing eases, leading up toward the main corner system (some loose rock). The quality of the rock improves considerably by the third pitch, which leads to a good belay near a small tree. The **fourth pitch** follows the corner to a belay stance below the largest roof (5.8). The **fifth pitch** begins with a balance move right across a narrow ledge and into a steep crack (5.9) to a good stance below the chimney/off-width crack. The **sixth pitch** climbs into the off-width crack (5–6 inches wide) past an old, questionable 1/4-inch bolt (5.9). Once in the chimney, the climbing eases, but protection is scarce. The **seventh and eighth pitches** continue up cracks to a ledge system that traverses left toward the summit.

Descent: Descend the scree gully west to the Blue Lake Trail leading to the highway 1 mile west of Washington Pass.

63 TOOTH AND CLAW GRADE III+; 5.12

This is a hard climb put up on lead. The first ascent involved an adventure into the unknown on a largely blank slab, bolting while standing on super-thin holds. Exposed climbing on beautifully clean slabs makes this aesthetic rock route a good choice for those up to its 5.12 standard. Many climbers descend this route via rappels from the top of the sixth pitch, where the climbing eases considerably.

First ascent ▲ Steve Risse and Bryan Burdo, 1988
Elevation ▲ 7,560 feet
Difficulty ▲ Grade III+; 5.12
Time ▲ 6–8 hours one-way from the base
Equipment ▲ Medium rack to 3 inches, quickdraws, 2 ropes for rappel descent
Season ▲ June–October

Approach (Grade II): Follow the approach to below the east wall of Liberty Bell given for climb 62, East Face.

Route: The **first pitch** climbs class 3–4 rock to the large ledge with a tree. The climbing begins in earnest on **pitch 2,** climbing up and left to a series of bolts on 5.11a face climbing to a belay near a small tree (full rope length). **Pitch 3** ascends straight up on 5.10+ face climbing with bolts for protection to another tree belay. The **fourth pitch** involves more of the same with a 5.11+ move at mid-pitch, ending at a belay shared with the East Face route. **Pitch 5** climbs up under a roof (passed on the left) up a crack to a larger roof (passed on the right) via crack climbing (5.9). The **sixth pitch** leads to a bolt ladder and 5.12 climbing to another tree belay. The **seventh pitch** ascends a 5.7 crack system. The **eighth pitch** continues up a now rotten crack (5.8). Easy climbing leads off to the left.

Descent: Descend the scree gully west to the Blue Lake Trail leading to the highway 1 mile west of Washington Pass—or rappel the climbing route.

Matt Kearns on Tooth and Claw (Photo by Dan Cauthorn)

MINUTEMAN TOWER _____

▲ *East Face*

Not really a summit in its own right but more a feature on Concord Tower, Minuteman is, however, separate enough to have its own identity. It is prominent and distinctive, ending in a summited tower but attached to and buttressing the higher Concord.

Squeezed between and dwarfed by the big east face on Liberty Bell and the big East Face on Lexington, this by comparison smaller route on Minuteman ascends mostly cracks to its pseudo summit, the elevation of which has never been actually measured but only estimated. The east walls of Concord loom above, impressive and as yet unclimbed.

Rock-climbing at Washington Pass continues to grow ever more popular. Routes like this, as well as the better-known favorites on bigger peaks, become irresistible when combined with the ease of access and good weather found here. Beware the bug season in midsummer, and the lack of water later in the season.

Special Considerations: Permits are not at present required for climbing at Washington Pass, which is in the Okanogan National Forest; camping is prohibited at the pass itself, but bivouacking at the base of some routes is permitted. For information and up-to-date regulations, call the Methow Valley Ranger District, which recently moved from Twisp to Winthrop (509-996-2266). Since parking for this route is on the highway, the Northwest Forest Pass is not required.

64 EAST FACE GRADE III; 5.10

This 5.10 rock climb in the heart of the Early Winters group has a lot going for it, but it is probably a little too hard to be a really popular rock climb. Other reasons the route does not see a lot of ascents include the fact that it is a relatively short climb in an area surrounded by bigger, steeper, more attractive walls. Still, Minuteman's East Face offers challenging climbing on solid rock, especially higher up. Expect some loose rock on the first pitch, which catches the debris coming out of a nearby gully, but the rock above is quite good.

First ascent ▲ Scott Davis and Bill Lingley, July 1967
Elevation ▲ 7,000 feet
Difficulty ▲ Grade III; 5.10
Time ▲ 6–8 hours round trip
Equipment ▲ Medium rack to 3 inches
Season ▲ June-October

Approach (Grade I+): Follow the approach to below the east wall of Liberty Bell given for climb 62, East Face. Minuteman Tower's East Face is just to the left of Liberty Bell; look for the broad apron ending in a tower against Concord Tower.

Route: The climbing route begins at the left edge of the face adjacent to the Minuteman-Lexington gully and very close to it. **Pitch 1** starts out in a corner system (5.7–5.8). **Pitch 2** traverses to the right on thin face moves through roofs into another gully/corner (5.8; long runouts). **Pitch 3** continues up a crack system to a belay at the top of the large apron. **Pitch 4** traverses to the right below roofs to

Minuteman Tower from the east (Photo by Jim Nelson)

Gary Brill on Minuteman's East Face, pitch 5 (Photo by Jim Nelson)

a belay on the right edge of the apron. **Pitch 5:** Above the belay, ascend a flake that turns into a nice hand crack on brittle, light-colored rock (5.10) to a belay. **Pitch 6** begins in a wide crack (formed by a flake) and continues up the hand crack on the final slab (5.8).

    Descent: Descend off the north side of the tower via four or five rappels using slings and tree anchors.

LIBERTY BELL

▲ *Beckey Route/Southwest Face* ▲ *Overexposure/South Face* ▲ *Serpentine Crack/ West Face* ▲ *Northwest Face* ▲ *Liberty Crack* ▲ *Thin Red Line*

Washington Pass is destined to become increasingly known as a center for Northwest alpine rock climbing in the years to come, more so than even the Stuart Range. Ease of access combined with rich alpine ambience make this area unique as a rock climbing destination. No mountain in the area boasts more or better routes than Liberty Bell. This giant piece of granite, with 1,200 feet of relief from the base of the east wall to the summit, has good rock, diverse routes, and interesting climbs, all in the heart of the Washington Pass climbing action. Proximity to the highway and ease of approach complete the attractions of this unsurpassed climbing area. Routes recommended on Liberty Bell range from short, low-5th-class climbs to multipitch bigwall routes.

Special Considerations: Permits are not at present required for climbing at Washington Pass, which is in the Okanogan National Forest; camping is prohibited at the pass itself, but bivouacking at the base of some routes is permitted. For information and up-to-date regulations, call the Methow Valley Ranger District (which recently moved from Twisp to Winthrop) of the Okanogan National Forest (509-996-2266). Northwest Forest Pass required at Blue Lake trailhead; not required for routes approached from highway parking.

65 BECKEY ROUTE/SOUTHWEST FACE GRADE II; 5.6

One of the shortest and most moderate routes in the whole Liberty Bell group, this was also the first climb of the peak. Climbers today, who virtually drive up to the mountain, can hardly imagine the miles covered on foot by the original climbers in the pre-highway days. That 16-mile approach is a far cry from the short walk climbers now use to reach this route.

First ascent ▲ Fred Beckey, Jerry O'Neil, Charles Welch, September 1946; first winter ascent: Fred Dunham and Gene Prater, March 29, 1972

Elevation ▲ 7,720 feet

Difficulty ▲ Grade II; 5.6

Time ▲ 3–5 hours one-way, car to summit

Equipment ▲ Small rack to 3 inches

Season ▲ May-October

Approach (Grade II): Drive State Highway 20 (North Cascades Highway) to 1 mile west of Washington Pass and park at the Blue Lake trailhead (5,200 feet).

Hike the trail 1.5 miles into a small meadow beneath granite slabs directly below Liberty Bell. Find the climbers path on the left (north) side of the slabs, and ascend until able to traverse right (south) across the slabs to open benches. Find the climbers path and ascend up and left; the path continues up from the slabs, and then left (north) into the gully between Liberty Bell and the first tower on the right (south), which is Concord Tower.

Climb the gully (usually snow-filled until late June). Once the snow is gone, the

Liberty Bell from the west (Photo by Jim Nelson)

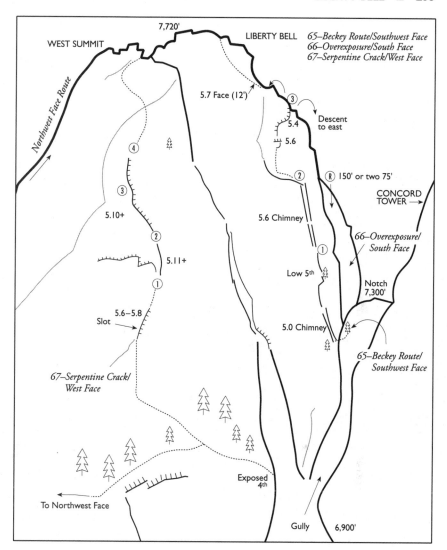

WEST SUMMIT

7,720'

LIBERTY BELL

65–Beckey Route/Southwest Face
66–Overexposure/South Face
67–Serpentine Crack/West Face

Northwest Face Route

5.7 Face (12')

③

Descent
to east

5.4

5.6

④

③

5.10+

②

5.11+

①

Slot

5.6–5.8

②

①

5.6 Chimney

Ⓡ 150' or two 75'

CONCORD
TOWER →

66–Overexposure/
South Face

Low 5th

Notch
7,300'

5.0 Chimney

65–Beckey Route/
Southwest Face

67–Serpentine Crack/
West Face

Exposed
4th

To Northwest Face

Gully   6,900'

potential for party-inflicted rockfall is high. If there are parties already in the gully, the best course of action is to cling to the left-hand wall or, safer, wait until the higher party reaches the Liberty Bell–Concord notch before proceeding. Climb the gully to within approximately 30 feet below the obvious notch, to the point where the climb actually begins at a small tree.

Route: From the tree, the **first pitch** traverses left and into a chimney/gully (low-5th-class climbing), under a chockstone, past ledges and small trees, to a belay at the base of a steeper chimney. The **second pitch** climbs this chimney (5.6) to a large ledge. The **third pitch** climbs low-angle rock to a crack leading to a small roof where the rock steepens and there is a fixed piton. A difficult move left (5.6) leads past the roof, then up and right, followed by friction climbing below a good crack.

Climber Andrew Oakley on the Beckey Route/Southwest Face, Liberty Bell
(Photo by Andreas Schmidt)

This leads around the corner to ledges at a shoulder—this shoulder is the false summit when viewed from the approach trail. A 12-foot friction slab (5.7) is followed by a **full pitch** of 5.0 climbing leading to the top.

Descent: Down-climb to the shoulder, below the friction slab, approximately 200 feet below the summit. Climb down left (east) through trees (class 3) 100 feet until able to walk right (west) to the end of an exposed ledge below a steep wall, where there are bolts for rappel anchors. Two 165-foot ropes reach the Liberty Bell–Concord notch from these anchors, or two single-rope rappels also work. This rappel route descends the Overexposure/South Face climbing route (climb 66) to the notch and gully.

66 OVEREXPOSURE/SOUTH FACE GRADE II; 5.8

This is the shortest route to the summit of Liberty Bell, and one commonly used as the descent route. This moderate, early route has two good, short pitches—each with a nice bit of crack climbing—but it starts with some unprotected and hard-to-find climbing on loose holds.

First ascent ▲ Ron Burgner and Don McPherson, August 1966
Elevation ▲ 7,720 feet
Difficulty ▲ Grade II; 5.8
Time ▲ 1–2 hours one-way, car to summit
Equipment ▲ Small rack to 2½ inches
Season ▲ May-October

Approach (Grade II): Follow the approach to the Liberty Bell–Concord notch given for climb 65, Beckey Route/Southwest Face.

Route: The route begins at the notch at the top of the approach gully. The **first pitch,** 80 feet long, begins with steep face climbing (5.8 initially) with some friable holds and poor protection; the pitch eases to low 5th class fairly quickly. The **second pitch,** also 80 feet, climbs two 30-foot corner cracks (5.8). Move right on a ledge past trees, up a tree-filled gully to the shoulder and the Beckey Route. The last pitch of the Beckey Route/Southwest Face (climb 65) leads to the summit.

Descent: Follow the descent given for climb 65, Beckey Route/Southwest Face.

67 SERPENTINE CRACK/WEST FACE GRADE III; 5.11+

This fine route features difficult crack climbing on solid rock. While the first-ascent party climbed predominantly on aid (using thirty pitons), the climb is now a popular free climb, although it is not uncommon for many climbers to "hangdog" this difficult climb. The route features a hard fist crack and a steep, awkward dihedral.

First ascent ▲ Fred Beckey, Doug Lean, David Wagner, July 1967
Elevation ▲ 7,720 feet
Difficulty ▲ Grade III; 5.11+
Time ▲ 3–5 hours one-way, car to summit
Equipment ▲ Medium rack to 4 inches
Season ▲ June-October

Approach (Grade II): Follow the approach to the gully between Liberty Bell and the first tower on the right (south), which is Concord Tower, given for climb 65, Beckey Route/Southwest Face.

Climb the gully to where it forks, approximately 200 feet before the Liberty Bell–Concord notch. A short bit of 4th-class climbing leads left (northwest) onto ledges high on Liberty Bell's West Face. Climb slabs to the base of a deep V-groove at the right-center of the West Face.

Route: The **first pitch** of Serpentine Crack/West Face climbs the groove (5.6–5.8) for a full pitch to a belay below a roof. The **second pitch** climbs past the roof on its right side via a very steep and awkward 5.11+ fist crack (short pitch). The **third pitch** climbs the corner crack (1–3½ inches wide), where a slab intersects a steep wall (5.10+; long pitch). **Another pitch** of mid-5th-class climbing leads to easier climbing and the false (west) summit. Scrambling leads to the true summit.

Descent: Follow the descent given for climb 65, Beckey Route/Southwest Face.

68 NORTHWEST FACE GRADE II+; 5.8

A short route leading to the western summit, the Northwest Face is similar in length and quality to Serpentine Crack (climb 67). The Northwest Face has an exceptionally long, sustained, well-protected dihedral pitch that is a highlight of the route.

First ascent ▲ Hans Kraus and John Rupley, August 1956; first free ascent: Sandy Bill, Ron Burgner, Ian Martin, Frank Tarver, August 1966

Elevation ▲ 7,720 feet

Difficulty ▲ Grade II+; 5.8

Time ▲ 3–5 hours one-way, car to summit

Equipment ▲ Medium rack to 2½ inches

Season ▲ June-October

Approach (Grade II): Follow the approach to the gully fork approximately 200 feet below the Liberty Bell–Concord notch given for climb 67, Serpentine Crack/West Face.

Where the gully forks, climb left (northwest) onto a large ledge. Continue all

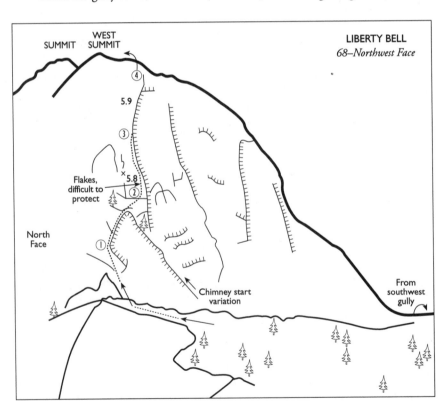

the way across (past the chimney/gully) to the northwest ridge, where the climber can look down and across the north face.

Route: The **first two pitches** ascend left (north) of the ridge crest (mid-5th class) leading to a large ledge below a steep wall. The **third pitch** climbs right of two steep face cracks, climbing a series of flakes (poor protection) leading to a strenuous lieback flake (5.8). The **fourth pitch** climbs the long, clean dihedral (thin crack; 5.9). Easier climbing soon leads to the false (west) summit and on to the true summit.

Descent: Follow the descent given for climb 65, Beckey Route/Southwest Face.

69 LIBERTY CRACK GRADE V; 5.9 AND A2

A classic Grade V big-wall climb on good rock, Liberty Crack is set in the heart of the Washington Pass climbing action. The rock is smooth and sound and, for the first 800 feet, completely devoid of significant ledges. This feature adds impact to the climb's exposure and enhances its big-wall feel.

Though the route is traditionally done with a lot of aid, a free ascent was claimed in 1992 at 5.13b; for most parties, however, the climb remains a combination of aid and free climbing. Of the twelve total pitches, seven will be aid for the 5.8+ climber, the 5.9–5.10 climber will have four short aid pitches, and the 5.10+ climber will have about three short aid sections. Both strong free climbers with basic aid-climbing skills and experienced aid climbers with mediocre free-climbing abilities will be able to finish the route in a long day. Less-experienced parties or those desiring a more relaxed pace should plan on a bivouac.

The nature of the route makes it popular, so be prepared to be delayed by slow-moving parties or passed by fast free-climbing parties.

Except for a 60-foot section of rock on the second and third pitches, the route consists entirely of crack climbing. This blank section above the Lithuanian Lip, where one crack system fades out and another soon begins, forms the crux of the climb. It is also the section where the greatest amount of fixed protection, bashies, and bolts are to be found.

The climber's rack size depends on the amount of free-climbing to be done. The rack should include mostly small to medium pieces, with only one or two pieces to 3½ inches. Although the route has been done clean by using the existing fixed gear, one or two pitons are recommended, because the amount of fixed gear is subject to change.

First ascent ▲ Steve Marts, Don McPherson, Fred Stanley, July 1965; first winter ascent: Jamie Christenson, Matt Christenson, Dale Farnham, John Znamierowski, February 1977

Elevation ▲ 7,720 feet

Difficulty ▲ Grade V; 5.9 and A2

Time ▲ 1–2 days round trip

Equipment ▲ Medium to large rack to 3½ inches; 1–2 pitons

Season ▲ May–October

Approach (Grade II): Drive State Highway 20 (North Cascades Highway) to 0.2 mile east of Washington Pass and park (5,400 feet).

Liberty Bell group from the east: A. Liberty Crack (climb 69); B. Thin Red Line (climb 70) (Photo by Jim Nelson)

From a small pond, several paths climb through woods leading to talus (snow in early season) below the east wall of Liberty Bell. Reach the start of the route by some 4th-class scrambling 40 feet to a ledge.

Route: **Pitch 1** begins from the right side of the ledge; an awkward right-facing corner (A2) leads to a straightforward face crack (A1) and to a good stance below the obvious roof; this pitch goes free at 5.10+ or 5.11. **Pitch 2** climbs the left-facing corner to the roof (known as the Lithuanian Lip) past a bolt and over the roof (A2) to a small crack, then ascends a bolt ladder to a good belay stance. **Pitch 3** ascends small cracks (A2) with some fixed gear (bolts and bashies) to the left edge of a roof where the crack system improves. Very steep climbing (A2) continues to a nice belay ledge. Free-climbing, this pitch is solid 5.11.

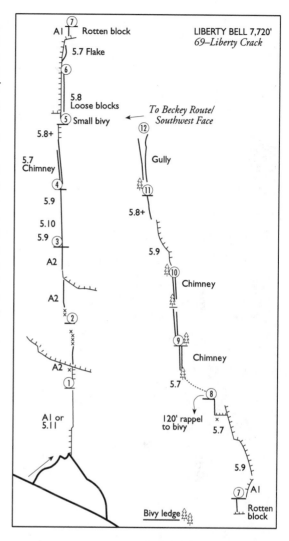

Pitch 4 ascends a straight-in face crack (5.10 or A1) to a ledge/belay below a chimney. **Pitch 5** climbs the chimney (5.7), which becomes a left-facing corner (5.8+), leading to a small ledge on the right—a possible but poor bivy site. **Pitch 6** (probably should be combined with pitch 7) ascends a right-facing corner (5.8) with several loose blocks leading to a belay/alcove. **Pitch 7** climbs a 5.7 lieback flake leading to a rotten-block roof. The rotten block is fixed with angle pitons (A1), taking the climber to the belay ledge on top of the block (very short pitch).

Pitch 8 begins with an awkward move right (A1 or hard free move) leading to a nice left-facing corner (5.9). Continue up, then left, across a slab, then up again to a belay ledge. From here a 120-foot rappel can be made to a very good bivy ledge. **Pitch 9** begins with a tricky traverse left (5.7) to easier tree-covered ledges and a short chimney (low class 5). **Pitch 10** is low to mid-5th class, following a chimney system

Climbers on the second and third pitches of Liberty Crack (Photo by Cliff Leight)

Marshall Balick leads to the base of the Lithuanian Lip pitch, Liberty Crack, Liberty Bell. (Photo by Tim Matsui)

Aiding past the Lithuanian Lip on Liberty Crack (Photo by Jim Nelson)

to a good ledge. **Pitch 11:** This long pitch climbs the left-facing corner (5.9) until the climber is able to move left into another system (5.8+) leading to a sandy ledge below a large tree. **Pitch 12** climbs the gully past the tree (low 5th class) leading to 4th-class ground. Continue up on moderate ground until it is possible to traverse left toward the standard descent route near the rappel bolts.

Descent: Follow the descent given for climb 65, Beckey Route/Southwest Face.

70 THIN RED LINE GRADE V; 5.9 AND A3

A classic big-wall route taking a bold, direct line up the middle of Liberty Bell's huge east face, this route features significantly more aid climbing and less free climbing than other routes on the mountain. A highlight of the climb is the long, strenuous pitch near midway, climbing through roofs and past other obstacles, beginning with a 5.9 mantel with a big-wall rack. As on some popular aid climbs, there is a lot of fixed gear on the first five pitches, including a lot of bashies.

First ascent ▲ Jim Madsen and Kim Schmitz, July 1967
Elevation ▲ 7,720 feet
Difficulty ▲ Grade V; 5.9 and A3
Time ▲ 1–2 days round trip
Equipment ▲ Large rack to 3 inches, mostly small to medium pieces; several pitons to ⅝ inch
Season ▲ May-October

Approach (Grade II): Follow the approach to below the east wall of Liberty Bell given for climb 69, Liberty Crack.

Kit Lewis on the Thin Red Line route on Liberty Bell (Photo by Dave Bale)

Route: The climb starts in the center of the face at the lowest point of the wall, not far (right) from Liberty Crack. **Pitch 1** begins with not particularly obvious face climbing, ascending (5.8) until the climber is able to traverse left to a small ledge. **Pitch 2** climbs up over a small roof (A3, with some free moves) to a ledge below a large, left-facing corner. Continue up the corner (A1) to a hanging belay at the left edge of the first roof. **Pitch 3** climbs up and left under a larger roof (A1). Continue climbing (A2) to the right side of another roof, which is passed via loose blocks. Move right to a small belay stance. **Pitch 4** ascends a crack (5.6) that leads to an arch (A2; pitons recommended here) leading to a hanging belay.

Pitch 5 starts from the belay with a pendulum right and mantel (5.9) leading to a crack through a small roof (A2+), followed by a larger roof. Belay at a tree above this roof. **Pitch 6** ascends via A1 and much free climbing (5.8) up and right to a belay ledge above a large block, a possible bivy site for a party of two. **Pitch 7** begins on aid (A2) until the climber is able to step left into a dihedral leading to a hanging belay below a small roof (free moves and aid). **Pitch 8** is a short pitch that leads past the roof to a large ledge (M&M Ledge, a good bivy site).

From the right end of the ledge, **pitch 9** ascends a crack leading up and left (5.8) into a chimney leading to a belay at large blocks. **Pitch 10** climbs through the loose blocks (5.7) to slabs below large roofs. **Pitch 11** climbs right, across the slabs (below

LIBERTY BELL 7,720'
70–Thin Red Line

Dave Bale on the second pitch of Thin Red Line (Photo by Kit Lewis)

roofs) and around a corner to the belay (5.7). **Pitch 12** climbs a short flake (5.8) leading to loose class 4 ground and then easier climbing to the top.

Descent: Follow the descent given for climb 65, Beckey Route/Southwest Face.

BURGUNDY SPIRE _____

▲ *North Face*

One of the highest summits in the range requiring sustained 5th-class climbing, Burgundy Spire by its North Face offers invigorating and challenging rock climbing and the reward of good views. Liberty Bell and Early Winters Spires stand close by to the west, viewed from an unusual eastern vantage, and from Burgundy Spire's airy 8,400-foot summit, the peaks of Cascade Pass and the Dome Peak area are visible above and beyond.

Wine Spires from the west (Photo by Jim Nelson)

Fred Beckey considers Burgundy Spire—along with Nooksack Tower—among the most technically difficult summits to attain in the Cascades. With only three ascents as of 1965, this is an outstanding peak that is gaining repeat customers among climbers in the know.

Special Considerations: Permits are not at present required for climbing at Washington Pass, which is in the Okanogan National Forest; camping is prohibited at the pass itself, but bivouacking at the base of some routes is permitted. For information and up-to-date regulations, call the Methow Valley Ranger District, which recently moved from Twisp to Winthrop (509-996-2266). Since parking for this route is on the highway, the Northwest Forest Pass is not required.

71 NORTH FACE GRADE II+; 5.8

The climb begins with several hundred feet of moderate climbing on good, broken rock leading to two honest pitches of steep 5.8, followed by a stretch of exposed 5.8 on a narrow ridge crest. Awkward chimney and off-width cracks finish the route.

Because the route faces north, the temperatures on this climb tend to be cool early or late in the season, a characteristic that makes the route a pleasant alpine rock climb on a hot summer day. Lovely campsites lie among big beautiful larch trees and

Kit Lewis descending in a storm from Burgundy Spire (Photo by Jim Nelson)

Winter camp below the Wine Spires: Chablis, Pernod, Chianti, Burgundy
(Photo by Jim Nelson)

Kevin Joiner on Burgundy Spire (Photo by Jim Nelson)

boulders on a bench (6,400 feet) below the west faces of the Wine Spires (the water dries up in late season); good bivy sites can be found at Burgundy Col.

First ascent ▲ Fred Beckey, Michael Hane, John Parrott, August 1953; first winter ascent: Kit Lewis, Jim Nelson, Kevin Joyner, December 1985

Elevation ▲ 8,400 feet

Difficulty ▲ Grade II+; 5.8

Time ▲ 1–2 days round trip; 2–4 hours one-way from col

Equipment ▲ Medium rack to 3½ inches; ice ax in early season

Season ▲ June-September

Approach (Grade III+): Drive State Highway 20 (North Cascades Highway) to 4 miles east of Washington Pass and park at the wide shoulder (4,250 feet) where a sign points to Silver Star Mountain. Burgundy Spire is visible directly above, as is much of the approach route. The climbers trail is located left (north) of the stream (Burgundy Creek) that drains the basin below the west faces of the Wine Spires. The location of the stream is important, because it is the best landmark for finding the climbers trail.

From the road, descend along the edge of talus 300 feet; cross Early Winters Creek on a log or ford. The trail can be found just left (north) of Burgundy Creek, approximately 300 feet uphill from where it flows into Early Winters Creek, at a spot where the slope steepens as it leaves the valley bottom.

The trail climbs steeply, staying well left (north) of the creek. A bench at 6,400 feet provides good early-season camping with water. (By midsummer, the area is buggy; by late summer, water is scarce or nonexistent.) From here, near the base of Burgundy Spire's west face, a long gully (with a small stream in early season) leads to Burgundy Col (7,950 feet). Burgundy Col makes a good bug-free bivy site in all seasons. Immediately east of the col is the Silver Star Glacier, providing a year-round water source.

Route: From Burgundy Col, climb approximately 200 feet of mostly 4th-class rock to ledges near Paisano Pinnacle. Climb left and up into a crack system (5.8) two pitches to a large ledge. From here, there are several options:

Option 1: Traverse west on ledge systems and then down to another roomy ledge on the west side of the spire 150 feet below the summit; from there, climb crack and flake systems directly up to the summit (5.8)—or *Option 2:* take the right-hand crack system beside the steep slab (5.7) to the summit block.

Option 3: Make a direct ascent up the narrow, exposed ridge crest (past a bolt) to below the summit block. Drop down 10 feet, crossing to the west side, and climb wide cracks (5.7), which are difficult to protect, to the summit.

Descent: Descend by rappelling to the col.

CHIANTI SPIRE
▲ *East Face*

This is a scenic climb on high-quality rock with straightforward routefinding. The unrelenting steepness of the route, combined with the impressive backdrop of glaciers and spires, gives the climb the flavor of high-mountain remoteness. This is a fun route in an appealing area, with genuine technical difficulties and outrageous alpine ambience.

Views while on the climb are down to the Silver Star Glacier and the jagged ridges on Silver Star Mountain itself. From the top, the successful climber gazes out to the numerous Washington Pass peaks, the foothills surrounding the Methow Valley, and farther east to the vast, sparsely populated open spaces of eastern Washington.

Special Considerations: Permits are not at present required for climbing at Washington Pass, which is in the Okanogan National Forest; camping is prohibited at the pass itself, but bivouacking at the base of some routes is permitted. For information and up-to-date regulations, call the Methow Valley Ranger District, which recently moved from Twisp to Winthrop (509-996-2266). Since parking for this route is on the highway, the Northwest Forest Pass is not required.

72 EAST FACE GRADE III; 5.10

The climb features some challenging crack climbing, ranging from finger-size to 4 inches. A short pitch of 5.7 face climbing on the final summit block leads to the tiny (1-foot-by-2-foot) summit. "Rebel yells," yodels of joy, and shouts of exhilaration have been known to ring out over the glaciers and rock towers of the Wine Spires as climbers on this fine route find expression for their feelings.

Jim Nelson on the Chianti summit block (Photo by Carl Diedrich)

Chianti Spire's East Face (Photo by Jim Nelson)

Tim Wilson on the fifth pitch of Chianti Spire's East Face (Photo by Dave Bale)

First ascent ▲ Mark Bebie, Carl Diedrich, Jim Nelson, Heather Paxson, June 1986, and 1987

Elevation ▲ 8,380 feet

Difficulty ▲ Grade III; 5.10

Time ▲ 1–2 days round trip; 5-7 hours one-way from col

Equipment ▲ Medium rack to 4 inches; 2 ropes; ice ax in early season

Season ▲ Mid-June–September

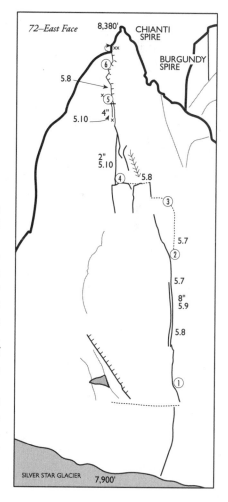

Approach (Grade III+): Follow the approach to Burgundy Col (7,950 feet) given for climb 71, North Face.

From Burgundy Col, descend 200–300 feet on moderate snow (25 degrees) until able to traverse below Burgundy Spire; continue traversing right (south) and slightly uphill until access to the upper Silver Star Glacier is gained. Chianti Spire is the first spire south of Burgundy Spire, and the route can be seen clearly from here.

Route: The climb begins in a wide crack in the left-facing corner in the center of the face. A distinct buttress borders the lower right-hand (north) side of the face; begin left (south) and uphill of this feature.

255

Climb the wide crack in **two pitches** with a combination of crack and face climbing (5.9) to ledges and easier climbing on **pitch 3.** On **pitch 4,** small cracks and face climbing lead up a short way until the climber is able to climb left around a blind corner (5.8). Continue left 15 feet (exposed) to a nice ledge at the base of the upper crack system. For **pitch 5,** climb the 2-inch crack (5.10) to a hanging stance where the crack widens to 4 inches. Climb the 4-inch crack (5.10) to a small stance. **Pitch 6** continues up the crack system (5.8) to the final rock obstacles. Fifteen feet of 5.7 face climbing on the summit block leads to the top.

Descent: Rappel the climbing route, beginning at the east end of the summit block. Two ropes are recommended to make four double-rope rappels down the face.

SILVER STAR MOUNTAIN ─────────────────────
▲ *Silver Star Glacier*

This is a superb nontechnical snow climb to a high and rewarding summit with outstanding views. At just under 9,000 feet, Silver Star Mountain is one of the highest peaks in the Washington Pass/Methow region. Its position east of the Cascades crest gives Silver Star Mountain reliably better weather, which makes it a good alternative when poor weather discourages climbing farther west. The climbing season itself starts a good month earlier over here; in May, wet snow or rain on the Cascades crest often means—at worst—dry snow flurries around Silver Star Mountain. Because of this early access, Silver Star Mountain is a good conditioning climb.

Special Considerations: Permits are not at present required for climbing at Washington Pass, which is in the Okanogan National Forest; camping is prohibited at the pass itself, but bivouacking at the base of some routes is permitted. For information and up-to-date regulations, call the Methow Valley Ranger District, which recently moved from Twisp to Winthrop (509-996-2266). Since parking for this route is on the highway, the Northwest Forest Pass is not required.

73 SILVER STAR GLACIER GRADE II
The glacier route is not visible from the road. Instead, it is the mountain's rugged west face that dominates the view eastward from Washington Pass. Access to the climbing route on the Silver Star Glacier is gained by ascending to the prominent notch (Burgundy Col) at the north (left) end of Silver Star Mountain's jagged ridge crest.

First ascent ▲ Fred Beckey, Joe Hieb, Herb Staley, Don Wilde, May 1952
Elevation ▲ 8,876 feet
Difficulty ▲ Grade II; class 3; 30-degree snow
Time ▲ 1–2 days round trip
Equipment ▲ Ice ax; crampons in late season
Season ▲ May–October

Approach (Grade III): Follow the approach to Burgundy Col (7,950 feet) given for climb 71, North Face.

Silver Star Creek approach to Silver Star Mountain (Photo by Gordy Skoog)

Lowell Skoog makes turns on the Silver Star Glacier. (Photo by Gordy Skoog)

Burgundy
Col

Silver Star Mountain from the north, showing the Silver Star Glacier
(Photo by Jim Nelson)

Route: From Burgundy Col, descend 200–300 feet on moderate snow (25 degrees) until able to traverse below Burgundy Spire; continue traversing right (southeast) slightly uphill until access to the upper Silver Star Glacier is gained. Once on the glacier, traverse right (south) below the Wine Spires and past a rock buttress, climbing to the top of the small glacier at a broad col (8,600 feet). The summit is reached by a short 3rd-class scramble eastward.

Descent: Descend the climbing route.

JUNO TOWER

▲ *Clean Break*

This is another find by Bryan Burdo, a climber who has been so active in the Cascades for so long, and who has proven adept at uncovering exceptional routes. Clean Break is an extraordinary alpine rock climb in a scenic but out-of-the-way part of the North Cascades. With superb pitches on excellent rock, the challenging alpine route ascending Vasiliki Ridge via a pronounced arête is already becoming a classic.

Burdo discovered the route while on his way to attempt another route on Burgundy Spire in 1984, going by way of Silver Star Creek (an alternative to the usual Burgundy approach, which leaves the highway closer to Washington Pass). Before him was a long buttress soaring up the "back side" of Vasiliki Ridge. He tried the first few pitches of the route on his way out, and finding them "beautiful," returned the next year with Yann "Rope Rocket" Merrand to finish the climb.

Special Considerations: Permits are not at present required for climbing at Washington Pass, which is in the Okanogan National Forest; camping is prohibited at the pass itself, but bivouacking at the base of some routes is permitted. For information and up-to-date regulations, call the Methow Valley Ranger District, which recently moved from Twisp to Winthrop (509-996-2266). Since parking for this route is on the highway, the Northwest Forest Pass is not required.

Juno Tower

Vasiliki Ridge and Juno Tower, with the Clean Break arête (Photo by Mark Kroese)

74 CLEAN BREAK GRADE IV+; 5.10B/C, OR 5.10A AND A1

From start to finish, Clean Break is interesting and challenging. The lower portion of the route is flagged by a 100-foot-long rock scar—the "Clean Break"—on the second pitch. And getting to that point is half the fun, according to Burdo, who calls the moves in the first-pitch crack some of the best on the climb: "It is an incredible 2-inch splitter crack that would have a major waiting queue in Yosemite." The route finishes with a steep and spectacular—but short—hand crack up an exposed headwall, ending at the summit of a feature known as Juno Tower.

The route is long enough, at thirteen pitches of strenuous climbing, that some parties fix the lower pitches, then do the route the following day. For others, Clean Break is a day climb.

First ascent ▲ Bryan Burdo and Yann Merrand, August 1985
Elevation ▲ 7,920 feet
Difficulty ▲ Grade IV+; 5.10b/c, or 5.10a and A1
Time ▲ 1–2 days round trip
Equipment ▲ Ice ax; large rack to 2 inches, including small wires and cams, 1 each half sizes 2.5 to 4; jumars if fixing first two pitches
Season ▲ June–September

Approach (Grade II+): Drive State Highway 20 (North Cascades Highway) to 7 miles east of Washington Pass and park at Silver Star Creek (3,450 feet).

From the road, follow a path along the east side of the creek for about 2 miles through open but log-strewn forest. At a meadow with large boulders (5,000 feet), where the valley opens up, head toward the stream in the woods and cross to the west side. The route is visible from here. Follow the woods up and right through

Joe Puryear on the amazing first pitch of Clean Break (Photo by Mark Westman)

talus and slabs that take you up and westward toward Sunset Col, a notch at the north end of Vasiliki Ridge (5,400 feet), avoiding the brush at the head of the valley. When the terrain opens up, traverse toward the base of the climb, where good bivouac sites are available. The route ascends the prominent arête on the northeast side of Vasiliki Ridge.

Route: The route is easy to identify by the giant rock scar on the second pitch. **Pitch 1:** Climb an easy chimney, then negotiate the "Paragon," a challenging 2-inch crack (5.10c, or 5.10a and A1). **Pitch 2:** The "Break" or rock scar is surmounted directly via the slab cracks (avoid the loose corner to the left), which after 20 feet works leftward (5.10b–c, or 5.10a and A1). An easy ledge allows a bypass left of the original harder line, which worked directly up the flaring corner of the break's left margin. Either way works, and leads to a small tree belay. The **third pitch** traverses right and gains cracks to a belay among large flakes. **Pitch 4:** A thin crack is then followed 20–30 feet to a fixed pin; a delicate face traverse (5.10a) gains the next crack on the left, then runs a full rope length to the belay, with one more traverse back right near the end. **Pitch 5:** Continue up easy steps (5.6) to a lean white wall with a steep, widening crack. The **sixth pitch** follows the 4-inch crack until a rightward slab traverse leads to a thin corner (5.10a) and up to the next stance. **Pitch 7:** From there, exit right and gain the arête (5.8), which is followed on its crest or along its right side, until the final pitch. **Pitches 8–12** follow along the crest of the arête in a series of short pitches of more quality climbing interspersed with sections of scramblings until **pitch 13:** a short, steep hand crack (5.10a) up an exposed headwall provides the exhilarating finish. Other options allow access to the ridge directly, bypassing the summit, but are loose and not as aesthetic.

Descent: Down-climb Juno Tower on the southwest side, then work north below the ridge to Sunset Col, which leads back to Silver Star Creek.

MOUNT HARDY
▲ *Northeast Buttress—The Disappearing Floor*

By all rights, the Northeast Buttress of Mount Hardy should be a well-known climb. Located less than 2 miles from the North Cascades Highway, the Northeast Buttress of Mount Hardy is a long climb on high-quality rock that ascends an obvious route up a prominent face. One of the most heavily trafficked trails in the Cascades passes through open meadows at the base of the route. So why did this striking line remain virtually unknown until 2001?

The route might still be unclimbed had not the first-ascent party accidentally stumbled on the climb. Mount Hardy is located between Rainy Pass and Harts Pass, and thousands of hikers pass below it every summer on the Pacific Crest Trail. Methow Pass, the low point on the ridge connecting Hardy and Golden Horn, is reached via 10 long trail miles of switchbacks. What most hikers never realize, however, is that the trail actually trends back toward State Highway 20 (North Cascades Highway). At Methow Pass, in fact, the trail is separated from the highway by a single ridge: that of Mount Hardy. The first-ascent party came across the route while on what they thought was a remote backcountry adventure. Research revealed the surprising truth: only a few hours of very moderate off-trail travel separate the base of the route from the highway. As a result, the first ascent was done car-to-car in a single day. With an easy walk-off descent, and unusual views north into the Pasayten Wilderness, this route has the makings of a modern-day classic.

Special Considerations: Mount Hardy lies on the border between Mount Baker–Snoqualmie National Forest and Okanagan National Forest. Permits are not required to hike or camp here; however, climbers may register for the route at the North Cascades National Park ranger station, officially known as the Wilderness Information Center, in Marblemount (360-873-4500). Northwest Forest Pass required.

75 NORTHEAST BUTTRESS—THE DISAPPEARING FLOOR
GRADE IV; 5.10c

A moderate lower apron leads to six pitches of superb climbing on a steep headwall in a very scenic part of the Cascades. Several more rope lengths of exposed climbing on a long, classic knife-edge lead directly to the summit. The upper ridge is reminiscent of more traveled climbs such as the North Ridge of Mount Stuart (climb 20), albeit without the massive glaciers that add to that route's ambience. The name of the route, "The Disappearing Floor," comes from the title of the nineteenth installment in the Hardy Boys mystery series, published in 1940.

First ascent ▲ Dan Aylward and Forrest Murphy, August 2001

Elevation ▲ 8,080 feet

Difficulty ▲ Grade IV; 5.10c

Time ▲ 1–2 days round trip

Equipment ▲ Medium rack to 5 inches with doubles in smaller sizes; ice ax in early season

Season: May-September

Approach (Grade III+): From Interstate 5 near Burlington, take the Cook Road exit (exit 232) east approximately 5 miles to where it joins Highway 20 in Sedro Woolley, and drive approximately 91.5 miles to the Easy Pass trailhead (6.2 miles west of Rainy Pass) on the west side of the highway (3,700 feet).

Return to the highway and hike 0.5 mile east along the shoulder before heading into the woods on the north side of the road and climbing directly up the wooded hillside. Mount Hardy is mislabeled on the USGS Mt. Arriva quadrangle (and all other maps based on USGS data, such as GreenTrails), with the name printed adjacent to a 7,197-foot summit. In fact, the true Mount Hardy is the highest point on the ridge between Mebee Pass and Methow Pass, 0.6 mile to the southeast.

The general goal of the approach is to cross a col between Point 7197 (the falsely labeled peak) and the next peak to the south (approximately 7,600 feet). There is no trail, but after the first few hundred yards, the slope becomes quite open. A series of parallel wooded ribs lead to a small plateau (around 6,400 feet), with the drier south-facing aspects providing the easiest travel. Once on the plateau, game trails lead easily to a short boulder field that in turn reaches the col at 7,260 feet in 2–3 hours from the car (good campsites here, but water may be scarce after early August).

Dan Aylward below the Northeast Buttress on Mount Hardy
(Photo by Forrest Murphy)

Mount Hardy's Disappearing Floor route from the east (Photo by Forrest Murphy)

Drop down the gully on the far side of the pass into the valley of the Methow River. This is fairly steep at first, but soon mellows out. About two-thirds of the way to the valley floor, the gully narrows where a permanent stream emerges from the boulders. Continue down until a few hundred feet above the river (around 5,400 feet), where the first full view of Mount Hardy appears around the shoulder, then leave the streambed and begin contouring southward. Open trees soon give way to boulder fields (snow in early season), which lead in 0.5 mile to the base of the route (5,700 feet; 1 hour from col). This approach may be much faster when snow covered, but an ice ax would be advisable for the gully descent.

Route: Begin on the left edge of a huge S-shaped gully that separates the Northeast Buttress from less distinct features to the left. **Pitches 1–3** follow the crest of the rib left of the gully to a point where the gully is constricted by a prominent chockstone. **Pitch 4** climbs over the chockstone, then directly up a short corner on the right side. After 20 feet (5.8), traverse right onto the lower-angled face. Continue up the depression, which turns into a V-groove on the right side of the buttress crest. Watch for loose blocks. **Pitch 5** climbs left out of the V-groove via steep, discontinuous cracks, reaching a major step in about 100 feet (5.9). **Pitch 6** now follows the crest of the ridge, which turns into an obvious pillar leaning against the main buttress. Easy climbing leads to where this pillar steepens (5.7). **Pitch 7** traverses 20 feet left onto the face, then up into the base of a wide gully/chimney, which is followed to its head, then climbs the steep right wall on positive handholds (5.8) and multicolored lichen to the top of the leaning pillar.

Pitch 8 is one of the most improbable on the route. Crossing the notch between the pillar and the wall above, climb directly upward for 25 feet on blocks, then make a rising leftward traverse across a blank-looking face, past a dihedral, and onto an arête. At 5.9, this traverse is much easier than it appears. On the arête, gain a beautiful finger crack (5.9), which reaches a broad, sandy ledge in 20 more feet. (*Note:* From the top of pitch 8, the first-ascent party climbed a full pitch directly upward, through the very obvious ear-shaped off-width above, encountering classic Yosemite-style 5.9+ climbing. Above this very physical pitch, the crack peters out into steep slabs, and climbing hammerless, they were forced to descend and look for another way. However, a direct finish on the headwall, linking with crack systems above, would be a spectacular addition to this route.)

Pitch 9 is almost horizontal: follow the sandy ledge 100 feet rightward, around the buttress crest, to a short, blocky corner, which leads in 25 feet to another comfortable ledge at the base of a massive, clean corner system (4th class). **Pitch 10** tackles the corner directly; the crux is turning a large flake about midway up the pitch (5.10a). After about 100 feet, make a short unprotected traverse right to a sickle-shaped ledge. **Pitch 11** climbs the 5-inch crack at the right side of the ledge to easier ground (5.10a). At the base of a bulging 8-inch crack, traverse rightward again around a corner to a small sandy ledge. **Pitch 12** is the crux of the route. Follow a shallow corner 100 feet, past a small roof (5.10a). Continue up the difficult finger crack above, where face holds to the left lead around a bulge to an alcove above (5.10c; nuts and small cams). Some aid was required here on the first ascent for cleaning, but the second was able to follow at the same grade. From the alcove, easier ground leads up and right to a huge terrace and the obvious end of the hard climbing. **Pitches 13–16** follow the buttress crest directly to the summit (low 5th class), generally on the crest or just right of it, with fabulous views down both sides. The summit block provides a sting in the tail (5.8), or traverse rightward below the summit to gain the ridgeline.

Descent: From the summit, descend loose talus and slabs 100 feet directly down the fall line, then begin a descending traverse parallel to the ridgeline, crossing several ribs. Whenever difficulties greater than 4th class arise, descend a bit before continuing to traverse. From the notch between Hardy and the 7,600-foot peak to the north

Dan Aylward leads on pitch 10 (5.10) of the Northeast Buttress on Mount Hardy
(Photo by Forrest Murphy)

(christened Nancy Drew by the first-ascent party), contour more flatly across lower-angled slopes, again crossing below any difficulties. After crossing several more rocky ribs, emerge onto a large boulder field on the north slope of Nancy Drew, which is descended directly to the col at 7,260 feet. Reverse the approach to the highway.

Mount Terror · Mount Degenhardt · The Pyramid · Inspiration Peak · West McMillan Spire · East McMillan Spire · Terror Glacier

West McMillan Spire's West Ridge route, with some of the Southern Pickets
(Photo by Jim Nelson)

WEST McMILLAN SPIRE

▲ West Ridge

Perhaps the easiest of all summits in the Southern Pickets to reach and to climb, this moderate route is frequently the one and only summit bagged by ambitious climbers venturing into that remote range. Approaches to the Pickets are notoriously difficult, and getting to West McMillan Spire is easy only in comparison to the difficulties of getting to the rest of the range. Expect to take 2 days on the approach to this route. In fact, very few climbers heading into the Picket Range accomplish their pre-trip plans of knocking off multiple summits. ("Well, we were going to do Luna and Terror and Fury, but we were so wasted by the time we got there . . . . ") The terrain is so rugged, the weather so changeable, and the approaches so taxing and time consuming that many parties feel fortunate to reach the summit of even one modest route.

Hence the great appeal of West McMillan Spire. Though not the finest route in the Pickets, the West Ridge is interesting, satisfying—and doable.

Special Considerations: Permits are required to camp in North Cascades National Park, anytime, anywhere, but at present there is no fee. For information and current park regulations, call the North Cascades National Park ranger station in Marblemount, officially known as the Wilderness Information Center (360-873-4500), or the National Park Service/U.S. Forest Service ranger station in Sedro Woolley, officially known as the North Cascades National Park Headquarters/U.S. Forest Service Mount Baker Ranger District (360-856-5700). Northwest Forest Pass not required.

76 WEST RIDGE GRADE II+

Characterized by mostly moderate climbing, the route does have a short section of steep snow and a final 800 feet of somewhat loose and unpleasant class 3 climbing that feels more like class 4. The West Ridge remains, however, a very reasonable climb on a peak set amid many difficult and challenging mountains.

First ascent ▲ Fred and Helmy Beckey, August 1940; first winter ascent: Mike Colpitts and Jaerl Secher-Jensen, March 1976

Elevation ▲ 8,000 feet

Difficulty ▲ Grade II+; exposed class 3; steep snow to 40 degrees

Time ▲ 2–3 days round trip; 2–5 hours one-way from high camp

Equipment ▲ Ice ax, crampons

Season ▲ June-September

Approach (Grade IV+): From Interstate 5 near Burlington, take the Cook Road exit (exit 232) east approximately 5 miles to where it joins State Highway 20 (North Cascades Highway) in Sedro Woolley. Drive 14 miles east of Marblemount to the west end of the town of Newhalem. Across Highway 20 from the Goodell Creek Campground (directly across from the North Cascades Park Visitors Center), turn north onto the road into the Goodell Creek drainage. Follow the road to a T intersection and turn left onto a gravel road (east of Goodell Creek). At a fork, take the right-hand (uphill) branch. Follow signs to the group campground (1 mile). A small parking lot (with room for just three or four cars) can be found at the north end of the campground (600 feet). The unmarked trail can be accessed northeast of the last campsite adjacent to the parking lot, or can be located about 300 feet south of the group campground. The trail ahead is unmaintained and often overgrown.

Follow the trail along a long-since abandoned logging road; at 4.5 miles (1,600 feet), just past a small creek crossing but before a small campsite, locate the climbers path leading right (east) and up the timbered ridge. (A large, arrow-shaped cairn may mark the path.) The way is fairly easy to follow until, about two-thirds of the way to timberline, the trail fades into huckleberry bushes in the last mile. (The usual bits of orange surveyors tape soon appear in the brush; it has been suggested by some that a more liberal use of the tape would establish one good trail as opposed to many faint ones that currently crisscross each other. Others see the stuff as being no good at all.) Things open up at last on a heather bench at 5,200 feet; water is available here until July most years, maybe later. Campsites can be found beyond the streams at 5,400 feet; the next decent camping is more than an hour away.

From the heather bench, begin traversing north, descending slightly at first, then traversing via a faint path for 2 miles to a big talus-filled gully. Ascend to a notch on a steep ridge (6,350 feet). From the notch, descend the ridge via steep scree and snow for 300–400 feet to a large, flat gravel and wildflower basin with many small streams (5,700 feet; good camping).

The approach continues traversing along benches, descending gradually 1 mile to the outlet of a high glacial lake (5,550 feet). From the lake outlet, climb slabs, moraine, and snow toward Terror Glacier below West McMillan Spire.

Route: From the glacier's edge, ascend directly toward the base of West McMillan

The view north from West McMillan Spire, showing Inspiration, Pyramid, Degenhardt, Baker, Terror, and Shukshan (Photo by Jim Nelson)

Spire's West Ridge. The final snow slopes narrow into a gully and become quite steep (to 40 degrees). Scree is followed by steep heather. Continue climbing up the ridge on scree and talus to the top; a short section of exposed, somewhat loose class 3 climbing is encountered just below the summit blocks.

Descent: Descend the climbing route.

Luna Peak

Luna Peak from the southeast (Photo by Jim Nelson)

LUNA PEAK
▲ Southwest Ridge

With a hard approach and a 3rd-class route on mediocre rock, the climb of Luna Peak has little to recommend it except the setting and the view—a view into what is probably the most rugged alpine wilderness in the Lower 48. Highest of the remote, almost mythical Picket Range, Luna Peak is not actually a part of either the McMillan Creek cirque wall (the Southern Pickets) or the Luna Creek cirque wall (the Northern Pickets). Instead, Luna Peak is the high point on the ridge dividing the two impressive cirques, thereby affording a view into both the Northern and Southern Pickets that is unmatched by any other vantage point. Luna is a truly fantastic view peak.

271

McMillan Creek cirque (Southern Pickets) from Luna Peak (Photo by Jim Nelson)

While the climb of Luna Peak itself is a simple affair, the approach is not. The lengthy and strenuous hike into Luna Peak requires a long walk through beautiful old-growth forest followed by an unsavory, classic North Cascades bushwhack to tree line and then steep alp slopes and talus—and even then the climber is only at the fringes of the wild and rugged Pickets.

Special Considerations: Permits are required to camp in North Cascades National Park, anytime, anywhere, but at present there is no fee. For information and current park regulations, call the North Cascades National Park ranger station in Marblemount, officially known as the Wilderness Information Center (360-873-4500), or the National Park Service/U.S. Forest Service ranger station in Sedro Woolley, officially known as the North Cascades National Park Headquarters/U.S. Forest Service Mount Baker Ranger District (360-856-5700). Northwest Forest Pass required.

From Ross Lake Resort (206-386-4437, reservations and current rates), it is possible to take a water taxi ($25 one-way for up to six people) up the lake to Big Beaver Creek.

77 SOUTHWEST RIDGE GRADE II

Luna Peak makes a worthwhile objective for any climber, particularly those with limited technical ability but a desire to experience a true wilderness climb. While Luna Peak is manageable with intermediate skills, offering a reasonable climb in this singular area, proceeding farther into the Picket Range is recommended only for those who have expert Cascades mountaineering skills.

Luna Creek cirque (Northern Pickets) from Luna Peak, with Baker and Shuksan in the distance (Photo by Jim Nelson)

First ascent ▲ Bill Cox and Will F. Thompson, September 1937; first winter ascent: John Roper, Russ Kroeker, Silas Wild, Paul Michelson, Jim Burcroof, December 1989
Elevation ▲ 8,285 feet
Difficulty ▲ Grade II; class 4
Time ▲ 3–5 days round trip; 2–3 hours one-way from high pass
Equipment ▲ Ice ax, crampons (for steep, wet heather and, possibly, log crossings)
Season ▲ June-September

Approach (Grade V): From Interstate 5 near Burlington, take the Cook Road exit (exit 232) east approximately 5 miles to where it joins State Highway 20 (North Cascades Highway) in Sedro Woolley. Drive Highway 20 about 20 miles to 3.8 miles east of Marblemount and the Ross Dam/Ross Lake Resort trailhead (2,100 feet).

Hike 0.8 mile down to Ross Lake (1,600 feet), a short distance above Ross Dam. Either hike 6 miles by trail along the west shore of Ross Lake to Big Beaver Creek, or take the water taxi from Ross Lake Resort (see Special Considerations, above).

From the point where the Big Beaver Trail leaves Ross Lake, hike up the trail approximately 11 miles. At this point, approximately 1.5 miles upstream (northwest) of Luna Camp on Big Beaver Trail, locate a major creek (known as Access Creek) across the valley to the west. It is necessary to ford Big Beaver Creek, or locate a suitable log crossing. Expect to spend some time locating a safe place to cross. Both sides of Access Creek (north and south) are reported to have similar obstacles, so ascend either side of the creek.

While there is no clear path, the going is reasonable (mostly through huckleberry bushes) for most of the way. Staying within earshot of the creek, continue up until the valley levels out (about 3,800 feet). When the slide alder and heavy brush become awkward and unpleasant, try moving along the creek or in the creekbed itself, water level permitting. Some unavoidable bushwhacking ends at last with talus and scree at the end of the valley (approximately 4,300 feet; good camping here).

Turn left (south) and climb steep scree slopes to a notch in the ridge (6,100 feet). From here the route traverses several steep basins along the south side of Luna Ridge and Luna Peak (this part of the route includes steep heather) to a high pass (7,200 feet; good bivy sites).

Route: From the high pass, the climb to the false or west summit takes about 1 hour and involves mostly talus with some class 3 rock near the top. The view from here is great, and for most, this is the end of the line. But if you have the time and moxie, do not stop here. Continue to the true (east) summit by traversing a somewhat time-consuming narrow ridge of exposed 3rd- and 4th-class rock.

Descent: Descend the climbing route.

MOUNT CHALLENGER ──────────────

▲ *Challenger Glacier*

A moderate snow-and-glacier climb finishing with a short section of 5th-class climbing on pretty good rock, Mount Challenger is a remote and highly satisfying climb that makes for an almost spiritual experience. Largely because of its location in the wild Picket Range, the route represents the best of traditional Cascades mountaineering. Guarded by long, rugged approaches that inflict real hardship on the climber, Mount Challenger (and the Pickets in general) inspires the imagination and offers rewards unsurpassed in the Cascades.

Those who appreciate the joys of alpine mountaineering will find Mount Challenger a symbol for the best the Cascades have to offer, and will enjoy the route despite the approach difficulties. Cliff Leight, a North Cascades climber and photographer who has summited on Mount Challenger numerous times, claims that it is the "perfect climb" in the range—once the long and arduous approach has been accomplished. Climbers will find Mount Challenger to be memorable, and very difficult to get to.

Special Considerations: Permits are required to camp in North Cascades National Park, anytime, anywhere, but at present there is no fee. For information and current park regulations, call the North Cascades National Park ranger station in Marblemount, officially known as the Wilderness Information Center (360-873-4500), or the National Park Service/U.S. Forest Service ranger station in Sedro Woolley, officially known as the North Cascades National Park Headquarters/U.S. Forest Service Mount Baker Ranger District (360-856-5700). Northwest Forest Pass required.

Mount Challenger from the north (Photo by Jim Nelson)

From Ross Lake Resort (206-386-4437, reservations and current rates), it is possible to take a water taxi up the lake to Big Beaver Creek ($25 one-way for up to six people) or to the Little Beaver Creek trailhead (approximately $60 for up to six people).

78 CHALLENGER GLACIER GRADE II; 5.7+

The final 2,000 feet of snow-and-glacier climbing is a picnic, a classic Cascades route on a large, gentle glacier. A final bit of rock gymnastics on better-than-average rock provides thrilling exposure and a suitable finish to so appealing a climb. The summit block provides an ideal perch from which to admire the Pickets and contemplate the isolation and beauty of these mountains.

First ascent ▲ Phillip Dickert, Jack Hossack, George MacGowan, September 1936; first winter ascent: climbers unknown, February 1977

Elevation ▲ 8,236 feet

Difficulty ▲ Grade II; 5.7+; snow or ice to 30 degrees, glacier travel

Time ▲ 3–5 days round trip; 3–6 hours one-way from high camp at east edge of glacier, 4–8 hours one-way from Perfect Pass

Equipment ▲ Ice ax, crampons, slings and carabiners for fixed pins or small rack to 1 inch

Season ▲ June-September

Approach: Located in North Cascades National Park, west of Ross Lake, Mount Challenger can be approached by several routes. Note that the approaches listed here are all quite arduous; none can be considered easier than the others. Each has its unique problems and punishment: Perfect Pass/Easy Ridge can involve the greatest elevation gain (6,500 feet, with 2,000 feet lost) and some exposed climbing. Big Beaver Creek valley/Wiley Ridge is the most direct route but has notorious and unsavory bushwhacking sections. Whatcom Pass/Whatcom Peak is technically difficult; it should be attempted by only experienced mountaineers.

Via Perfect Pass/Easy Ridge (Grade V+): Follow the approach to Hannegan Pass (5,066 feet) given for climb 83, Ruth Glacier. Camping can be found below the pass on both the west and east sides. Follow the trail down the east side of the pass into the Chilliwack Valley for 5 miles to where the river is crossed (2,750 feet). An old trail, which is deteriorating and may be difficult to find, branches off the trail here and leads through timber and alpine slopes to the top of Easy Ridge (5,190 feet). Continue along the crest of Easy Ridge for 2 to 3 miles to Easy Peak (6,613 feet). Just beyond Easy Peak, begin a descending traverse off Easy Ridge to the east, aiming to pass below a steep rock buttress on the southwest slopes of Whatcom Peak (somewhere between 5,200 to 5,400 feet), where cliffs, vegetation, and slabs bar the way to Perfect Pass. In addition to these difficulties, the "perfect impasse," a deep chimney/gully, is encountered, which bars the way. There are two options to reach Perfect Pass:

Option 1/the high route: Traverse under the steep rock buttress of Whatcom Peak (between 5,200 and 5,400 feet). Look for exposed ledges at approximately 5,400 feet that traverse into the deep gully and back out. Continue upward, navigating through bushes and slabs to Perfect Pass (6,300 feet). This option avoids the elevation loss of Option 2, but it is quite exposed, and the key ledges can be difficult and time consuming to find (note that these ledges are easier to find when traveling from west to east than they are east to west).

Option 2/the low route: This route requires descending approximately 1,600 feet to a point at which the deep gully can be crossed at 3,800 feet. From there, continue traversing below the cliffs on the right until you have passed them and moved into in a bushy gully and short section of timber that leads to easier ground and eventually to Perfect Pass (6,300 feet).

From Perfect Pass, descend to the east for 200 feet to the Challenger Glacier and begin an ascending traverse of the Challenger Glacier (rappels may be necessary). Ascend to the top of a rock island/rib at 6,400 feet. Continue to climb up and left for 1 more mile to the east side of the glacier (6,800 feet), 2–5 hours from Perfect Pass. Campsites are to the east of the glacier.

Via Big Beaver Creek valley/Wiley Ridge (Grade IV+): Follow the approach to the Big Beaver Trail given for Luna Peak, climb 77, Southwest Ridge. Hike up the trail 14 miles to Beaver Pass (3,620 feet). From the southern end of the pass, begin bushwhacking west through devils club and huckleberry bushes for 0.5 mile, heading for the left-hand (east-facing) timbered rib. Ascend to timberline at a flat bench at 5,700 feet; continue up the ridge to another bench (6,350 feet), where it is possible to begin a steep traverse to the left (west) across the south slope of Wiley Ridge. This traverse is somewhat unpleasant (particularly when wet) across steep heather. The

Jim Martin and Heather Paxson navigate crevasses on the Challenger Glacier, with Baker and Shuksan in the distance. (Photo by Jim Nelson)

traverse starts descending after crossing a gully; descend to approximately 6,000 feet until able to climb up a short way to easier ground. The route traverses across heather benches, a talus field, and more benches for approximately 1 mile.

From this point it is possible to continue traversing (steep in places) near tree line (6,200–6,400 feet), contouring at that altitude all the way to the Challenger Glacier, or for a more scenic alternative, climb to the ridge (approximately 6,600 feet).

Once on the ridge crest, continue climbing to 6,900 feet, above Eiley Lake. At this point, in small dense trees, begin a descent down to Eiley Lake (6,550 feet) and on to Wiley Lake (6,750 feet). Climb over the top of Point 7374, traversing through a notch at 7,250 feet on the south side of Point 7374 (or traverse around the north side of Point 7374 at 7,100 feet via the Wiley Ridge Glacier). Camp on rock at the eastern end of the Challenger Glacier (6,200 feet) directly below the peak.

Via Whatcom Pass/Whatcom Peak (Grade V): Whatcom Pass (5,206 feet) can be reached in 17 miles from the west via the Chilliwack River Trail and the Hannegan-Whatcom Trail (see Via Perfect Pass/Easy Ridge, above), or in 17 miles from the east via Little Beaver Trail from Ross Lake.

From Whatcom Pass, Whatcom Peak (7,574 feet) presents a formidable obstacle to reaching Perfect Pass and the Challenger Glacier. Whatcom Peak can be negotiated by two routes:

Option 1: Traverse the Whatcom Glacier, staying between 5,400 and 5,600 feet, depending on conditions (danger from falling and sliding ice), followed by a long ascending traverse across steep talus, scree, and rock slabs to Perfect Pass (6,300 feet).

Option 2: Climb over the summit of Whatcom Peak via the north ridge. Begin at Whatcom Pass proper, following the climbers path south, then climbing talus, rock slabs, and heather benches to the point at which the ridge narrows and steepens at 6,200 feet. The final 1,500 feet is 30-degree snow and 3rd-class rock. The rock is loose and extremely exposed. From the summit (7,574 feet), descend snow and ice to Perfect Pass (6,300 feet).

To reach the Challenger Glacier from Perfect Pass, see Via Perfect Pass/Easy Ridge, above.

Route: From the lower slopes of the Challenger Glacier, straightforward snow-and-glacier climbing lead to the upper slopes of the Challenger Glacier, traversing past the final bergschrund to a short snow arête leading west to the summit rocks. Third-class rock scrambling traverses west to a 40-foot-high step (5.7+) with fixed protection.

Descent: Descend the climbing route.

MOUNT BAKER ———————————————————
▲ *Easton Glacier* ▲ *North Ridge*

The third-highest mountain in the state of Washington, Mount Baker wears its heavy mantle of ice with exceptional beauty. And while not as massive or dominating as Mount Rainier or Mount Adams, Mount Baker has the more aesthetic shape, one that pops up surprisingly from many vantage points in the Cascades and around Puget Sound. Its high altitude and position far west of the Cascades crest—Baker is only 35 miles from tidewater—place it to receive the full wet blast of winter storms, feeding its dozen glaciers. Geologists warn that Mount Baker may be the next of the Cascades volcanoes to show eruptive activity. The Sherman Crater has historically exhibited continual signs of thermal activity. Those "steam eruptions" greatly increased in 1975 and remain at an increased level to this day.

Lying mostly in the Mount Baker Wilderness Area, the peak nonetheless has a pie-shaped wedge on the south slopes set aside as a recreation area, which is open to motorized vehicles. But Mount Baker is big enough to provide recreation for all. Recommended routes on Mount Baker include a technical snow-and-ice ridge route of exceptional quality, and one of the easiest of all glacier routes on a Cascades volcano.

Special Considerations: Climbers must share the pie-shaped area of the Mount Baker National Recreation Area on the south slopes of Mount Baker with snowmobiles. During daylight hours in late spring, expect to hear the whine of these machines. Do not do the route if this intrusion is going to aggravate you to the point of anger. Instead, go climb something else; you can also work with the snowmobilers and the Forest Service to manage this prime recreational area appropriately.

Permits are not currently required to climb and camp on the south slopes of Mount Baker (climb 79). Currently, permits are not required to climb and camp in the Mount Baker Wilderness Area; however, the proximity of the North Ridge (climb 80) to the very popular normal route for Mount Baker means that North Ridge climbers should take special care when camping. Choose sites in areas that will not damage the fragile alpine environment (pitch tents on snow or rocks) and take necessary precautions for the human-waste problem. For more information on both climbs 79 and 80, call the National Park Service/U.S. Forest Service ranger station in Sedro Woolley, officially known as the North Cascades National Park Headquarters/ U.S. Forest Service Mount Baker Ranger District (360-856-5700); for information on climb 79, call the Glacier Public Service Center in Glacier—a Forest Service ranger station that in the summer also houses National Park Service personnel (360-599-2714). Northwest Forest Pass required.

79 EASTON GLACIER GRADE II

One of the most moderate of all glacier routes on a Cascades volcano, the Easton Glacier shares with the Swift Glacier on Mount St. Helens and the South Rib route on Mount Adams the honor of being the least-technical volcano climb in the range. Draped with the heavy glaciation typical of Mount Baker, the south-facing Easton Glacier presents a route of surprising gentleness—so gentle, in fact, that in early season, snowmobiles frequently ascend to the 10,000-foot level of this crevassed, 20- to 30-degree slope. (The south slope's designation as part of the Mount Baker National Recreation Area makes the incursion by these machines legal.) The route has become a popular ski and snowboard outing in early season. The Easton Glacier is a true four-season climb for those with winter climbing skills.

While it is not steep, the Easton Glacier is nonetheless fraught with the usual dangers of long, high Cascades glacier routes—changeable weather (and its chief, related problem, poor visibility), crevasse danger, and altitude. Getting lost in a whiteout on any Cascades volcano is a thrill no one ever wants to experience. Carry a map and compass or, even better, those items in conjunction with an altimeter. Strong crevasse-rescue and glacier-travel skills, and good judgment, are required of climbers attempting even a moderate route such as this on a 10,700-foot mountain. Be aware that the Easton Glacier is also a long route; with a second-day elevation gain of approximately 5,000 feet (depending on the location of camp), the summit day can actually involve more climbing than some routes on Mount Rainier.

Snowboarder on the Easton Glacier, Black Buttes behind (Photo by John Erben)

Mount Baker from the south, showing the Easton Glacier route
(Photo by Austin Post, USGS)

First ascent ▲ Unknown
Elevation ▲ 10,781 feet
Difficulty ▲ Grade II; 30-degree snow and ice, glacier travel, altitude
Time ▲ 1–3 days round trip; 5–10 hours one-way from camp
Equipment ▲ Ice ax, crampons
Season ▲ May-August; year-round for experienced climbers

Approach (Grade II+): From Interstate 5 near Burlington, take the Cook Road exit (exit 232) east approximately 5 miles to where it joins State Highway 20 (North

Cascades Highway) in Sedro Woolley. Drive east 22.2 miles from I-5, turn north (left) on Baker Lake Road, and travel 12.5 miles to just beyond Rocky Creek bridge. Turn left onto Forest Road 3725 and begin following signs to the Mount Baker National Recreation Area and Schriebers Meadow. At 3 miles, turn right onto the Schriebers Meadow Road (FR 372), which ends in 6 miles at the trailhead (3,200 feet).

Follow the excellent trail through Schriebers Meadow, across the Easton Glacier stream (Sulphur Creek) on a suspension bridge, and then through old-growth timber to Morovitz Meadow (4,500 feet). In the upper meadows, take the right-hand fork to the Railroad Grade Trail.

Continue up the moraine on the Railroad Grade, so named because the moraine climbs gradually at a near-perfect 6 percent grade, for another mile, past the highest protected campsites in the trees (5,600 feet). Higher campsites can be found along the edge of the glacier on moraines at approximately 6,000 feet, with more sites at approximately 7,000 feet. The higher the camp, the better the views but the farther one has to carry a big pack.

Route: The 7,000-foot level is the point where most parties rope up for glacier travel and move out onto the Easton Glacier. (**Note:** In very early season, the Easton Glacier can be ascended directly from above the suspension bridge over Sulphur Creek, avoiding the summer trail in the big timber west of the glacier.)

From the 7,000-foot level, take the best route possible through crevasses, aiming for the base of Sherman Peak at a flat area at 9,600 feet, not far from the Sherman Crater steam vents. (A detour to look at the crater is well worth the effort.) From here, the route ascends the final 30-degree headwall to the summit plateau. The highest point is several hundred yards to the east.

Descent: Descend the climbing route.

80 NORTH RIDGE GRADE III+

One of the best of the technical snow-and-ice climbs on a Cascades volcano, the North Ridge of Baker is also one of the safest of the steep routes typically found on big mountains in the range. Being a ridge route, danger from icefall or avalanche is minimal. But the North Ridge remains a steep, committing climb with tricky routefinding and a long approach over a heavily crevassed glacier.

As with all snow-and-ice climbs in the Cascades, conditions play a large part in the difficulty of the climb. Cold temperatures overnight are welcomed—soft snow in early morning means a slower and more dangerous glacier crossing as well as a longer and more strenuous climb. If conditions are poor, consider the seldom-climbed Colfax Peak, East Ridge, as an alternative.

The climbing is, for the most part, on snow and ice to 40 degrees, with several ice pitches considerably steeper (60–70 degrees) higher up, providing the most spectacular climbing on the route. This ice step occurs at a point on the route where the ridge begins to merge onto the upper ice cap and snowfields. You will not mistake this exciting part of the route, nor will you miss the dramatic views down to the Roosevelt and Coleman Glaciers. The route can be quite icy later in the season, when it is suitable only for those comfortable on steep, hard ice.

The Roosevelt and Coleman Glaciers from the north, showing the North Ridge route
(Photo by Jim Nelson)

First ascent ▲ Fred Beckey, Dick and Ralph Widrig, August 1948
Elevation ▲ 10,781 feet
Difficulty ▲ Grade III+; 70+-degree snow and ice, glacier travel, altitude
Time ▲ 2 days round trip; 3–6 hours one-way from the base
Equipment ▲ Crampons, ice ax, second ice tool, 4–6 ice screws, snow
pickets or deadmen
Season ▲ May–early July

Approach (Grade II+): From Interstate 5 at Bellingham, drive the Mount Baker
Highway (State Highway 542) to 2 miles beyond the town of Glacier, to Glacier
Creek Road. Drive 8 miles and park at the Coleman Glacier/Heliotrope Ridge
trailhead (3,700 feet).

Hike the well-traveled trail as it traverses north into timber, crossing Kulshan
Creek over a bridge at 2 miles (4,500 feet). Near tree line, beyond the site of the old
Kulshan Cabin, the trail crosses a glacial stream; exercise caution, because in warm
weather the stream can be very fast with a large volume of water. This stream can be
difficult to cross.

Continue east through a final patch of forest, looking for the climbers trail
branching off uphill at approximately 5,400 feet, 3–4 hours from the road. (Another
trail, the trail to the lower Coleman Glacier, traverses east another 0.5 mile with

Helen Vrabel on Baker's North Ridge (Photo by Jim Nelson)

additional creek crossings that also can be troublesome in warm weather.) The steep and loose climbers trail follows a large moraine crest leading to benches and campsites below a western lobe of the Coleman Glacier (6,000 feet). Take necessary precautions to protect health; water contamination from human waste is a serious problem. Higher campsites can be found on Heliotrope Ridge at 7,200 feet or on the glacier itself at approximately 7,000 feet, 5–7 hours from the road.

Route: From the 7,000-foot camp, there are two possible starts, one high and one low.

Mount Baker from the north (Photo by Jim Nelson)

Lower option: Start east from the lower campsites and cross the Coleman Glacier at approximately 6,500 feet, climbing gradually until under the base of the route at approximately 7,500 feet. Continue beyond the base of a rock spur at 7,800 feet, climbing onto the broad, lower slopes of the North Ridge, bearing slightly right and ascending to where the ridge narrows and steepens (approximately 8,800 feet). This lower left-hand start to the route is not as steep as the higher start, and has less potential for rockfall hazard.

Higher option: The right-hand start is more direct, but much steeper (40-degree snow and ice) and more prone to rockfall from midseason on. Climb a spur ridge leading up and onto the crest of the North Ridge (well below the steep step) at approximately 8,800 feet.

From the point on the ridge where the two starts converge, climb 35- to 40-degree snow and ice until the lower slopes of the North Ridge narrow and steepen as the route leads onto a lobe of the summit ice cap. At the obvious, steep step (approximately 9,600 feet), climb two pitches of 60- to 70-degree snow and ice onto the upper shoulder, where the ridge opens up onto broader slopes. Continue climbing steep snow-and-ice slopes, navigating as necessary around crevasses, bearing slightly east (left), skirting large crevasses and on to the summit.

Dan McNerthney ice-climbing on Mount Baker's Coleman Glacier
(Photo by Jim Nelson)

Descent: Descend by traveling west across the broad summit plateau approximately 0.5 mile to the western edge of the plateau. Descend west-southwest down the 30-degree snow and ice of the Roman Wall of the Deming Glacier. Descend the western edge of the Deming Glacier near the pumice/scree ridge to where it ends at the Coleman Glacier–Deming Glacier col (9,000 feet). From the col, descend by traversing the Coleman Glacier west-northwest below the Black Buttes, eventually returning to Heliotrope Ridge.

MOUNT SHUKSAN
▲ Sulphide Glacier ▲ North Face

A dramatic, virtually year-round snow-and-ice route and an appealing glacier climb are both recommended climbs on Mount Shuksan, one of the most beautiful mountains in the Cascades. The massive and complex Mount Shuksan—whose handsome profile from Picture Lake has become a frequent photographic cliché—offers no less than five rugged faces, with four of them commonly climbed. Big, remote, interesting, and guarded by sometimes troublesome approaches, Mount Shuksan exerts a strong attraction for climbers drawn to its wilderness slopes and rugged beauty.

Sulphide Glacier

Crystal Glacier

Mount Shuksan from the south, showing the Sulphide Glacier route
(Photo by Jim Nelson)

Special Considerations: Permits are required to camp in North Cascades National Park, anytime, anywhere, but at present there is no fee. For information and current park regulations, call the North Cascades National Park ranger station in Marblemount, officially known as the Wilderness Information Center (360-873-4500); the National Park Service/U.S. Forest Service ranger station in Sedro Woolley, officially known as the North Cascades National Park Headquarters/U.S. Forest Service Mount Baker Ranger District (360-856-5700); or the Glacier Public Service Center in the town of Glacier (360-599-2714), which is staffed in summer by both National Park Service and Forest Service personnel. Northwest Forest Pass required.

81 SULPHIDE GLACIER GRADE II+

This aesthetic glacier climb is remarkable for its lack of technical difficulty and its position on this big, attractive mountain. Like Baker's Easton Glacier and Rainier's Emmons Glacier, the Sulphide Glacier is one of the outstanding moderate glacier routes on a Cascades peak. It is the least technical route to the summit of this rugged, heavily glaciated peak, and is certainly safer—and probably more appealing—than the Fisher Chimneys route, although that is a matter of opinion. Following the western edge of the largest of Mount Shuksan's half dozen glaciers, the Sulphide Glacier route is a straightforward glacier climb for most of its length, with brief stretches of steeper snow and ice. The route has become a favorite with the growing coterie of ski mountaineers, who enjoy the glacier's challenge through late June or early July most years.

The nature of this route (or any other glacier route) should not be construed as

a "hands in pockets" ascent, however, because Mount Shuksan is a big mountain harboring the usual potential for serious problems: rapidly changing weather, poor visibility, serious routefinding problems, and crevasse danger. And the final summit pyramid can present problems of falling rock, mostly party induced.

First ascent ▲ Unknown

Elevation ▲ 9,127 feet

Difficulty ▲ Grade II+; 30-degree snow or ice, glacier travel

Time ▲ 1–3 days round trip; 4–7 hours one-way from camp

Equipment ▲ Ice ax, crampons

Season ▲ May-August

Approach (Grade III): From Interstate 5 near Burlington, take the Cook Road exit (exit 232) east approximately 5 miles to where it joins State Highway 20 (North Cascades Highway) in Sedro Woolley. Drive east 22.2 miles to the Baker Lake Road and follow it 24.9 miles to Shannon Creek Campground. Turn left on Shannon Creek Road (Forest Road 1152) and drive 4.5 miles to the junction with FR 1152-014; turn right on FR 1152-014 and drive 1.6 miles to road end and a small parking area (2,500 feet).

The formerly unsigned trail now has a trailhead board with map, information on glacier composting toilets, and permits. And what used to be a badly overgrown trail, actually an overgrown extension of the old logging road, has been vigorously brushed by Forest Service hotshot crews in recent years and at present is in pretty good shape.

Hike the trail/road for approximately 2 miles to the base of an old clear-cut (3,200 feet), where the trail/road becomes a trail, unsigned but marked Shannon Ridge Trail No. 742 on USGS and Green Trails maps. Climb steeply up through the clear-cut to old-growth forest higher up, then onto the crest of the ridge (4,600 feet) and spectacular views of Mount Baker. Follow the trail as it turns right and continues up and down the open ridge, entering the national park at 4,700 feet, and reaching a small notch or col, and the last trees (5,400 feet). There are poor campsites here (lots of excrement near limited camping), but no water after midseason; better camping can be found higher up.

A steep traverse on snow or talus leads eastward and up, arriving at slabs below the Sulphide Glacier (5,700 feet) and campsites. The route reaches the glacier at 6,000 feet. High, scenic campsites can be found on the west edge of the glacier (6,500 feet). Both of these high campsites, which generally melt out in mid-July, have a composting toilet.

Route: From the high campsites, ascend the far west (left) side of Sulphide Glacier in a series of steps, navigating around crevasses as necessary. The route flattens out at 7,600 feet, continuing beyond a broad col (7,800 feet) leading west to upper Curtis Glacier (Hells Highway). Still keeping far west, the route steepens, leading to the summit pyramid. Climb the central gully slabs (class 3–4) of the summit pyramid.

Descent: Descend the climbing route.

Eric Bilski approaches Shuksan's summit pyramid via the Sulphide Glacier. (Photo by Cliff Leight)

Mount Shuksan from the north, showing the North Face route and the Price Glacier
(Photo by Jim Nelson)

82 NORTH FACE GRADE III–IV

This is a serious snow-and-ice route of moderate steepness on one of the most beautiful mountains in the Cascades. No route on Mount Shuksan is more dramatic than the seldom-done North Face, which ascends the snow- and glacier-clad shoulder dividing the White Salmon cirque from the Price Glacier cirque. This North Face route offers classic Mount Shuksan challenges: approach difficulties through a valley choked with slide alder, problems with routefinding on the complex peak, and the physical demands resulting from the sheer size of the mountain. But it is a rewarding and direct route to the summit with a satisfying feeling of openness and exposure, a sublime setting, and a view down to Price Lake, milky with glacial silt.

The climbing is 40- to 50-degree snow and ice. As with all such routes, snow conditions can be a major variable. Good snow (cold and hard) makes for a pleasant and enjoyable climb, while soft snow can make for a terrifying and possibly dangerous experience. Any climb of Mount Shuksan can be considered strenuous.

In winter, provided the Mount Baker Highway is plowed and open, this is one of the more accessible routes on the mountain, and winter snow conditions are often good. In spring (April-June), the climb and especially the descent can often be made quickly and easily. However, spring conditions are unpredictable and vary greatly—they can be among the best or the worst. In summer (July-August), a cold morning after a clear night can yield excellent cramponing conditions—at least on the ascent. If the snow has not hardened substantially during the night, consider abandoning the climb, because rockfall potential increases throughout the summer. Fall (late August–early October) is also a favorite season for this climb. Longer, colder nights, less snow, and more ice are all factors contributing to a classic ice climb. Sharp tools and crampons take care of the hard ice encountered this time of year.

An ascent of the North Face presents the classic descent dilemma: if snow conditions and experience level allow, one choice may be to descend back down the

North Face, eliminating the need to "carry over." But conditions that are good in the morning may become dangerous by midday, in which case the Fisher Chimneys (or possibly the White Salmon Glacier) is the recommended route for descent. Prior knowledge of the somewhat complicated Fisher Chimneys route is helpful. Besides, to carry over and bivy may be considered an added attraction to the total Mount Shuksan experience.

First ascent ▲ Rex Fassett, Elsa Hanft, Benton Thompson, August, 1927; first winter ascent: Bruce Blume and Dave Seman, December 1975; first ski descent: Gordy Skoog and Jens Kuljurgis, February 1988

Elevation ▲ 9,127 feet

Difficulty ▲ Grade III–IV; 40- to 50-degree snow or ice

Time ▲ 2–3 days round trip

Equipment ▲ Crampons, ice ax, snow pickets (winter and spring); ice screws, 2–3 pitons (late summer and fall)

Season ▲ Year-round

Approach (Grade III+): From Interstate 5 at Bellingham, drive the Mount Baker Highway (State Highway 542) to the town of Glacier; continue 19.5 miles to the White Salmon Lodge (3,650 feet) just before crossing Razor Hone Creek for the second time. The short access road to the lodge is usually gated, so park at the highway.

Steve May and Russ Dalton on the summit pyramid of Mount Shuksan
(Photo by Bruce Carter)

North
shoulder

The North Face route of Mount Shuksan (Photo by Jim Nelson)

The dirt road leading from the lodge toward the mountain ends in about 1 mile; from the road end (3,800 feet), cross the clear-cut into the forest and follow a traversing route toward the upper reaches of the White Salmon Valley. This can be difficult cross-country travel; avoid the worst of the brush by staying in heavy timber where possible.

Good campsites can be found on the moraines below the White Salmon Glacier (4,100 feet), or continue to the top of the ridge (5,500 feet) to enjoy the scenery and the frequent icefalls from the hanging glaciers on Shuksan's rugged North Face.

Route: The route traverses east and onto the small and relatively inactive hanging glacier remnant. At the head of this glacier (keep to the right) is a rock band with an even smaller piece of the glacier above. A short gully leads through the rocks (snow until late season), with some icefall threat from the hanging glacier above. As the season progresses, a bergschrund opens, defining the upper boundary of this glacier, which leads onto the upper convex snow or ice shoulder. This is the most exposed section of the climb, with dramatic views down to Price Lake and the forested valleys farther below. The summit is another 1–2 hours beyond the top of the shoulder, depending on snow conditions.

From the broad north shoulder col (8,400 feet) dividing the Hanging Glacier from the Crystal Glacier, traverse south around to the southeast slopes of the summit pyramid, eventually turning right (west) and heading upward toward the central depression on the south face of the final summit pyramid. The central gully system can be followed to the top (class 3). Another option is to take the more solid rock of the summit pyramid's southeast ridge (class 3–4).

Descent: One of the descent options for the North Face climbing route, the Curtis Glacier/Fisher Chimneys route, is somewhat complex. For climbers with no previous knowledge of the route, an altimeter is most useful. Set the altimeter to 9,127 feet at the summit. If poor weather prevents reaching the summit, set the altimeter for 8,400 feet at the north shoulder col before turning right (southwest).

From the southern base of the summit pyramid, descend south-southwest, keeping to the right-hand (west) edge of the Sulphide Glacier. At 7,800 feet, begin the descent right (west) down the 25-degree slopes of Hells Highway (mismarked on some USGS maps as the Hourglass). The slope leads to the gentle slopes of the upper Curtis Glacier. A rappel is sometimes needed here in late season. Begin a slightly rising traverse north until approximately 7,400 feet, halfway across the glacier. A slightly descending traverse northwest leads to a rock rib (class 3) leading down and right to the upper White Salmon Glacier, just above Winnies Slide (7,000 feet), also mismarked on the USGS quadrangle.

Continue down Winnies Slide, a relatively steep (40-degree) slope descended on its left (west) edge to 6,800 feet. At this point, a decision must be made: to descend the White Salmon Glacier (a more direct route back to the car), or to descend the Fisher Chimneys route (easier, perhaps, but more complicated and involving a 3-mile hike or hitchhike along the road to the car). Conditions on the White Salmon Glacier and prior knowledge (or lack of it) of the Fisher Chimneys route are important factors in choosing between these two options.

Via Fisher Chimneys: Bear left (west) across rocks, then snow, continuing down and west to 6,400 feet and a point on the ridge where the Fisher Chimneys begin. Look for a cairn and signs of foot traffic. The series of gullies that make up the Fisher Chimneys are class 3–4; they trend slightly left (east) at the top as they descend, gradually trending slightly right (west) farther down. About two-thirds of the way down, traverse right (west) several hundred feet on a scree bench until able to

Rob May on the North Face of Mount Shuksan (Photo by Andreas Schmidt)

continue down through the final gullies. At the base of the chimneys is a talus slope; traverse down and right (west) until able to pick up a climbers track (west) to Lake Ann. From Lake Ann, hike 4 miles of trail to the road at Austin Pass, 1 mile above the Mount Baker Ski Area. Hitchhike or walk the final 3 miles to the spur road leading to White Salmon Creek and the car.

Via White Salmon Glacier: From below Winnies Slide (6,800 feet), stay generally right until reaching the moraines and campsites. Descend north of White Salmon Creek, staying in heavy timber to avoid brush. Cross to the south side of the creek at the end of the logging road and return to the car.

NOOKSACK TOWER

▲ *Beckey-Schmidtke Route*

This is a remote and strenuous mixed alpine climb in a setting of wild, rugged grandeur. Since its first ascent in 1946, Nooksack Tower has proven to be a much-sought-after objective; views from the summit include Jagged Ridge of Mount Shuksan and intimate looks at the spectacularly broken East Nooksack and Price Glaciers. The climb is characterized by a troublesome and complicated approach and, once you get there, by medium- to poor-quality rock with a high potential for rockfall. For that reason the route is potentially dangerous.

Nooksack Tower and the east side of Mount Shuksan (Photo by Austin Post, USGS)

Special Considerations: Permits are required to camp in North Cascades National Park, anytime, anywhere, but at present there is no fee. For information and current park regulations, call the North Cascades National Park ranger station in Marblemount, officially known as the Wilderness Information Center (360-873-4500); the National Park Service/U.S. Forest Service ranger station in Sedro Woolley, officially known as the North Cascades National Park Headquarters/U.S. Forest Service Mount Baker Ranger District (360-856-5700); or the Glacier Public Service Center in the town of Glacier (360-599-2714), which is staffed in summer by both National Park Service and Forest Service personnel. Camping permits for this climb are best obtained at the Glacier Public Service Center. Northwest Forest Pass required.

83 BECKEY-SCHMIDTKE ROUTE GRADE IV

Nooksack Tower poses physical challenges and philosophical dilemmas for climbers selecting routes. Once the decision is made to tackle the route, many climbers report feeling on the summit a certain kinship with the mountain amid the rugged chaos of ice and rock that make its setting so exceptional. But those successful climbers also feel a certain abiding apprehension at the thought of descending the loose rock and steep snow.

First ascent ▲ Fred Beckey and Clifford Schmidtke, July 1946; first winter ascent: Jim Nelson, Kit Lewis, Greg Collum, Tim Wilson, February 1983

Elevation ▲ 8,268 feet (USGS quad: 8,285 feet)

Difficulty ▲ Grade IV; low-5th-class rock; moderate glacier travel, 40- to 50-degree snow and ice

Time ▲ 2–3 days round trip; 5–7 hours one-way from high camp (below glacier)

Equipment ▲ Ice ax, crampons, medium rack (mostly nuts) to 2 inches, pitons, 2 ropes

Season ▲ May–September

Approach (Grade III+): From Interstate 5 at Bellingham, drive State Highway 542 (Mount Baker Highway) east to the town of Glacier; continue 13.3 miles and just before the Mount Baker Highway crosses the Nooksack River, turn left on unpaved Nooksack River Road (Forest Road 402). Drive 1.5 miles to a fork; take the right fork onto FR 404. Continue 1 mile to where a bridge is out (2,400 feet).

Hike the overgrown abandoned road approximately 2.5 miles where the trail enters big timber; the next 0.5 mile of the approach is crucial and tricky. Many have become lost here. The idea is to cross the Nooksack River and find the trail to Price Lake along the left (east) side of Price Creek.

Upon entering the big timber, descend to the Nooksack River and find a log crossing or suitable ford. Once across the Nooksack River, look for the trail approximately 50 yards left (east) of Price Creek while avoiding the dense brush in the valley bottom. The path to Price Lake climbs steeply through timber, avoiding cliff bands, eventually arriving at spectacular Price Lake (3,900 feet). From the lake, the approach climbs the morainal ridge to the left (north) of the lake, with good campsites along the way (between 5,200 feet and the glacier). Ascend the glacier to the start of the couloir at the base of Nooksack Tower on the east side (7,400 feet).

Price Glacier

Nooksack Tower (Photo by Cliff Leight)

Kit Lewis on Nooksack Tower (Photo by Jim Nelson)

Route: Cross the bergschrund and climb the 40- to 50-degree snow couloir on the left (east) side of the Nooksack Tower. After 500–600 feet, below where the couloir narrows, it is possible to exit right (west) and traverse on ramps and ledges. The ledge system leads into a gully system; the route wanders up this central gully system leading to the summit. The rock climbing is moderate 4th and low 5th class, and the rock is mostly reasonable (with the ever-present danger of loose stones on ledges).

Descent: Descend the climbing route with a combination of rappels and down-climbing. Two ropes are useful for the lower rappels in the rockfall-prone snow couloir in late season. The descent is difficult and time consuming—climbers should plan for spending as much time on the descent (or more) as they spent climbing the tower.

Donna McBain skis Ruth Mountain (Photo by Steve Risse)

RUTH MOUNTAIN

▲ *Ruth Glacier*

Ruth Mountain is a gentle peak—a true walk-up—with some moderate snow slopes; a small glacier; and spectacular up-close views of the seldom-visited northeast faces of Mount Shuksan as well as glimpses into the nearby Chilliwack and Picket Ranges. The mountain was prospected in the nineteenth century and was possibly climbed at the time, although the first documented ascent was by a Mountaineers outing in 1916.

Special Considerations: Climbers usually camp on the Forest Service side of Ruth Mountain, for which no permit is required. Those who venture on to nearby

The Ruth Glacier route on Ruth Mountain, and Mount Shuksan above Hannegan Pass (Photo by Keith Gunnar)

Ice Peak (many climbers do) need a National Park Service permit to camp in North Cascades National Park. For information and current park regulations, call the North Cascades National Park ranger station in Marblemount, officially known as the Wilderness Information Center (360-873-4500); the National Park Service/ U.S. Forest Service ranger station in Sedro Woolley, officially known as the North Cascades National Park Headquarters/U.S. Forest Service Mount Baker Ranger District (360-856-5700); or the Glacier Public Service Center in Glacier—a Forest Service ranger station that in the summer also houses National Park Service personnel (360-599-2714). Northwest Forest Pass required.

84 RUTH GLACIER GRADE II

For novice climbers, Ruth Mountain makes a good outing; for all climbers, the route is a good conditioning hike and an outstanding introduction to and inspiration for the more difficult climbs into the peaks in the adjacent area. In early season (April-June), Ruth Mountain is popular as a ski outing.

Not only is the climb itself virtually without technical problems, the approach is made via established trails and mostly moderate terrain. A maintained Forest Service trail leads to Hannegan Pass; a climbers trail and snow slopes lead to the gentle but active glacier (take necessary precautions here) and on to the summit.

First ascent ▲ Mountaineers outing, 1916
Elevation ▲ 7,106 feet
Difficulty ▲ Grade II; 25-degree snow, glacier travel
Time ▲ 4–7 hours one-way; 2–3 hours one-way from Hannegan Pass
Equipment ▲ Ice ax, crampons
Season ▲ April-October

Approach (Grade II+): From Interstate 5 at Bellingham, drive State Highway 542 (Mount Baker Highway) east to the town of Glacier; continue 13.3 miles and turn left on unpaved Nooksack River Road just before the Mount Baker Highway crosses the Nooksack River. At 1.4 miles, take the uphill branch, which is Hannegan Pass Road (Forest Road 402), 4.2 miles to the Hannegan Pass trailhead and campground with rest rooms (3,100 feet).

Follow the trail as it traverses the north (left) side of the Ruth Creek valley, then switchbacks steeply up to Hannegan Pass (5,066 feet) at 4 miles. There are campsites before and below (west side of) the pass; camping at the pass itself is discouraged for impact reasons. Higher alpine camping can be found above the pass, past the exposed traverse described below.

Route: From 0.25 mile south of the pass, locate a climbers trail climbing directly up steep heather to a bench at 5,500 feet. Traverse left (east) on steep snow, and be careful here: this is the most exposed snow slope on the entire climb, because there is a cliff band below with no runout. This gradually ascending traverse (southeast) leads over a minor ridge as it continues southeast over talus or snow to a broad ridge (5,600 feet) leading south onto a long snow slope. This final snow slope of 20–25 degrees supports a small glacier. Although it is not normally heavily broken up, expect to see a few crevasses by midseason.

Descent: Descend the climbing route.

BEAR MOUNTAIN
▲ *North Buttress*

Legendary Bear Mountain is surprisingly nondescript and hard to pick out from the south. Its fame comes from the rarely seen great north wall and the long North Buttress. Although not as big as Slesse Mountain, this route holds an equal ability to psychout climbers. Exposure and position are unmatched in the Cascades. While belaying, contemplate the north wall and its 8-day direct ascent by pioneer wall climbers Pete Doorish and Dale Farnham. If you are looking to avoid some of the problems with the Beckey/Fielding start, the Direct North Buttress triples the amount of rock climbing (see climbers topo and route photo). Pioneered by Alan Kearney and Bobby Knight in September 1980, this climb compares favorably with the Northeast Buttress on Slesse (climb 86) and is one of the finest North Cascades rock climbs.

Special Considerations: Permits are required to camp in North Cascades National Park, anytime, anywhere, but at present there is no fee. For information and current park regulations, call the North Cascades National Park ranger station in Marblemount, officially known as the Wilderness Information Center (360-873-4500), or the National Park Service/U.S. Forest Service ranger station in Sedro Woolley, officially known as the North Cascades National Park Headquarters/U.S. Forest Service Mount Baker Ranger District (360-856-5700). The Sedro Woolley ranger station may be the only convenient place to obtain the permit, since most climbers approach via State Highway 9. The Park Service recognizes that it may be inconvenient to obtain a permit for this route, and in some instances a phone call to the Marblemount ranger station with trip dates may suffice for a permit.

A special note: This climb involves a backcountry crossing of the international border; for this and any other climb that crosses the border, climbers must call U.S. Customs in Blaine (360-332-5771) or Sumas (360-988-2971) for information.

85 NORTH BUTTRESS GRADE IV; 5.8–5.10A

The last of Fred Beckey's big projects in the Cascades, this imposing, abrupt route radiates invincibility. It goes at 5.8—unless the original A4 off-width crack is taken at 5.10a—with an awesome view into the heart of the magnificent north wall. The

North Buttress skirts the right-hand edge of the concave and overhanging north wall. The route climbs the steep central glacier directly below the wall (an unappealing section, because objective dangers exist) before traversing right across a prominent ramp leading to the crest of the buttress. From here the climb is disappointingly short: seven pitches—but what pitches they are!

First ascent ▲ Fred Beckey and Mark Fielding, July 1967; Direct North Buttress (Grade V; 5.10): Alan Kearney and Bobby Knight, September 1980

Elevation ▲ 7,942 feet

Difficulty ▲ Grade IV; 5.8–5.10a

Time ▲ 2–3 days round trip

Equipment ▲ Crampons, ice ax, large rack to 2½ inches

Season ▲ July-August

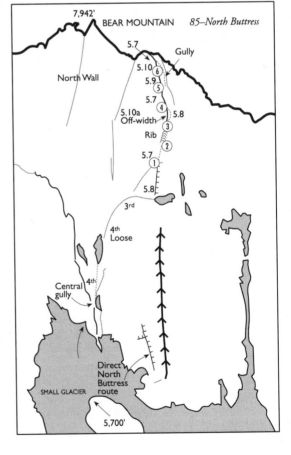

Bear Mountain from the north: A. original route; B. Direct North Buttress route
(Photo by Cliff Leight)

Approach (Grade IV): Drive Canada Highway 1 (Trans-Canada Highway) east from
Vancouver, British Columbia, to the Chilliwack-Sardis exit. Follow signs south to
Sardis on Vedder Road; in approximately 5 miles turn onto Chilliwack Lake Road
and drive to Depot Creek, along the east shore of Chilliwack Lake. Park here at the
gate (2,000 feet).

Walk the final 1.5 miles of road to the south end of Chilliwack Lake and locate
the Chilliwack River Trail. Follow good trail through tremendous old-growth forest
along the Chilliwack River. Once across the border into the United States, the trail is
infrequently maintained and can be slow going due to windfall.

Leave the trail at Bear Creek and ascend a timbered spur to the northwest, with
minimal bushwhacking but steep going. At the tree line, climb through huckleberry

Joe Puryear in the crux dihedral on the North Buttress route of Bear Mountain
(Photo by Mark Westman)

bushes for several hundred feet before coming into meadowland above Ruta Lake. Continue along the divide, then traverse the south slopes, crossing a rock rib onto bivy sites at a col (6,400 feet). A descent from the col into the Bear Creek drainage leads to the base of the north face.

Route: Staying fairly high in the cirque, traverse snow slopes to below the base of the North Buttress. Climb the glacier to reach a flat area below the central couloir on the east side of the buttress. The couloir should be mostly filled with snow, but a

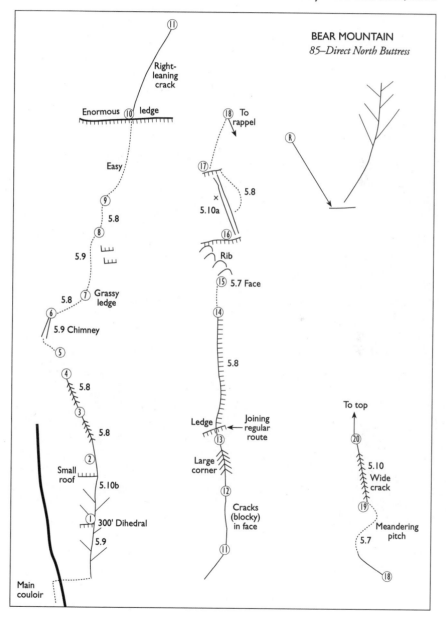

BEAR MOUNTAIN
85–Direct North Buttress

Jim Nelson on the North Buttress of Bear Mountain (Photo by Dave Bale)

short section of rock may be preferable to any unstable-looking snow blocks. Ascend several pitches on slabby, debris-covered rock (4th class; reasonable protection) to unpleasantly loose, sandy ledges. Ascend an easy ramp (a right-leading ledge) to the crest of the North Buttress.

The **first pitch** climbs a steep corner system just left of the crest (5.8). The **second pitch** lies on the crest (mid-5th class). The **third pitch** climbs steep rock left of the crest (5.8) to a nice ledge on the crest below the off-width crack. The **fourth pitch** climbs the off-width crack (5.10a), or goes slightly right of the buttress crest (5.8). The **fifth pitch** is another moderate one along the crest (5.7) that leads to an exposed belay below a steep step. The **sixth pitch** goes on the crest (5.9); an alternative is to down-climb (5.7) and tension-traverse down and right into a chimney (4th class) that leads back to the crest above the step. The **final pitch** (5.7) leads to the top of the buttress a short distance from the summit.

Descent: From the summit, begin descending toward the Chilliwack River (west), keeping left (south). Access into the basin below is blocked by a steep rock band at 7,300 feet. Stay left (south) until able to down-climb a short rock gully (3rd class) leading north and back to camp. This descent is direct and straightforward, requiring 1 hour from the summit.

SLESSE MOUNTAIN ───────────────

▲ *Northeast Buttress*

Slesse Mountain is located in the rugged Chilliwack region a few miles north of the U.S.–Canadian border. This long, intimidating route is in a rugged area that challenges the climber's skills and psychological state but rewards him or her with spectacularly exposed summit pitches on steep rock. This route on Slesse Mountain is truly a classic, one of the most challenging in the range.

Upon first view, the Northeast Buttress is a sobering sight. No photograph can convey the feeling one gets standing at the bottom of this tremendous route, long considered one of the most serious of the big alpine climbs in the Cascades. By now, greater knowledge of the route and advances in rock climbing standards have contributed to reduce much of the climb's mystique. Still, one can only imagine the anticipation and anxiety the first-ascent party must have felt at the bottom, contemplating the unknown.

Special Considerations: At present, permits are not required for this route. This climb involves beginning on one side of the mountain and finishing on the other. A somewhat unorthodox but sensible approach alternative is to arrange for helicopter transport between the two sides of the mountain; contact Highland Helicopters in Agassiz, British Columbia (604-796-9610). This alternative intrudes on no wilderness and makes this once-formidable climb into a strenuous day trip in the mountains.

86 NORTHEAST BUTTRESS GRADE V; 5.9+

The buttress can be divided into three distinct sections. The rock on the lower section is solid and glacier polished but also quite brushy. Climbers may wish to bypass this section, recognizing the spectacular summit pitches as the most enjoyable climbing. The bottom third of the route can be bypassed by traversing across the top of the pocket glacier on the east side of the buttress. The pocket glacier, perched on steep slabs, forms annually from winter snows avalanching down the east wall. By

The dramatic Northeast Buttress of Slesse Mountain (Photo by Jim Nelson)

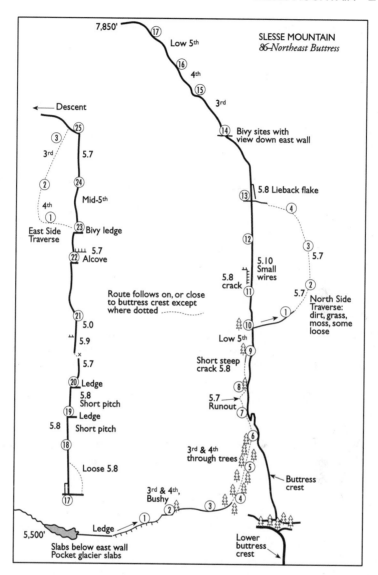

7,850'

Low 5th

SLESSE MOUNTAIN
86–Northeast Buttress

4th

3rd

← Descent

Bivy sites with
view down east wall

3rd 5.7

5.8 Lieback flake

4th Mid-5th

East Side
Traverse Bivy ledge

5.7
Alcove

5.10
Small
wires

5.8
crack

Route follows on, or close
to buttress crest except
where dotted ......

North Side
Traverse:
dirt, grass,
moss, some
loose

5.0

5.9

Low 5th

x 5.7

Ledge
5.8
Short pitch
Ledge
Short pitch

Short steep
crack 5.8

5.7
Runout

5.8

Loose 5.8

3rd & 4th
through trees

Buttress
crest

3rd & 4th,
Bushy

Ledge

5,500'

Slabs below east wall
Pocket glacier slabs

Lower
buttress
crest

April an impressive amount of ice has formed here. In recent years this glacier has been sliding off the slabs in its entirety, usually by late July, filling the lower basin with a large pile of ice cubes. (It is here in the lower basin where debris from the 1953 crash of a DC-7 is still evident.) Once the pocket glacier has avalanched, the slabs that once held the pocket glacier can be climbed directly to bypass the lower third of the route.

The middle third of the route also presents options: the buttress crest appeals to those with solid rock climbing skills, while the north side bypass (5.7) appeals to those who wish an easier route and do not mind a fair amount of dirt and vegetation.

The magnificent final pitches—the real reason for doing the climb—follow the buttress crest with sustained mid-5th-class climbing on solid rock, steep and exposed.

First ascent ▲ Fred Beckey, Steve Marts, Eric Bjornstad, August 1963; first winter ascent: Jim Nelson and Kit Lewis, 1986

Elevation ▲ 7,850 feet

Difficulty ▲ Grade V; 5.9+

Time ▲ 1–3 days round trip

Equipment ▲ Medium rack to 3 inches, chocks, 2 ropes

Season ▲ June-September

Approach: Start by leaving your vehicle at the Slesse Mountain trailhead for the return trip after you finish the climb. Drive Canada Highway 1 (Trans-Canada Highway) east of Vancouver, British Columbia, to the Chilliwack-Sardis exit. Follow signs south to Sardis on Vedder Road; in approximately 5 miles turn onto Chilliwack River Road and continue 13.2 miles to Slesse Creek Road. Turn right (south) on Slesse Creek Road; at 4.2 miles, turn left and follow the logging road on the east side of Slesse Creek; at 6.8 miles from Chilliwack River Road, reach a small creek at the base of the Slesse Mountain Trail. This is the spot to leave your car (or a bicycle, for about a 9-mile ride back to the starting point).

Then there are two options for getting to the starting point on Nesakwatch Creek Road: using a second vehicle for a shuttle, or arranging a helicopter pickup.

Via vehicle shuttle (Grade III): Drive a second car back to Chilliwack River Road and drive approximately 6 miles south to the Centre Creek/Nesakwatch Creek Road. This road begins at the Riverside Campground and crosses the Chilliwack River in 100 yards, then forks in another 100 yards. Take the right fork, which leads to Nesakwatch Creek and Slesse Mountain. Drive 2.5 miles to the gate and park.

Cross to the west side of Nesakwatch Creek and hike the spur road 1–2 miles to the basin below the pocket glacier (approximately 4,000 feet).

Via helicopter (Grade 0): Arrange for a helicopter (see Special Considerations, above) to meet you near the Slesse Mountain trailhead and transport you to the base of the route on the north side of Slesse Mountain.

Route: In early season, traverse onto the pocket glacier from the far left (east) by climbing timbered slopes (snow in early season) for approximately 600 feet. (This route avoids avalanche danger from the pocket glacier.) From the top of the pocket glacier, traverse right **three pitches** (3rd and 4th class), then up **three more pitches** to gain the crest of the buttress. (If the pocket glacier is completely gone, the slabs where the glacier used to be can be safely ascended directly from the lower basin to the crest of the buttress, 3rd and 4th class.)

To climb the complete buttress from the toe of the buttress, as per the original "direct" ascent, involves several hard free pitches on good to excellent rock (glacier polished) along with much dirty, unpleasant climbing and scrambling to reach the point on the buttress where the direct variation intersects the main route (pitch 6 on the climbers topo).

Once on the crest of the buttress, a **pitch** of 4th-class climbing is followed by a runout **pitch** (5.7) and a **pitch** with a short, steep crack (5.8), then by **another pitch** of low-5th-class climbing. At dirt ledges near the base of the first step (**pitch 10** on the climbers topo), the climber can either follow the crest or take the North Side Traverse.

To follow the crest, climb four pitches—**pitches 11–14**—(mostly mid-5th class); the second of these pitches, however (pitch 12 on the climbers topo), is the crux of the whole climb and goes 5.10.

North Side Traverse variation: From dirt ledges near the base of the first step (pitch 10 on the climbers topo), it is possible to bear right (north) one pitch, and then up gullies and corners (to 5.7) three to four more pitches to the large bench on top of the ridge at half height (at the top of pitch 13 on the climbers topo). There is a snow patch here in early season that is a possible water source for bivying, but also makes this variation a wet one for part of the season.

From the large bench at the top of pitch 14, **three pitches** (3rd through low 5th class) continue to the base of the final headwall. From here (**pitch 17**), eight outstanding pitches lead up the crest to the summit. The Northeast Buttress broadens here and blends with the north face, making the crest difficult to distinguish. Climb straight up, following

Kit Lewis on the first winter ascent of the Northeast Buttress on Slesse Mountain (Photo by Jim Nelson)

your instincts as to where the crest lies. The first, **pitch 18,** is loose (5.8). The second, **pitch 19,** continues up and slightly left (5.8). The fourth pitch (**pitch 21**) is the steepest of the upper section and starts in a crack, climbs past a bolt, and goes through a small roof (5.9). **Two more pitches** continue up to a good ledge on the crest (5.7). From here, the climber has two options.

The main route ascends the final **two pitches (24 and 25)** and climbs cracks to the summit ridge (5.7).

East Side Traverse variation: From the ledge on the crest at pitch 23, traverse east a full pitch before continuing up 3rd- and 4th-class rock another two or three pitches to the summit.

Descent: Getting down from Slesse Mountain is a long, dry piece of work. From the true summit, walk south along the crest several hundred feet, turning slightly west of the crest until able to rappel toward a gully identified by a slender gendarme.

Climbers on the polished slabs of Slesse Mountain (approaching the Northeast Buttress); these slabs are where the pocket glacier lies until it slides off. (Photo by Gordy Skoog)

Max Block and Mike Boyle on the Northeast Buttress of Slesse Mountain
(Photo by Jim Nelson)

Variation: Instead of making the rappel, continue moving south, following ledge systems back and forth, down-climbing (3rd and 4th class) until able to climb back west and into the gully identified by the slender gendarme.

The gully steepens lower down; stay high and traverse northwest across several more gullies until the steep rock below is outflanked. Once off the mountain, continue traversing northwest over a wooded ridge and then descend southwest along the ridge to the Slesse Mountain Trail and many steep switchbacks to Slesse Creek.

INDEX

THE AUTHORS

Jim Nelson, a native Northwesterner, is a professional mountain guide, climber, and mountain-shop owner. He has spent thirty-two years climbing year-round in the Cascades, the past twenty-one of those teaching, guiding, and advising on equipment. Nelson has guided clients of all abilities up diverse routes in virtually every corner of the range during all seasons. He has established more than a dozen first ascents in the Cascades.

His experience climbing in the Cascades amounts to decades of exhaustive research for *Selected Climbs in the Cascades, Volume I.* He is uniquely qualified to assess and evaluate the relative merits of the thousands of routes in the range.

Nelson is also a photographer whose mountain images have graced catalog covers and appeared in books and magazines. He has climbed in the Sierra Nevada; the Coast, Purcell, Selkirk, and Rocky Mountain Ranges of British Columbia; the Karakoram; and Alaska, where he made the second ascent of Infinite Spur on Mount Foraker.

Photo by Patricia Vadasy

Peter Potterfield is a journalist and author with a twenty-seven-year publishing career in newspapers, magazines, books, and online publishing. Potterfield has made a specialty of covering mountaineering and wilderness adventure and has written on these subjects for *Outside, Reader's Digest, Summit, Backpacker, Conde Nast Traveler,* and other national publications. Potterfield's book, the critically acclaimed *In the Zone* (The Mountaineers, 1996), is a compilation of mountaineering survival stories and epic climbs. His latest book is *The High Himalaya* (The Mountaineers, 2001). Potterfield currently is editor and publisher of MountainZone.com, a web-based mountain-sports site, where he pioneered live reporting of Everest expeditions and other real-time mountaineering events. For more than a decade, he served as editor-in-chief of *Pacific Northwest* Magazine, where he was named a finalist for the National Magazine Award for General Excellence.

An avid weekend climber, Potterfield has climbed extensively since 1978 in the mountains of the Northwest; he has also climbed in Alaska, Canada's Coast Range, Nepal, Patagonia, New Zealand, Antarctica, the Sierra Nevada, and the Rockies of New Mexico and Colorado.

Photo by James Martin

Climber on a winter ascent of Nooksack Tower (Photo by Jim Nelson)

THE MOUNTAINEERS, founded in 1906, is a nonprofit outdoor activity and conservation club, whose mission is "to explore, study, preserve, and enjoy the natural beauty of the outdoors . . . . " Based in Seattle, Washington, the club is now the third-largest such organization in the United States, with 15,000 members and five branches throughout Washington State.

The Mountaineers sponsors both classes and year-round outdoor activities in the Pacific Northwest, which include hiking, mountain climbing, ski touring, snow-shoeing, bicycling, camping, kayaking and canoeing, nature study, sailing, and adventure travel. The club's conservation division supports environmental causes through educational activities, sponsoring legislation, and presenting informational programs. All club activities are led by skilled, experienced volunteers, who are dedicated to promoting safe and responsible enjoyment and preservation of the outdoors.

If you would like to participate in these organized outdoor activities or the club's programs, consider a membership in The Mountaineers. For information and an application, write or call The Mountaineers, Club Headquarters, 300 Third Avenue West, Seattle, Washington 98119; 206-284-6310.

The Mountaineers Books, an active, nonprofit publishing program of the club, produces guidebooks, instructional texts, historical works, natural history guides, and works on environmental conservation. All books produced by The Mountaineers fulfill the club's mission.

Send or call for our catalog of more than 500 outdoor titles:

The Mountaineers Books
1001 SW Klickitat Way, Suite 201
Seattle, WA 98134
800-553-4453
mbooks@mountaineers.org
www.mountaineersbooks.org

Other titles you might enjoy from The Mountaineers Books

Available at fine bookstores and outdoor stores, by phone at (800) 553-4453, or on the Web at *www.mountaineersbooks.org*

Mountaineering: The Freedom of the Hills, 6th edition, by The Mountaineers. $24.95 paperbound. 0-89886-427-5.

Extreme Alpinism: Climbing Light, High, and Fast by Mark Twight. $27.95 paperbound. 0-89886-654-5.

Fifty Favorite Climbs: The Ultimate North American Tick List by Mark Kroese. $32.95 paperbound. 0-089886-811-4.

Climbing: Training for Peak Performance by Clyde Soles. $18.95 paperbound. 0-89886-898-X.

Selected Climbs in the Cascades, Volume II: Alpine Routes, Sport Climbs, & Crag Climbs by Jim Nelson and Peter Potterfield. $26.95 paperbound. 0-89886-561-1.

Mount Rainier: A Climbing Guide by Mike Gauthier. $16.95 paperbound. 0-89886-655-3.

Cascade Alpine Series, Volume I: Columbia River to Stevens Pass, 3rd edition, by Fred Beckey. $34.95 paperbound. 0-89886-577-8.

Cascade Alpine Series, Volume II: Stevens Pass to Rainy Pass, 3rd edition, by Fred Beckey. $29.95 paperbound. 0-8986-838-6.

Cascade Alpine Series, Volume III: Rainy Pass to Fraser River, 2nd edition, by Fred Beckey. $29.95 paperbound. 0-89886-423-2.

Alaska: A Climbing Guide by Mike Wood and Colby Coombs. $24.95 paperbound. 0-89886-724-X.

Denali's West Buttress: A Climber's Guide to Mt. McKinley's Classic Route by Colby Coombs and Bradford Washburn. $16.95 paperbound. 0-89886-516-6.

The High Sierra: Peaks, Passes, and Trails, 2nd edition, by R. J. Secor. $29.95 paperbound. 0-90886-625-1.

Climbing California's Fourteeners: 183 Routes to the Fifteen Highest Peaks by Stephen Porcella and Cameron Burns. $19.95 paperbound. 0-89886-555-7.

Idaho: A Climbing Guide, 2nd edition, by Tom Lopez. $35.00 paperbound. 0-89886-608-1.

Selected Climbs in the Desert Southwest: Colorado & Utah by Cameron M. Burns. $22.95 paperbound. 0-89886-657-X.

Selected Climbs in North Carolina by Yon Lambert and Harrison Shull. $24.95 paperbound. 0-89886-855-6.